CREATED BY MITCH SCHAUER

MITCH SCHAUER

Script and pencils

MIKE VOSBURG

Inking

**MICHAEL LESSA &
JUSTIN YAMAGUCHI**

Color and lettering

Produced by LINCOLN BUTTERFIELD, LLC

FANTAGRAPHICS BOOKS, INC.
WWW.FANTAGRAPHICS.COM

LINCOLN BUTTERFIELD, LLC
WWW.LINCOLNBUTTERFIELD.COM

Associate Publisher: Eric Reynolds
Publishers: Gary Groth & Kim Thompson
Rip M.D. logo and book design: Adam Grano

 To receive a free catalogue of fine comics and books, call 1-800-657-1100 or visit Fantagraphics Books' website. | Distributed in the U.S. by W.W. Norton and Company, Inc. (212-354-5500) | Distributed in Canada by the Canadian Manda Group (416-516-0911) | Distributed in the UK by Turnaround Distribution (208-829-3009) | Distributed to comics stores by Diamond Comics Distributors (800-452-6642) | First printing July, 2010 | ISBN: 978-1-60699-369-9 | Printed in Singapore

TRUTH BE TOLD, THINGS GO BUMP
IN THE NIGHT BECAUSE THEY CAN'T SEE
WHERE THE HECK THEY'RE GOING.

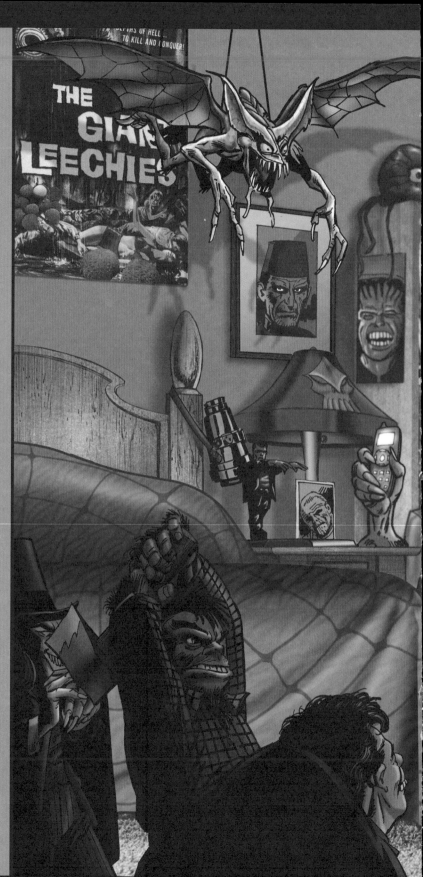

SINCE THE AGE OF SIX, RIPLEY PLIMPT HAS LOVED CLASSIC MOVIE MONSTERS. FROM THE FIRST TIME HE WATCHED FRANKENSTEIN'S MONSTER GENTLY SMILE, CAREFULLY PICK UP AND CARRY THE YOUNG GIRL, CLOESTINE, ONTO A ROOF TO RESCUE HER BALL IN 1942'S *THE GHOST OF FRANKENSTEIN*, RIPLEY HAS BEEN HOOKED. "THESE CLASSIC MONSTERS AREN'T MONSTERS!", RIP REALIZED, "THEY'RE JUST LIKE US, SORT OF. THEY MAY BE REALLY SCARY-LOOKING AND USE STRANGULATION AS A COMMUNICATION SKILL, BUT THEY DO HAVE FEELINGS, THEY CAN BE HURT AND MOST OF THE TIME, THEY DON'T REALLY WANT TO BE MONSTERS AT ALL!"

FROM *DAS CABINET DES DR. CALIGARI*, DIRECTED BY ROBERT WIENE IN 1920, RIGHT UP TO JOSEPH GREEN'S *THE BRAIN THAT WOULDN'T DIE* RELEASED IN 1962, RIP HAS COLLECTED THEM ALL — MONSTER DVDS, MONSTER TOYS, MONSTER BOOKS, MONSTER CLOTHES — ANYTHING RELATING TO THE MYRIAD OF MISUNDERSTOOD CREATURESOF THE NIGHT WHO ORIGINALLY STOMPED, OOZED OR CREEPED THEIR WAY ACROSS MOVIE SCREENS. NOW, AT THE AGE OF ELEVEN, RIPLEY PLIMPT'S HEARTFELT OBSESSION AND VAST KNOWLEDGE OF MOVIE MONSTERS HAVE CONVINCED HIM THAT MONSTERS JUST MIGHT EXIST FOR REAL, IN THE REAL WORLD!

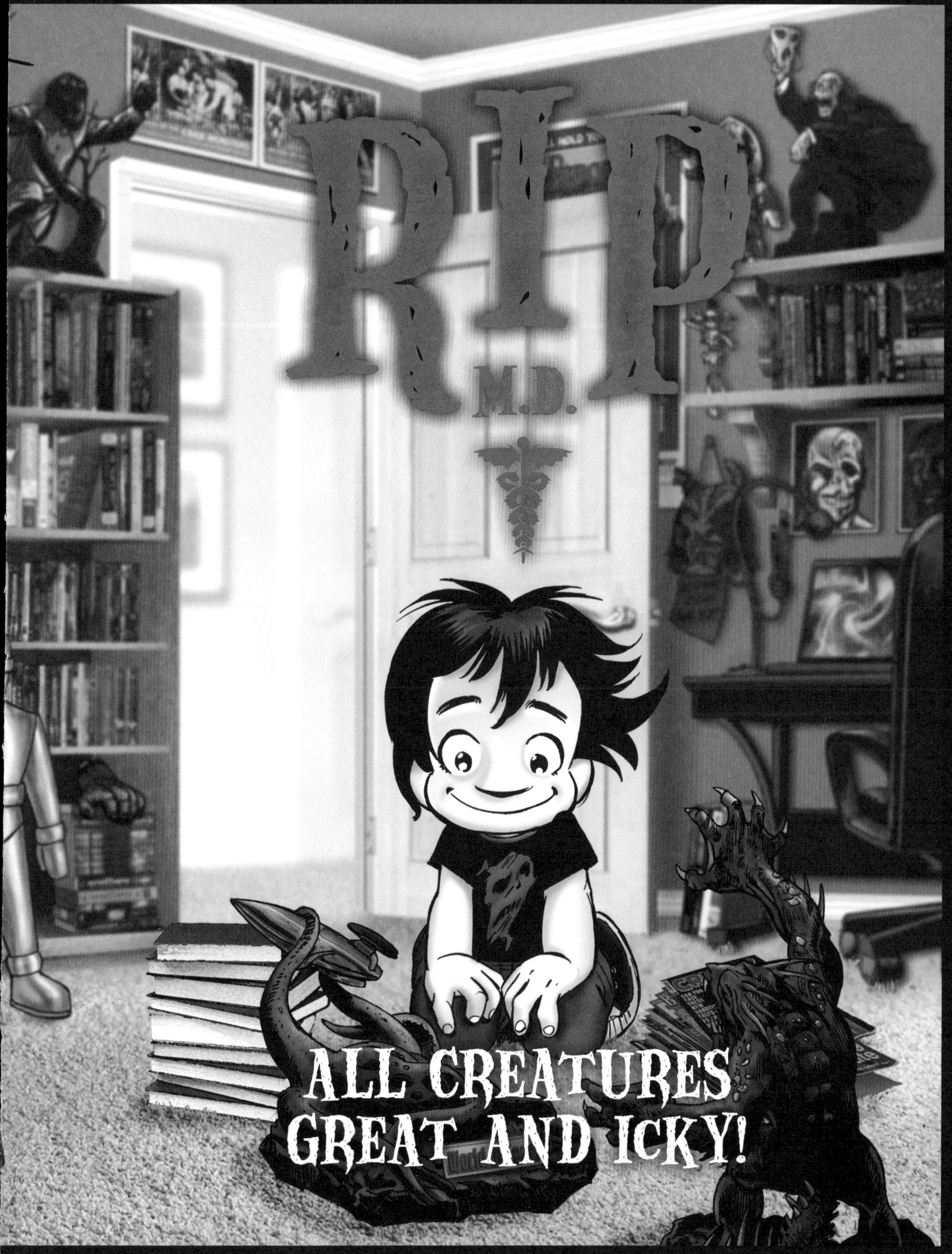
RIP M.D.
ALL CREATURES GREAT AND ICKY!

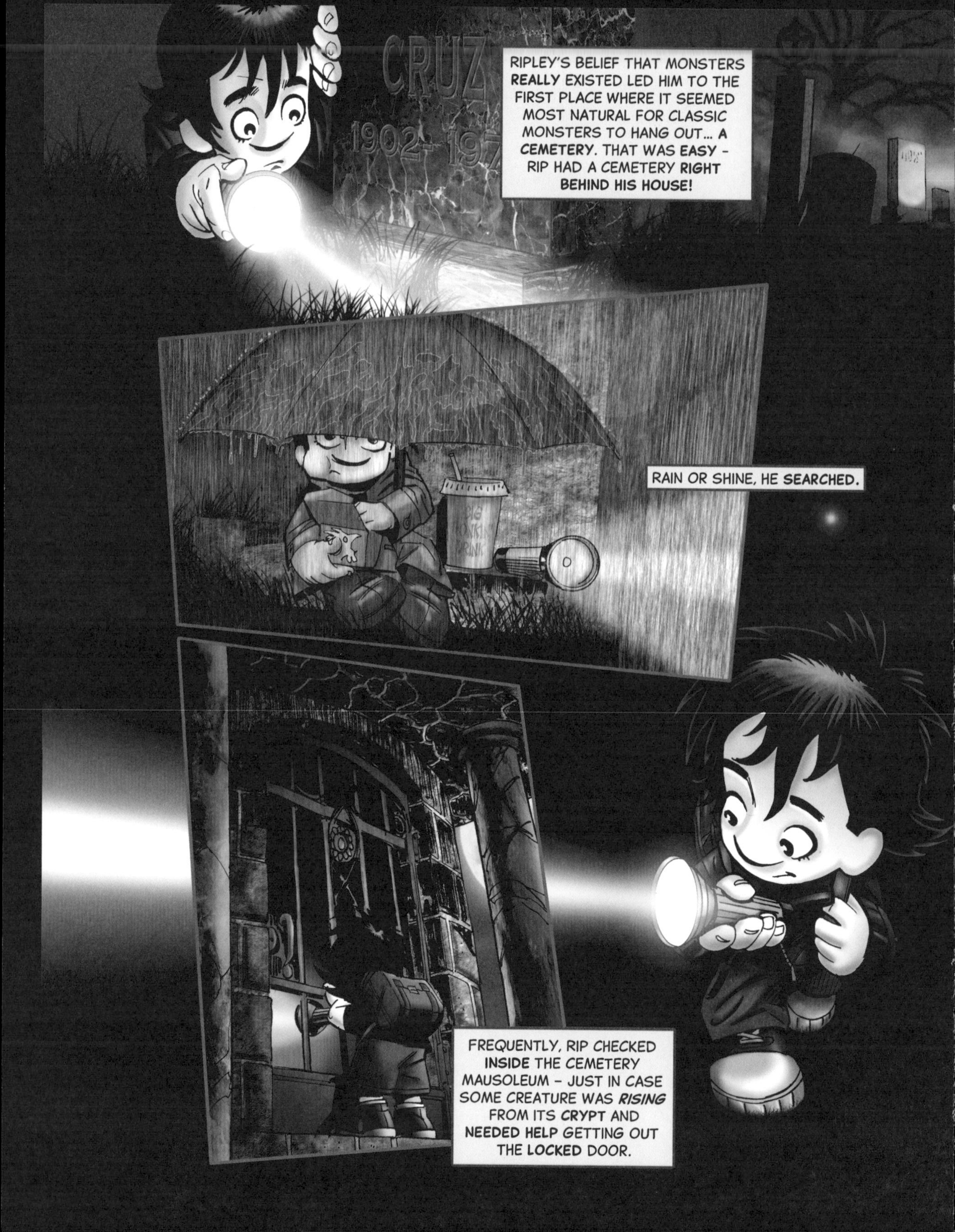
CRUZ
1902- 197
RIPLEY'S BELIEF THAT MONSTERS REALLY EXISTED LED HIM TO THE FIRST PLACE WHERE IT SEEMED MOST NATURAL FOR CLASSIC MONSTERS TO HANG OUT... A CEMETERY. THAT WAS EASY - RIP HAD A CEMETERY RIGHT BEHIND HIS HOUSE!
RAIN OR SHINE, HE SEARCHED.
FREQUENTLY, RIP CHECKED INSIDE THE CEMETERY MAUSOLEUM - JUST IN CASE SOME CREATURE WAS RISING FROM ITS CRYPT AND NEEDED HELP GETTING OUT THE LOCKED DOOR.

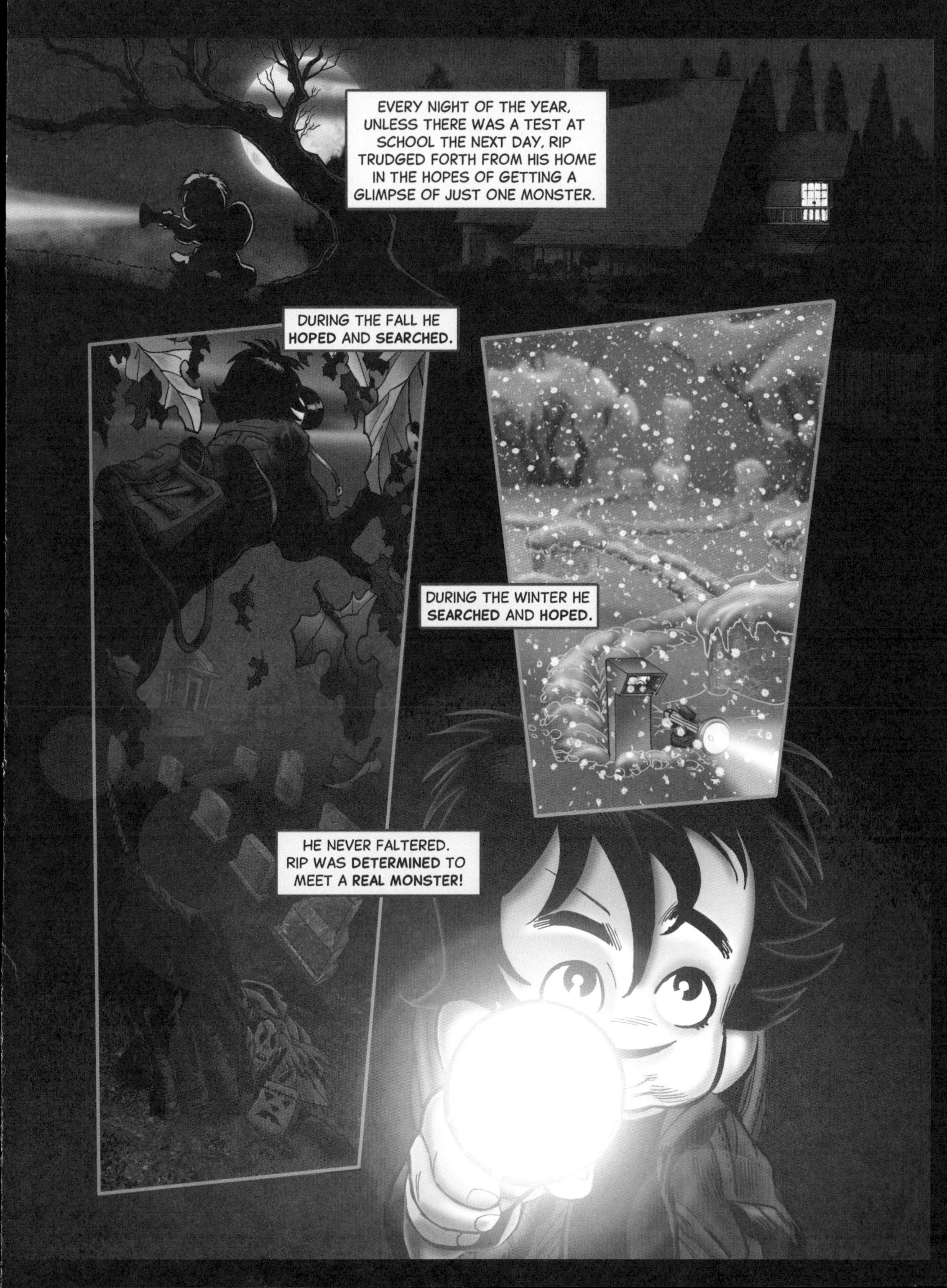
EVERY NIGHT OF THE YEAR, UNLESS THERE WAS A TEST AT SCHOOL THE NEXT DAY, RIP TRUDGED FORTH FROM HIS HOME IN THE HOPES OF GETTING A GLIMPSE OF JUST ONE MONSTER.
DURING THE FALL HE HOPED AND SEARCHED.
DURING THE WINTER HE SEARCHED AND HOPED.
HE NEVER FALTERED. RIP WAS DETERMINED TO MEET A REAL MONSTER!

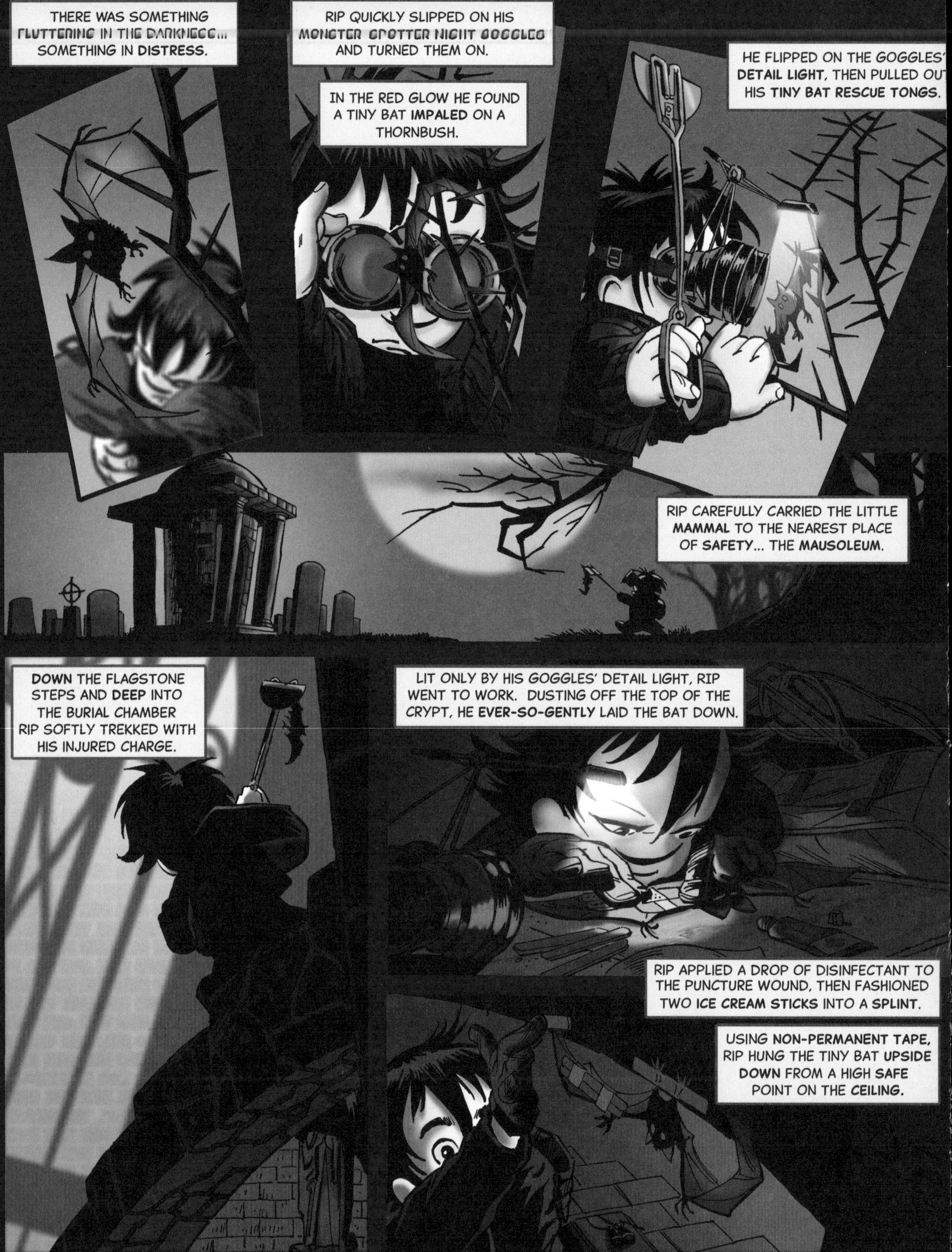
THERE WAS SOMETHING FLUTTERING IN THE DARKNESS... SOMETHING IN DISTRESS.
RIP QUICKLY SLIPPED ON HIS MONSTER SPOTTER NIGHT GOGGLES AND TURNED THEM ON.
IN THE RED GLOW HE FOUND A TINY BAT IMPALED ON A THORNBUSH.
HE FLIPPED ON THE GOGGLES' DETAIL LIGHT, THEN PULLED OUT HIS TINY BAT RESCUE TONGS.
RIP CAREFULLY CARRIED THE LITTLE MAMMAL TO THE NEAREST PLACE OF SAFETY... THE MAUSOLEUM.
DOWN THE FLAGSTONE STEPS AND DEEP INTO THE BURIAL CHAMBER RIP SOFTLY TREKKED WITH HIS INJURED CHARGE.
LIT ONLY BY HIS GOGGLES' DETAIL LIGHT, RIP WENT TO WORK. DUSTING OFF THE TOP OF THE CRYPT, HE EVER-SO-GENTLY LAID THE BAT DOWN.
RIP APPLIED A DROP OF DISINFECTANT TO THE PUNCTURE WOUND, THEN FASHIONED TWO ICE CREAM STICKS INTO A SPLINT.
USING NON-PERMANENT TAPE, RIP HUNG THE TINY BAT UPSIDE DOWN FROM A HIGH SAFE POINT ON THE CEILING.

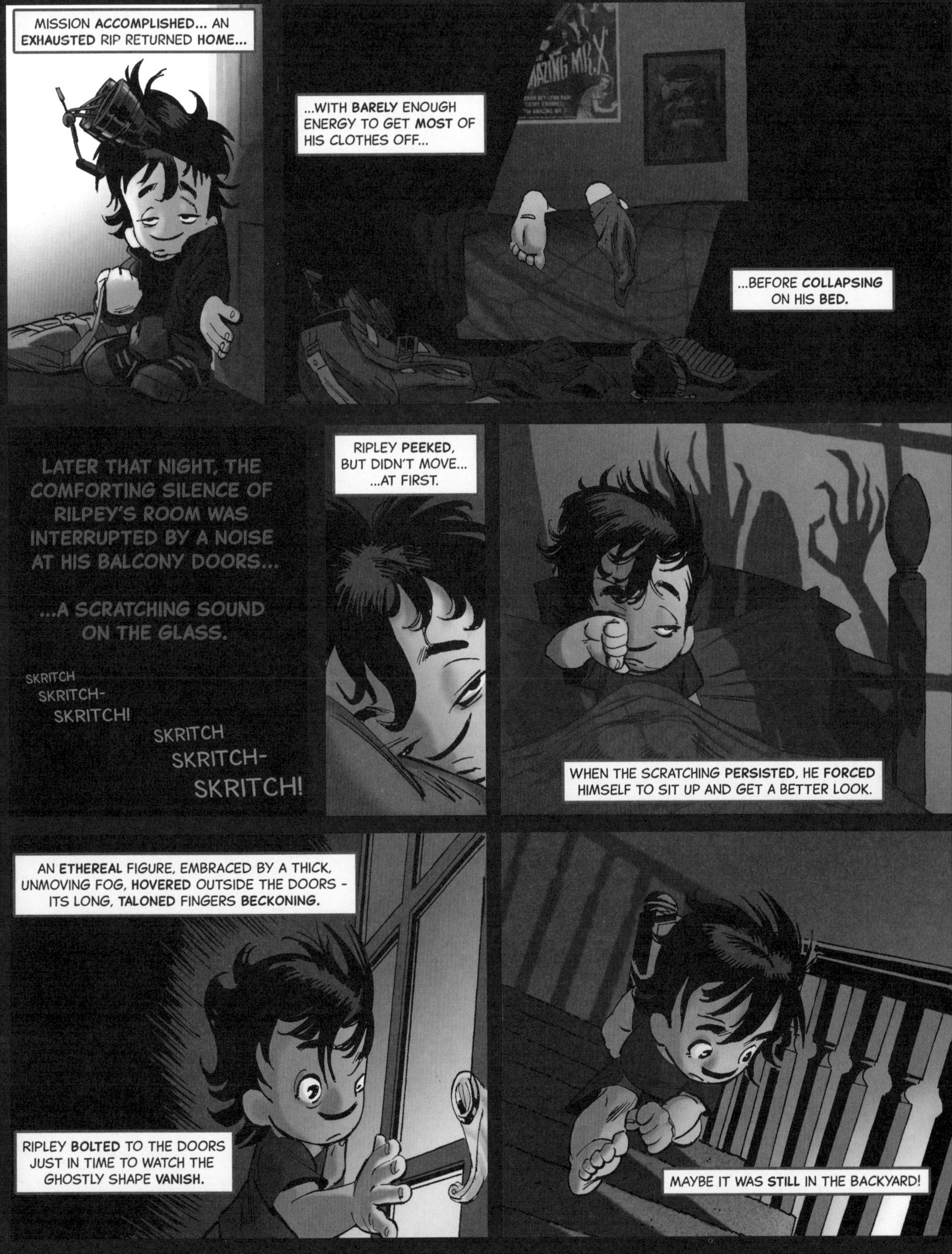

MISSION ACCOMPLISHED... AN EXHAUSTED RIP RETURNED HOME...
...WITH BARELY ENOUGH ENERGY TO GET MOST OF HIS CLOTHES OFF...
...BEFORE COLLAPSING ON HIS BED.
LATER THAT NIGHT, THE COMFORTING SILENCE OF RILPEY'S ROOM WAS INTERRUPTED BY A NOISE AT HIS BALCONY DOORS...
...A SCRATCHING SOUND ON THE GLASS.
SKRITCH SKRITCH-SKRITCH!
SKRITCH SKRITCH-SKRITCH!
RIPLEY PEEKED, BUT DIDN'T MOVE... ...AT FIRST.
WHEN THE SCRATCHING PERSISTED, HE FORCED HIMSELF TO SIT UP AND GET A BETTER LOOK.
AN ETHEREAL FIGURE, EMBRACED BY A THICK, UNMOVING FOG, HOVERED OUTSIDE THE DOORS - ITS LONG, TALONED FINGERS BECKONING.
RIPLEY BOLTED TO THE DOORS JUST IN TIME TO WATCH THE GHOSTLY SHAPE VANISH.
MAYBE IT WAS STILL IN THE BACKYARD!

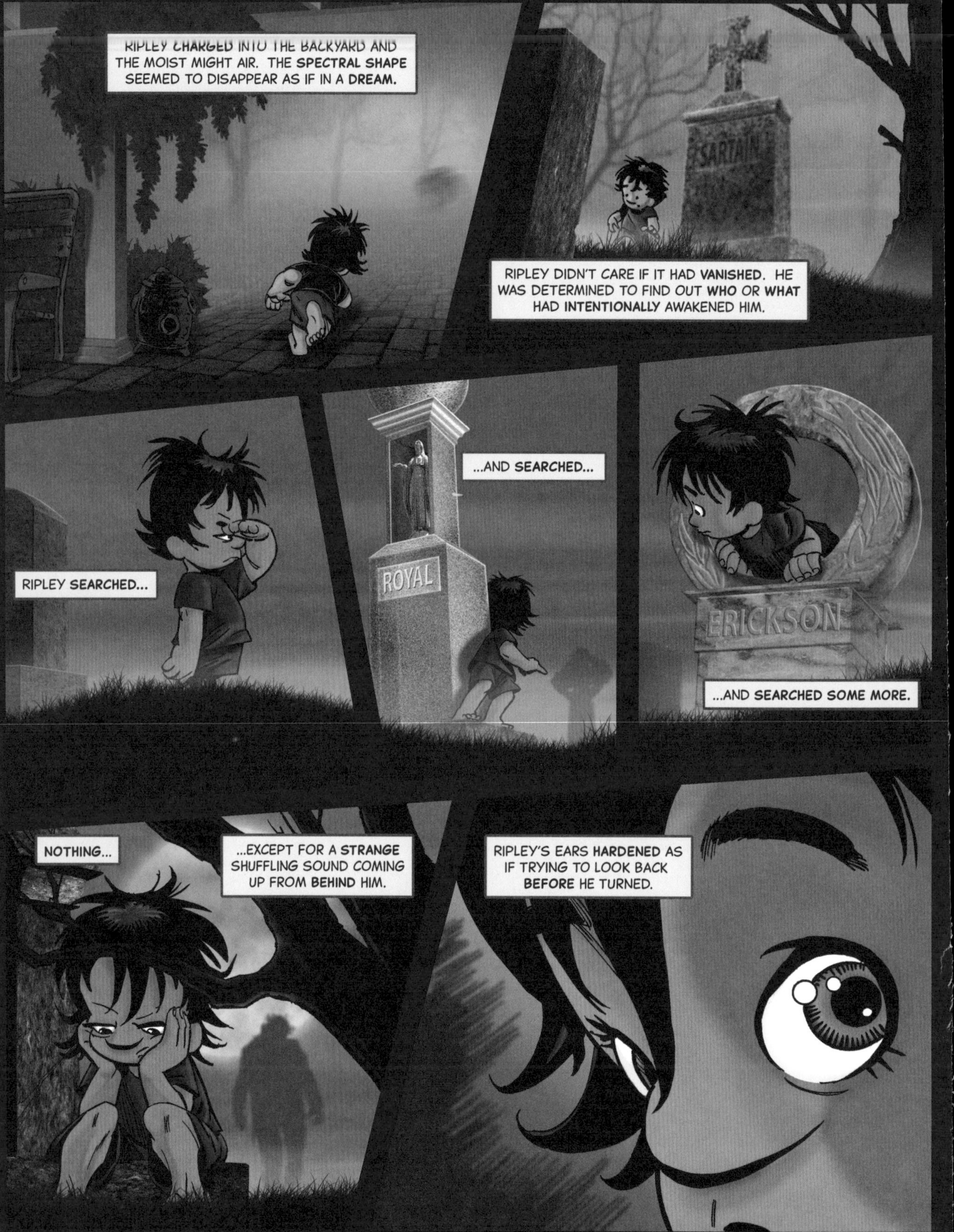
RIPLEY CHARGED INTO THE BACKYARD AND THE MOIST MIGHT AIR. THE SPECTRAL SHAPE SEEMED TO DISAPPEAR AS IF IN A DREAM.
SARTAIN
RIPLEY DIDN'T CARE IF IT HAD VANISHED. HE WAS DETERMINED TO FIND OUT WHO OR WHAT HAD INTENTIONALLY AWAKENED HIM.
RIPLEY SEARCHED...
...AND SEARCHED...
ROYAL
ERICKSON
...AND SEARCHED SOME MORE.
NOTHING...
...EXCEPT FOR A STRANGE SHUFFLING SOUND COMING UP FROM BEHIND HIM.
RIPLEY'S EARS HARDENED AS IF TRYING TO LOOK BACK BEFORE HE TURNED.

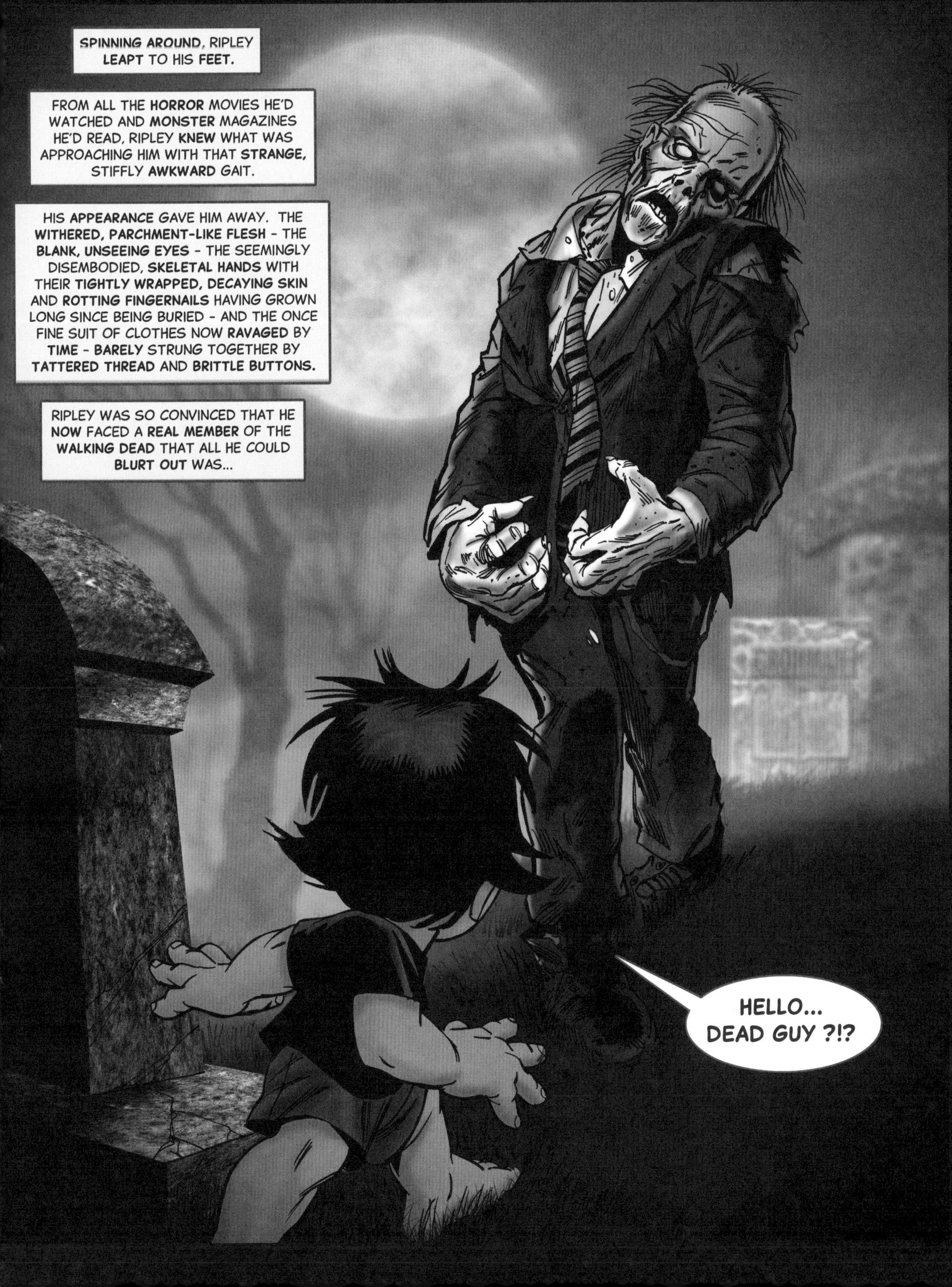
SPINNING AROUND, RIPLEY LEAPT TO HIS FEET.
FROM ALL THE HORROR MOVIES HE'D WATCHED AND MONSTER MAGAZINES HE'D READ, RIPLEY KNEW WHAT WAS APPROACHING HIM WITH THAT STRANGE, STIFFLY AWKWARD GAIT.
HIS APPEARANCE GAVE HIM AWAY. THE WITHERED, PARCHMENT-LIKE FLESH - THE BLANK, UNSEEING EYES - THE SEEMINGLY DISEMBODIED, SKELETAL HANDS WITH THEIR TIGHTLY WRAPPED, DECAYING SKIN AND ROTTING FINGERNAILS HAVING GROWN LONG SINCE BEING BURIED - AND THE ONCE FINE SUIT OF CLOTHES NOW RAVAGED BY TIME - BARELY STRUNG TOGETHER BY TATTERED THREAD AND BRITTLE BUTTONS.
RIPLEY WAS SO CONVINCED THAT HE NOW FACED A REAL MEMBER OF THE WALKING DEAD THAT ALL HE COULD BLURT OUT WAS...
HELLO... DEAD GUY ?!?

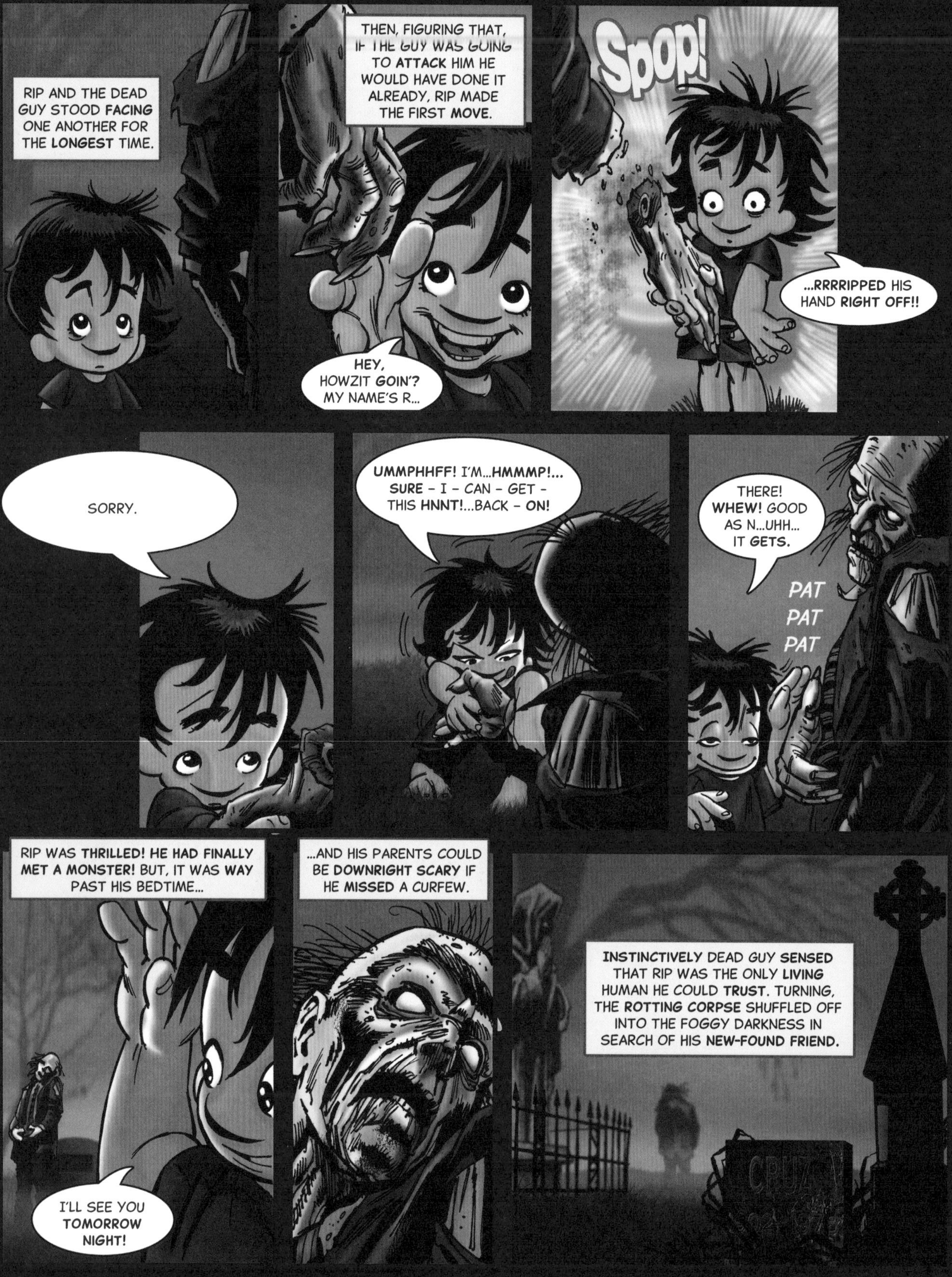
RIP AND THE DEAD GUY STOOD FACING ONE ANOTHER FOR THE LONGEST TIME.
THEN, FIGURING THAT, IF THE GUY WAS GOING TO ATTACK HIM HE WOULD HAVE DONE IT ALREADY, RIP MADE THE FIRST MOVE.
HEY, HOWZIT GOIN'? MY NAME'S R...
SPOP!
...RRRRIPPED HIS HAND RIGHT OFF!!
SORRY.
UMMPHHFF! I'M...HMMMP!... SURE – I – CAN – GET – THIS HNNT!...BACK – ON!
THERE! WHEW! GOOD AS N...UHH... IT GETS.
PAT PAT PAT
RIP WAS THRILLED! HE HAD FINALLY MET A MONSTER! BUT, IT WAS WAY PAST HIS BEDTIME...
I'LL SEE YOU TOMORROW NIGHT!
...AND HIS PARENTS COULD BE DOWNRIGHT SCARY IF HE MISSED A CURFEW.
INSTINCTIVELY DEAD GUY SENSED THAT RIP WAS THE ONLY LIVING HUMAN HE COULD TRUST. TURNING, THE ROTTING CORPSE SHUFFLED OFF INTO THE FOGGY DARKNESS IN SEARCH OF HIS NEW-FOUND FRIEND.

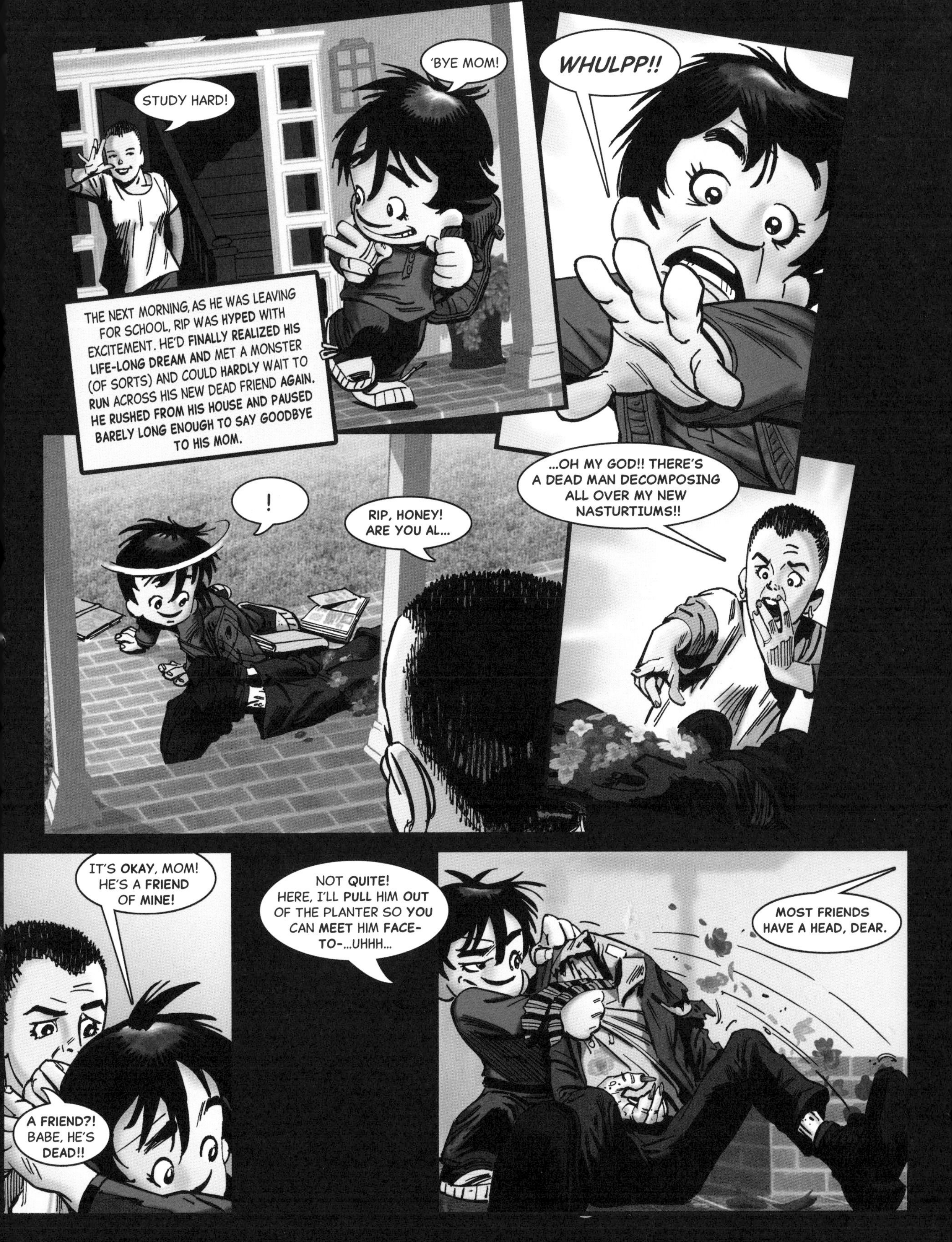
STUDY HARD!
'BYE MOM!
THE NEXT MORNING, AS HE WAS LEAVING FOR SCHOOL, RIP WAS HYPED WITH EXCITEMENT. HE'D FINALLY REALIZED HIS LIFE-LONG DREAM AND MET A MONSTER (OF SORTS) AND COULD HARDLY WAIT TO RUN ACROSS HIS NEW DEAD FRIEND AGAIN. HE RUSHED FROM HIS HOUSE AND PAUSED BARELY LONG ENOUGH TO SAY GOODBYE TO HIS MOM.
WHULPP!!
!
RIP, HONEY! ARE YOU AL...
...OH MY GOD!! THERE'S A DEAD MAN DECOMPOSING ALL OVER MY NEW NASTURTIUMS!!
IT'S OKAY, MOM! HE'S A FRIEND OF MINE!
A FRIEND?! BABE, HE'S DEAD!!
NOT QUITE! HERE, I'LL PULL HIM OUT OF THE PLANTER SO YOU CAN MEET HIM FACE-TO-...UHHH...
MOST FRIENDS HAVE A HEAD, DEAR.

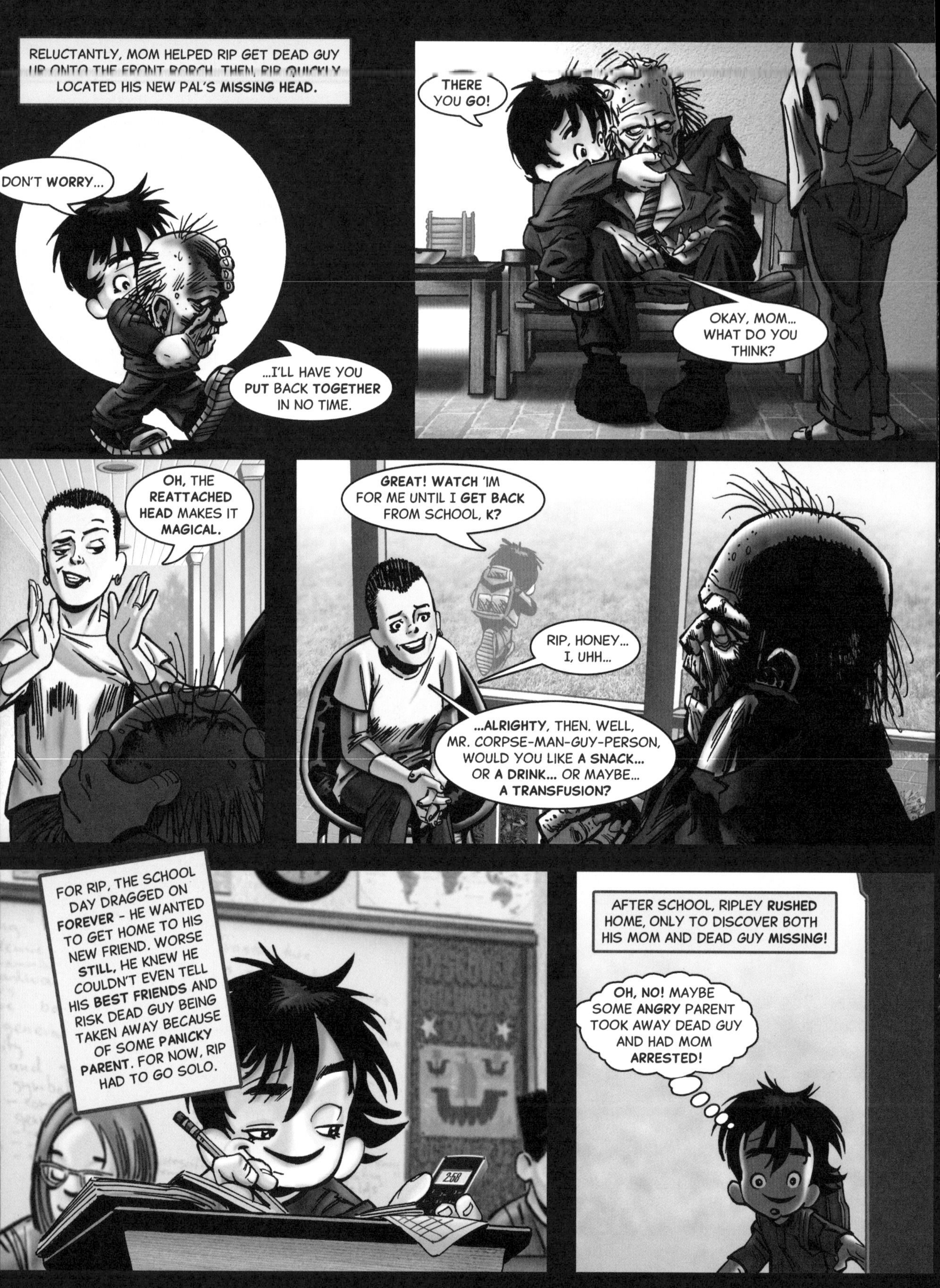
RELUCTANTLY, MOM HELPED RIP GET DEAD GUY UP ONTO THE FRONT PORCH. THEN, RIP QUICKLY LOCATED HIS NEW PAL'S MISSING HEAD.
DON'T WORRY...
...I'LL HAVE YOU PUT BACK TOGETHER IN NO TIME.
THERE YOU GO!
OKAY, MOM... WHAT DO YOU THINK?
OH, THE REATTACHED HEAD MAKES IT MAGICAL.
GREAT! WATCH 'IM FOR ME UNTIL I GET BACK FROM SCHOOL, K?
RIP, HONEY... I, UHH...
...ALRIGHTY, THEN. WELL, MR. CORPSE-MAN-GUY-PERSON, WOULD YOU LIKE A SNACK... OR A DRINK... OR MAYBE... A TRANSFUSION?
FOR RIP, THE SCHOOL DAY DRAGGED ON FOREVER - HE WANTED TO GET HOME TO HIS NEW FRIEND. WORSE STILL, HE KNEW HE COULDN'T EVEN TELL HIS BEST FRIENDS AND RISK DEAD GUY BEING TAKEN AWAY BECAUSE OF SOME PANICKY PARENT. FOR NOW, RIP HAD TO GO SOLO.
2:58
AFTER SCHOOL, RIPLEY RUSHED HOME, ONLY TO DISCOVER BOTH HIS MOM AND DEAD GUY MISSING!
OH, NO! MAYBE SOME ANGRY PARENT TOOK AWAY DEAD GUY AND HAD MOM ARRESTED!

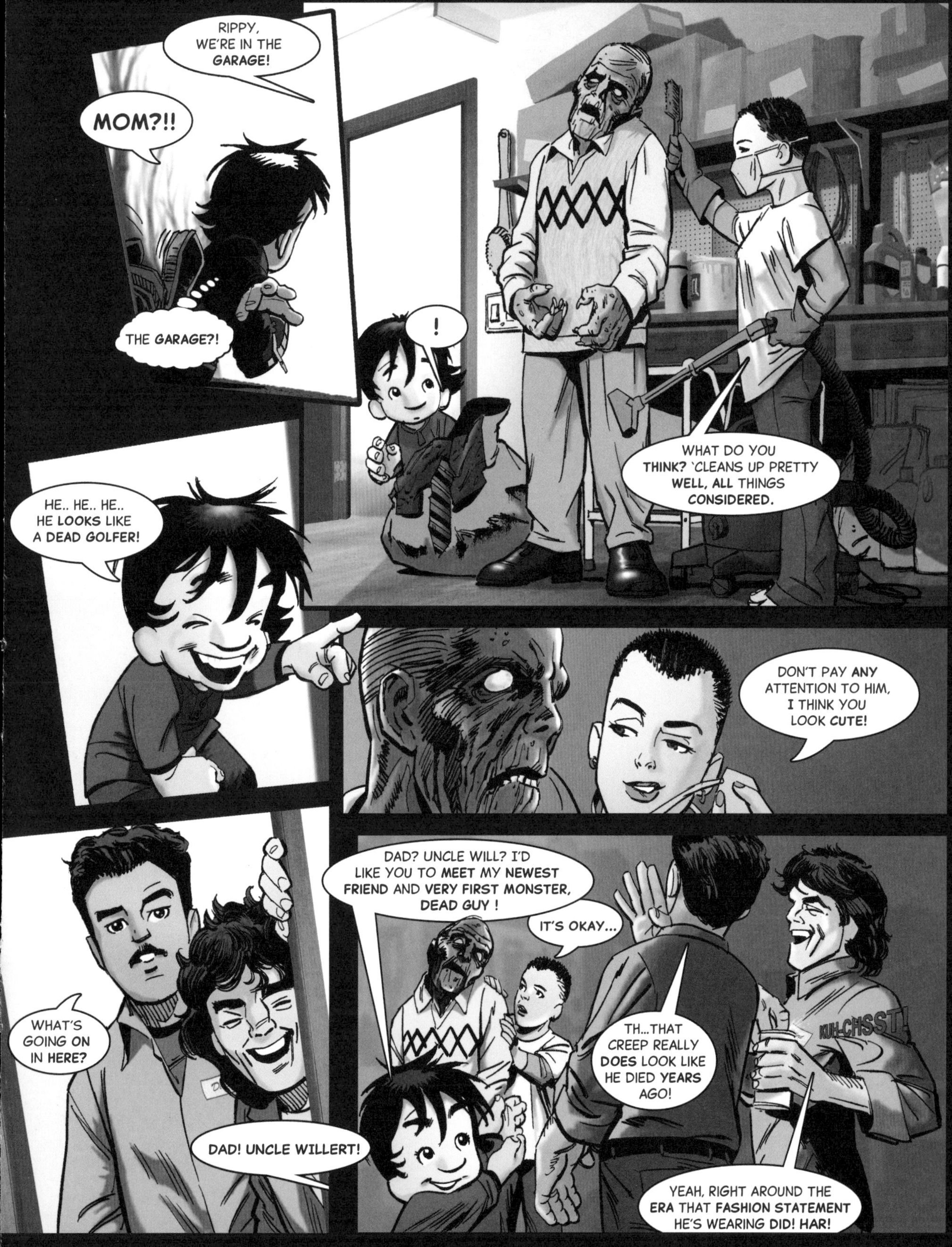
RIPPY, WE'RE IN THE GARAGE!
MOM?!!
THE GARAGE?!
!
WHAT DO YOU THINK? 'CLEANS UP PRETTY WELL, ALL THINGS CONSIDERED.
HE.. HE.. HE.. HE LOOKS LIKE A DEAD GOLFER!
DON'T PAY ANY ATTENTION TO HIM, I THINK YOU LOOK CUTE!
WHAT'S GOING ON IN HERE?
DAD! UNCLE WILLERT!
DAD? UNCLE WILL? I'D LIKE YOU TO MEET MY NEWEST FRIEND AND VERY FIRST MONSTER, DEAD GUY !
IT'S OKAY...
TH...THAT CREEP REALLY DOES LOOK LIKE HE DIED YEARS AGO!
KUH-CHSST!
YEAH, RIGHT AROUND THE ERA THAT FASHION STATEMENT HE'S WEARING DID! HAR!

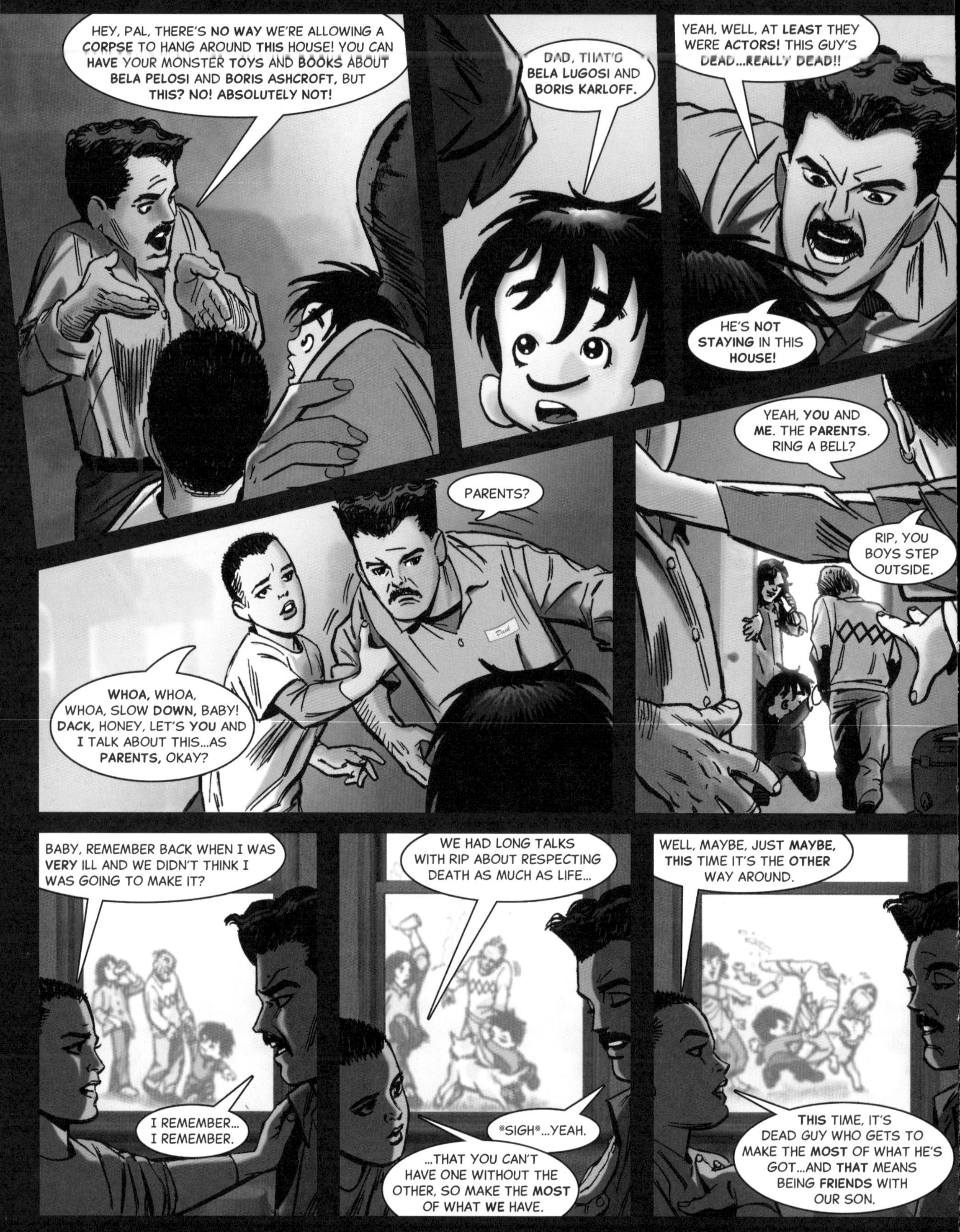
HEY, PAL, THERE'S NO WAY WE'RE ALLOWING A CORPSE TO HANG AROUND THIS HOUSE! YOU CAN HAVE YOUR MONSTER TOYS AND BOOKS ABOUT BELA PELOSI AND BORIS ASHCROFT, BUT THIS? NO! ABSOLUTELY NOT!
DAD, THAT'S BELA LUGOSI AND BORIS KARLOFF.
YEAH, WELL, AT LEAST THEY WERE ACTORS! THIS GUY'S DEAD...REALLY DEAD!!
HE'S NOT STAYING IN THIS HOUSE!
WHOA, WHOA, WHOA, SLOW DOWN, BABY! DACK, HONEY, LET'S YOU AND I TALK ABOUT THIS...AS PARENTS, OKAY?
PARENTS?
YEAH, YOU AND ME. THE PARENTS. RING A BELL?
RIP, YOU BOYS STEP OUTSIDE.
BABY, REMEMBER BACK WHEN I WAS VERY ILL AND WE DIDN'T THINK I WAS GOING TO MAKE IT?
I REMEMBER... I REMEMBER.
WE HAD LONG TALKS WITH RIP ABOUT RESPECTING DEATH AS MUCH AS LIFE...
...THAT YOU CAN'T HAVE ONE WITHOUT THE OTHER, SO MAKE THE MOST OF WHAT WE HAVE.
SIGH...YEAH.
WELL, MAYBE, JUST MAYBE, THIS TIME IT'S THE OTHER WAY AROUND.
THIS TIME, IT'S DEAD GUY WHO GETS TO MAKE THE MOST OF WHAT HE'S GOT...AND THAT MEANS BEING FRIENDS WITH OUR SON.

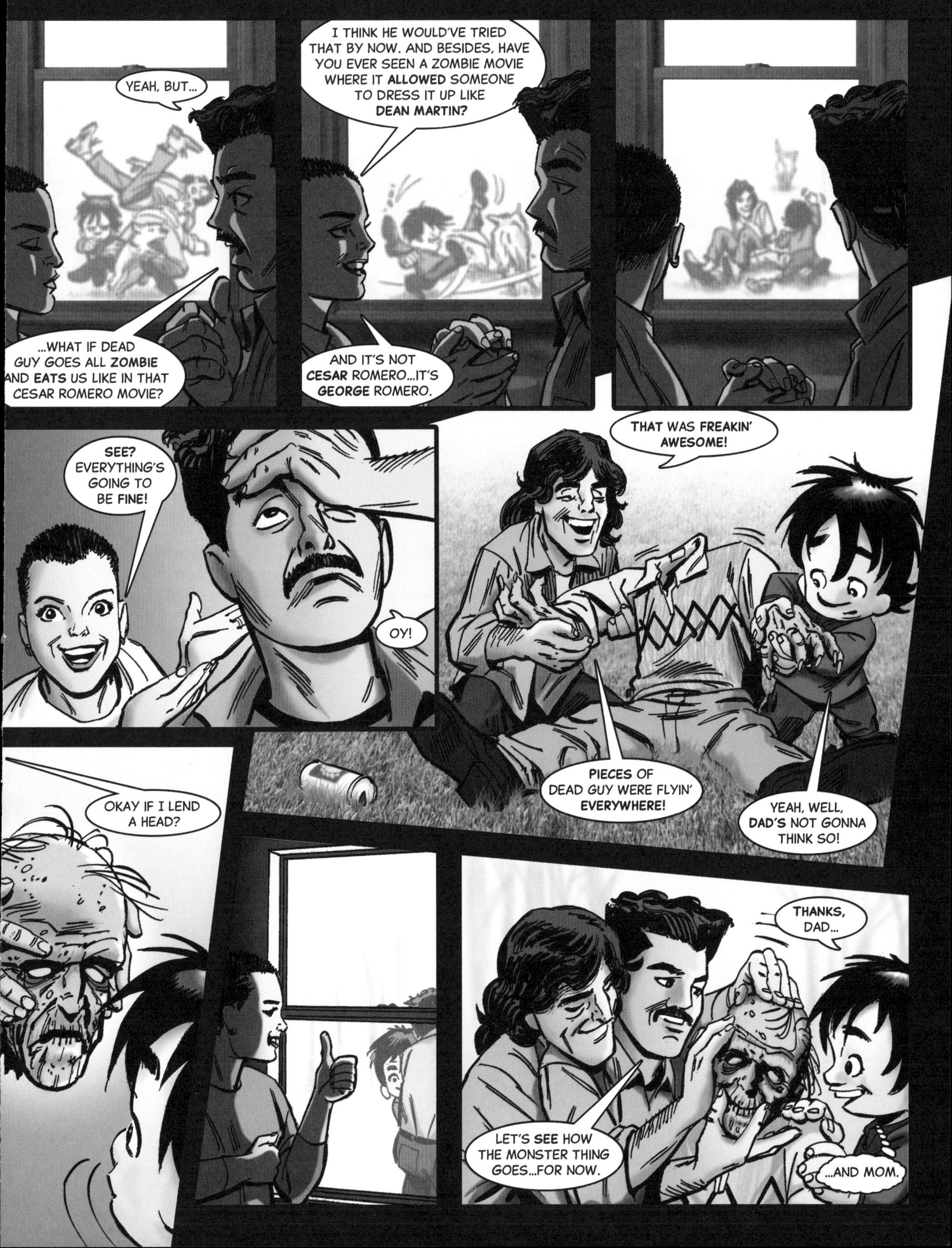
YEAH, BUT...
...WHAT IF DEAD GUY GOES ALL ZOMBIE AND EATS US LIKE IN THAT CESAR ROMERO MOVIE?
I THINK HE WOULD'VE TRIED THAT BY NOW. AND BESIDES, HAVE YOU EVER SEEN A ZOMBIE MOVIE WHERE IT ALLOWED SOMEONE TO DRESS IT UP LIKE DEAN MARTIN?
AND IT'S NOT CESAR ROMERO...IT'S GEORGE ROMERO.
SEE? EVERYTHING'S GOING TO BE FINE!
OY!
THAT WAS FREAKIN' AWESOME!
PIECES OF DEAD GUY WERE FLYIN' EVERYWHERE!
YEAH, WELL, DAD'S NOT GONNA THINK SO!
OKAY IF I LEND A HEAD?
THANKS, DAD...
LET'S SEE HOW THE MONSTER THING GOES...FOR NOW.
...AND MOM.

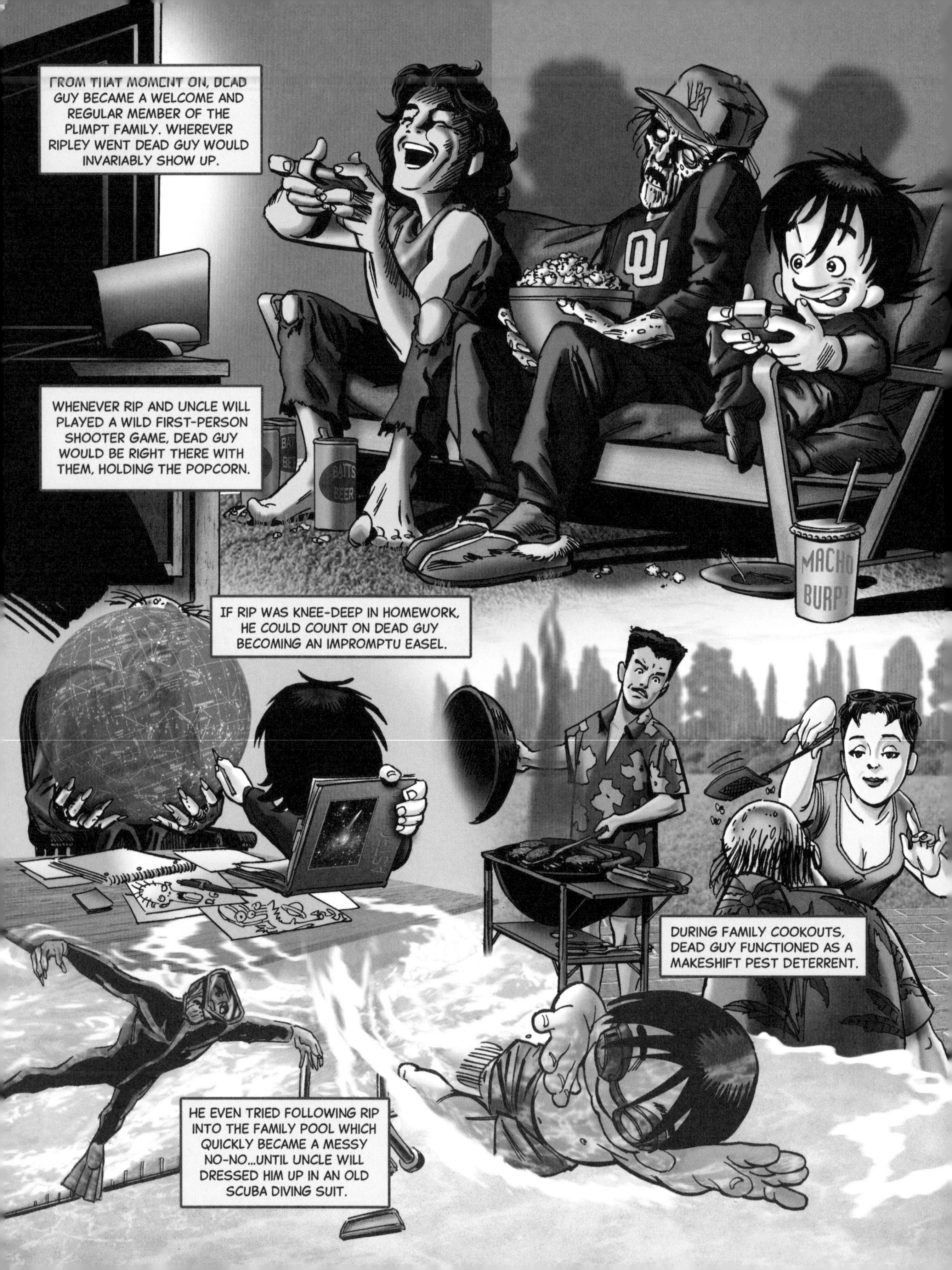
FROM THAT MOMENT ON, DEAD GUY BECAME A WELCOME AND REGULAR MEMBER OF THE PLIMPT FAMILY. WHEREVER RIPLEY WENT DEAD GUY WOULD INVARIABLY SHOW UP.
WHENEVER RIP AND UNCLE WILL PLAYED A WILD FIRST-PERSON SHOOTER GAME, DEAD GUY WOULD BE RIGHT THERE WITH THEM, HOLDING THE POPCORN.
BATTS BEER
MACHO BURP!
IF RIP WAS KNEE-DEEP IN HOMEWORK, HE COULD COUNT ON DEAD GUY BECOMING AN IMPROMPTU EASEL.
DURING FAMILY COOKOUTS, DEAD GUY FUNCTIONED AS A MAKESHIFT PEST DETERRENT.
HE EVEN TRIED FOLLOWING RIP INTO THE FAMILY POOL WHICH QUICKLY BECAME A MESSY NO-NO...UNTIL UNCLE WILL DRESSED HIM UP IN AN OLD SCUBA DIVING SUIT.

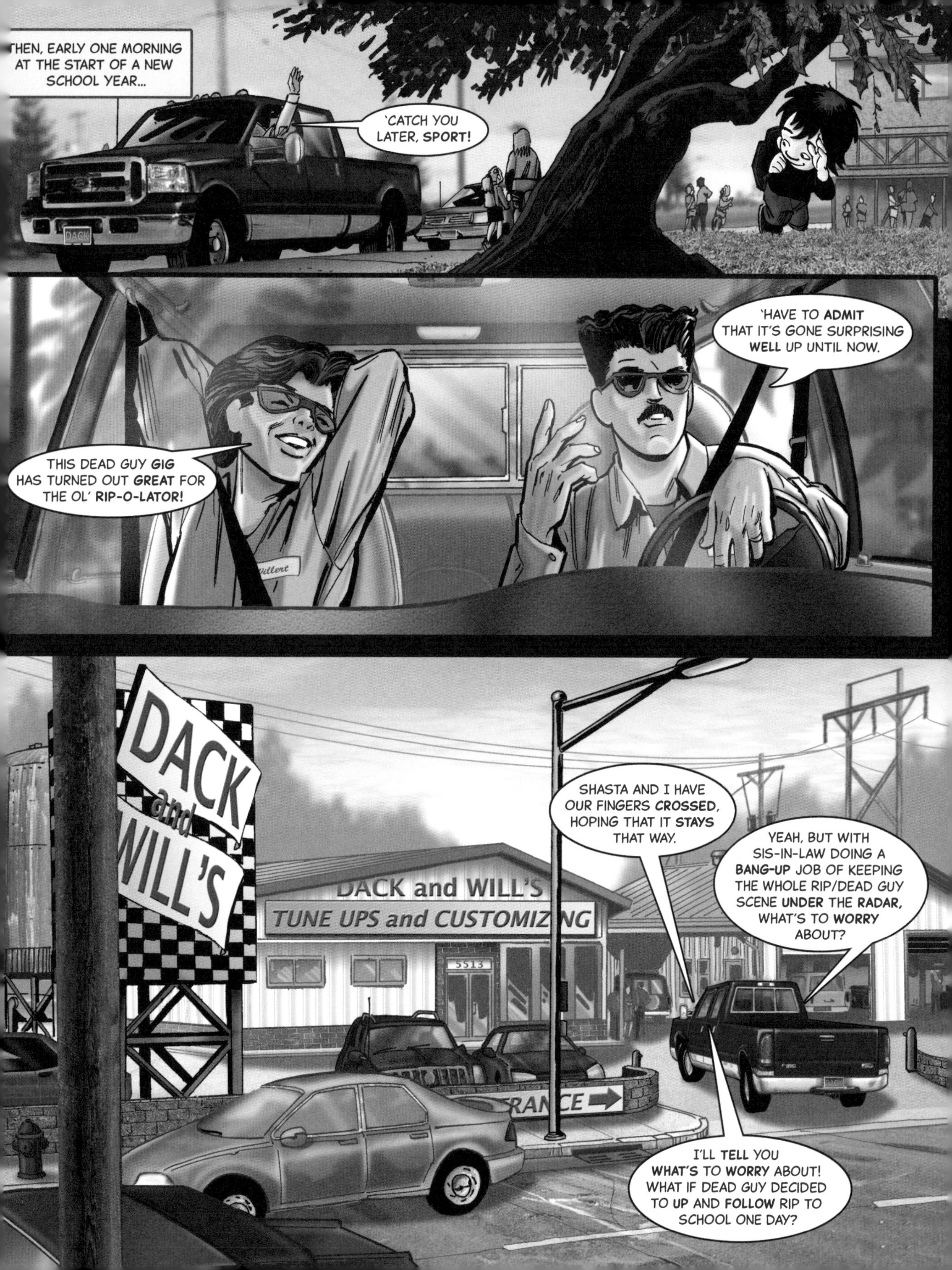
THEN, EARLY ONE MORNING AT THE START OF A NEW SCHOOL YEAR...
'CATCH YOU LATER, SPORT!
DACK
'HAVE TO ADMIT THAT IT'S GONE SURPRISING WELL UP UNTIL NOW.
THIS DEAD GUY GIG HAS TURNED OUT GREAT FOR THE OL' RIP-O-LATOR!
Willert
DACK and WILL'S
SHASTA AND I HAVE OUR FINGERS CROSSED, HOPING THAT IT STAYS THAT WAY.
DACK and WILL'S
TUNE UPS and CUSTOMIZ NG
5513
YEAH, BUT WITH SIS-IN-LAW DOING A BANG-UP JOB OF KEEPING THE WHOLE RIP/DEAD GUY SCENE UNDER THE RADAR, WHAT'S TO WORRY ABOUT?
RANCE
I'LL TELL YOU WHAT'S TO WORRY ABOUT! WHAT IF DEAD GUY DECIDED TO UP AND FOLLOW RIP TO SCHOOL ONE DAY?

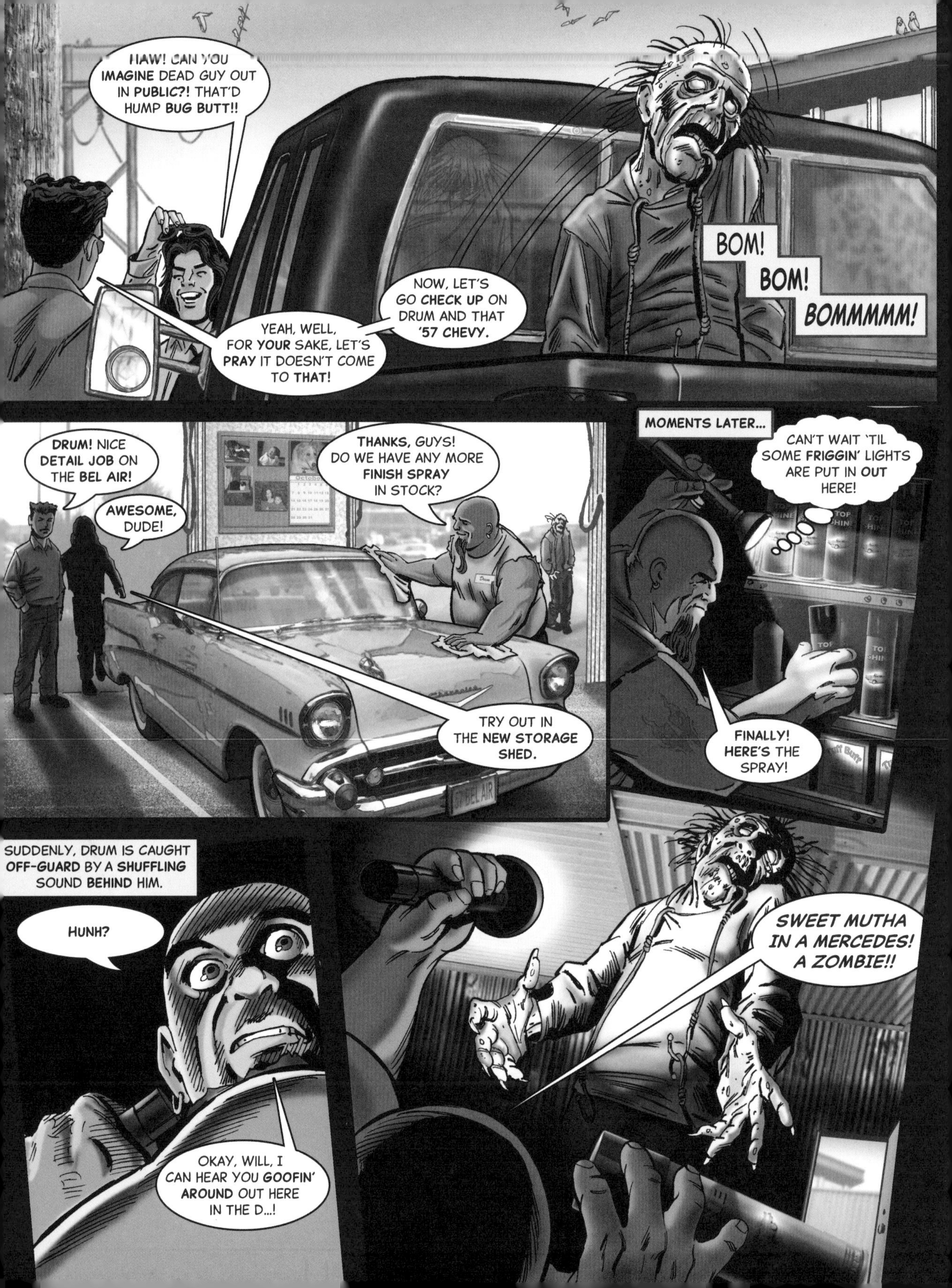
HAW! CAN YOU IMAGINE DEAD GUY OUT IN PUBLIC?! THAT'D HUMP BUG BUTT!!
YEAH, WELL, FOR YOUR SAKE, LET'S PRAY IT DOESN'T COME TO THAT!
NOW, LET'S GO CHECK UP ON DRUM AND THAT '57 CHEVY.
BOM!
BOM!
BOMMMMM!
DRUM! NICE DETAIL JOB ON THE BEL AIR!
AWESOME, DUDE!
THANKS, GUYS! DO WE HAVE ANY MORE FINISH SPRAY IN STOCK?
TRY OUT IN THE NEW STORAGE SHED.
MOMENTS LATER...
CAN'T WAIT 'TIL SOME FRIGGIN' LIGHTS ARE PUT IN OUT HERE!
FINALLY! HERE'S THE SPRAY!
SUDDENLY, DRUM IS CAUGHT OFF-GUARD BY A SHUFFLING SOUND BEHIND HIM.
HUNH?
OKAY, WILL, I CAN HEAR YOU GOOFIN' AROUND OUT HERE IN THE D...!
SWEET MUTHA IN A MERCEDES! A ZOMBIE!!

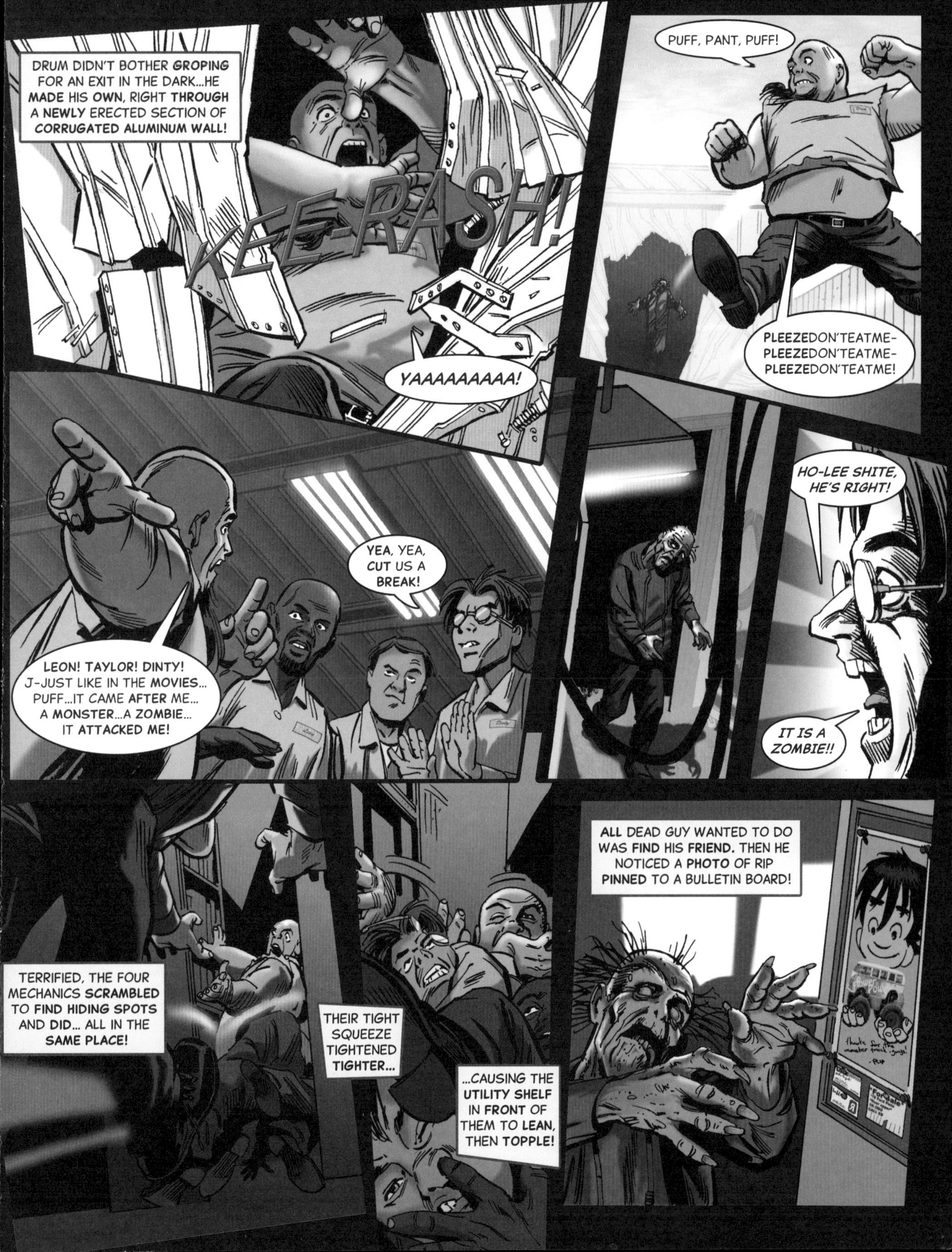
DRUM DIDN'T BOTHER GROPING FOR AN EXIT IN THE DARK...HE MADE HIS OWN, RIGHT THROUGH A NEWLY ERECTED SECTION OF CORRUGATED ALUMINUM WALL!
KEE-RASH!
YAAAAAAAAA!
PUFF, PANT, PUFF!
PLEEZEDON'TEATME-PLEEZEDON'TEATME-PLEEZEDON'TEATME!
LEON! TAYLOR! DINTY! J-JUST LIKE IN THE MOVIES... PUFF...IT CAME AFTER ME... A MONSTER...A ZOMBIE... IT ATTACKED ME!
YEA, YEA, CUT US A BREAK!
HO-LEE SHITE, HE'S RIGHT!
IT IS A ZOMBIE!!
TERRIFIED, THE FOUR MECHANICS SCRAMBLED TO FIND HIDING SPOTS AND DID... ALL IN THE SAME PLACE!
THEIR TIGHT SQUEEZE TIGHTENED TIGHTER...
...CAUSING THE UTILITY SHELF IN FRONT OF THEM TO LEAN, THEN TOPPLE!
ALL DEAD GUY WANTED TO DO WAS FIND HIS FRIEND. THEN HE NOTICED A PHOTO OF RIP PINNED TO A BULLETIN BOARD!

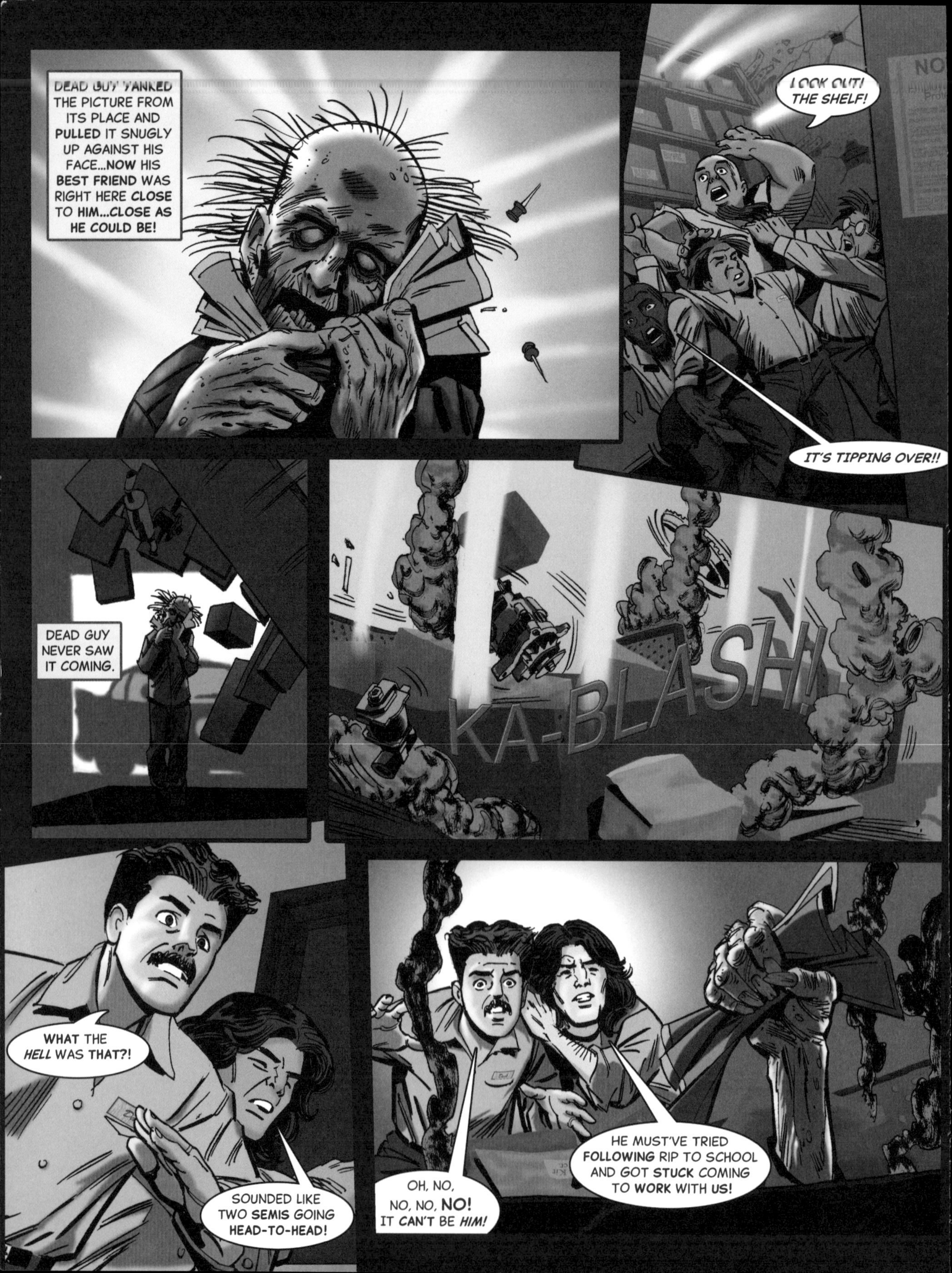

DEAD GUY YANKED THE PICTURE FROM ITS PLACE AND PULLED IT SNUGLY UP AGAINST HIS FACE...NOW HIS BEST FRIEND WAS RIGHT HERE CLOSE TO HIM...CLOSE AS HE COULD BE!
LOOK OUT! THE SHELF!
IT'S TIPPING OVER!!
DEAD GUY NEVER SAW IT COMING.
KA-BLASH!
WHAT THE HELL WAS THAT?!
SOUNDED LIKE TWO SEMIS GOING HEAD-TO-HEAD!
OH, NO, NO, NO, NO! IT CAN'T BE HIM!
HE MUST'VE TRIED FOLLOWING RIP TO SCHOOL AND GOT STUCK COMING TO WORK WITH US!

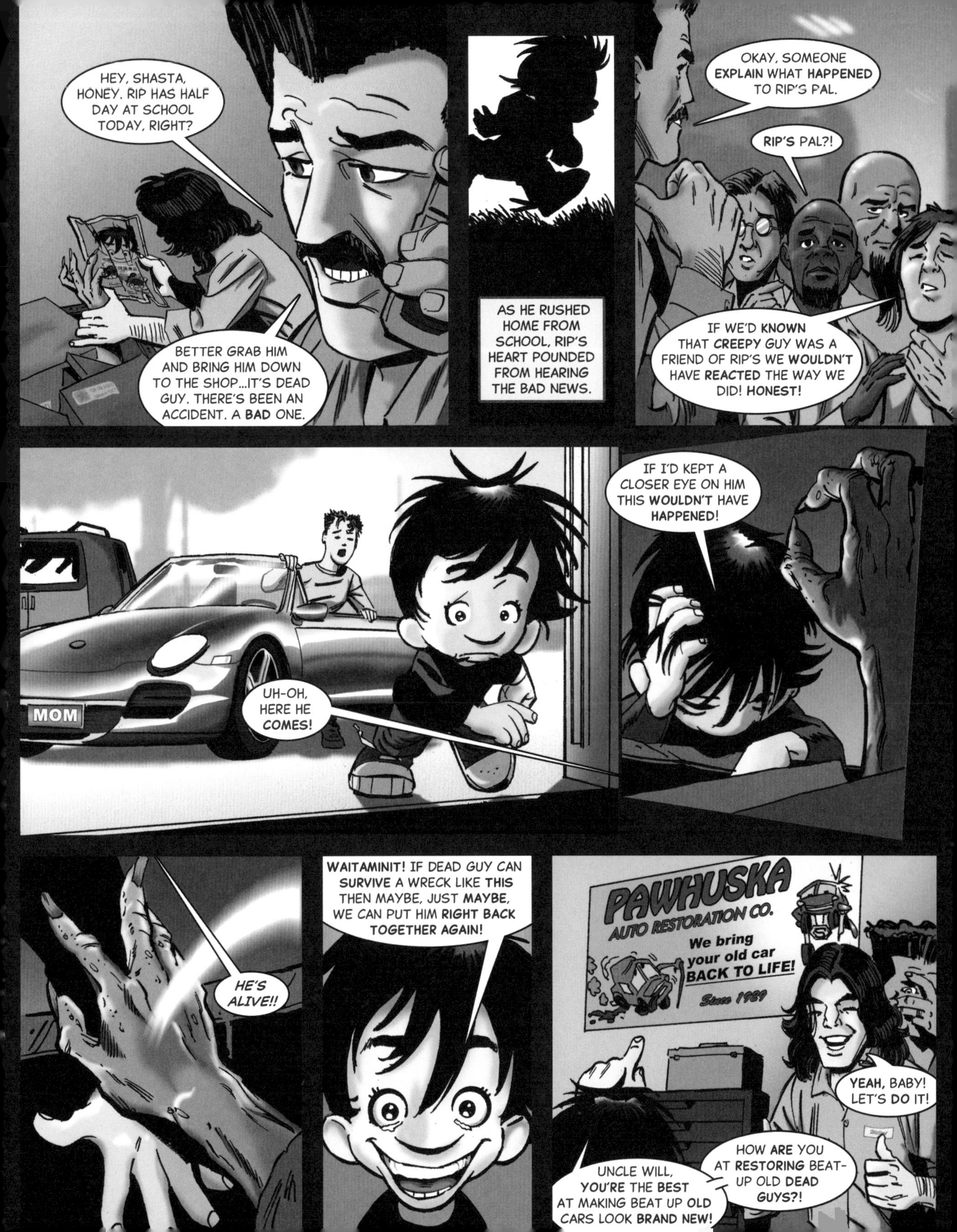
HEY, SHASTA, HONEY. RIP HAS HALF DAY AT SCHOOL TODAY, RIGHT?
BETTER GRAB HIM AND BRING HIM DOWN TO THE SHOP...IT'S DEAD GUY. THERE'S BEEN AN ACCIDENT. A BAD ONE.
AS HE RUSHED HOME FROM SCHOOL, RIP'S HEART POUNDED FROM HEARING THE BAD NEWS.
OKAY, SOMEONE EXPLAIN WHAT HAPPENED TO RIP'S PAL.
RIP'S PAL?!
IF WE'D KNOWN THAT CREEPY GUY WAS A FRIEND OF RIP'S WE WOULDN'T HAVE REACTED THE WAY WE DID! HONEST!
MOM
UH-OH, HERE HE COMES!
IF I'D KEPT A CLOSER EYE ON HIM THIS WOULDN'T HAVE HAPPENED!
HE'S ALIVE!!
WAITAMINIT! IF DEAD GUY CAN SURVIVE A WRECK LIKE THIS THEN MAYBE, JUST MAYBE, WE CAN PUT HIM RIGHT BACK TOGETHER AGAIN!
PAWHUSKA AUTO RESTORATION CO.
We bring your old car BACK TO LIFE!
Since 1989
YEAH, BABY! LET'S DO IT!
UNCLE WILL, YOU'RE THE BEST AT MAKING BEAT UP OLD CARS LOOK BRAND NEW!
HOW ARE YOU AT RESTORING BEAT-UP OLD DEAD GUYS?!

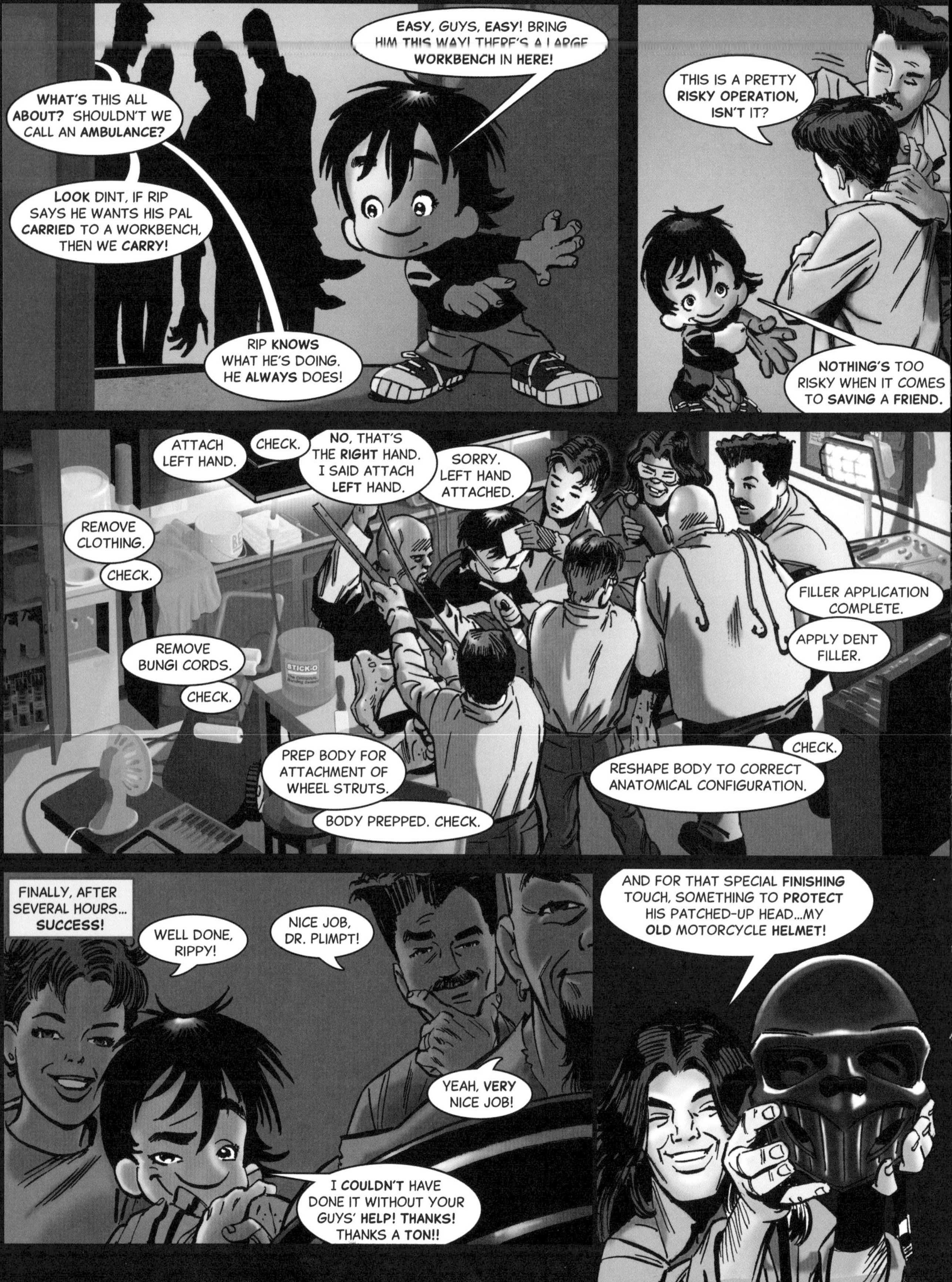
WHAT'S THIS ALL ABOUT? SHOULDN'T WE CALL AN AMBULANCE?
EASY, GUYS, EASY! BRING HIM THIS WAY! THERE'S A LARGE WORKBENCH IN HERE!
LOOK DINT, IF RIP SAYS HE WANTS HIS PAL CARRIED TO A WORKBENCH, THEN WE CARRY!
RIP KNOWS WHAT HE'S DOING. HE ALWAYS DOES!
THIS IS A PRETTY RISKY OPERATION, ISN'T IT?
NOTHING'S TOO RISKY WHEN IT COMES TO SAVING A FRIEND.
ATTACH LEFT HAND.
CHECK.
NO, THAT'S THE RIGHT HAND. I SAID ATTACH LEFT HAND.
SORRY. LEFT HAND ATTACHED.
REMOVE CLOTHING.
CHECK.
REMOVE BUNGI CORDS.
CHECK.
STICK-O
PREP BODY FOR ATTACHMENT OF WHEEL STRUTS.
BODY PREPPED. CHECK.
RESHAPE BODY TO CORRECT ANATOMICAL CONFIGURATION.
CHECK.
APPLY DENT FILLER.
FILLER APPLICATION COMPLETE.
FINALLY, AFTER SEVERAL HOURS... SUCCESS!
WELL DONE, RIPPY!
NICE JOB, DR. PLIMPT!
YEAH, VERY NICE JOB!
I COULDN'T HAVE DONE IT WITHOUT YOUR GUYS' HELP! THANKS! THANKS A TON!!
AND FOR THAT SPECIAL FINISHING TOUCH, SOMETHING TO PROTECT HIS PATCHED-UP HEAD...MY OLD MOTORCYCLE HELMET!

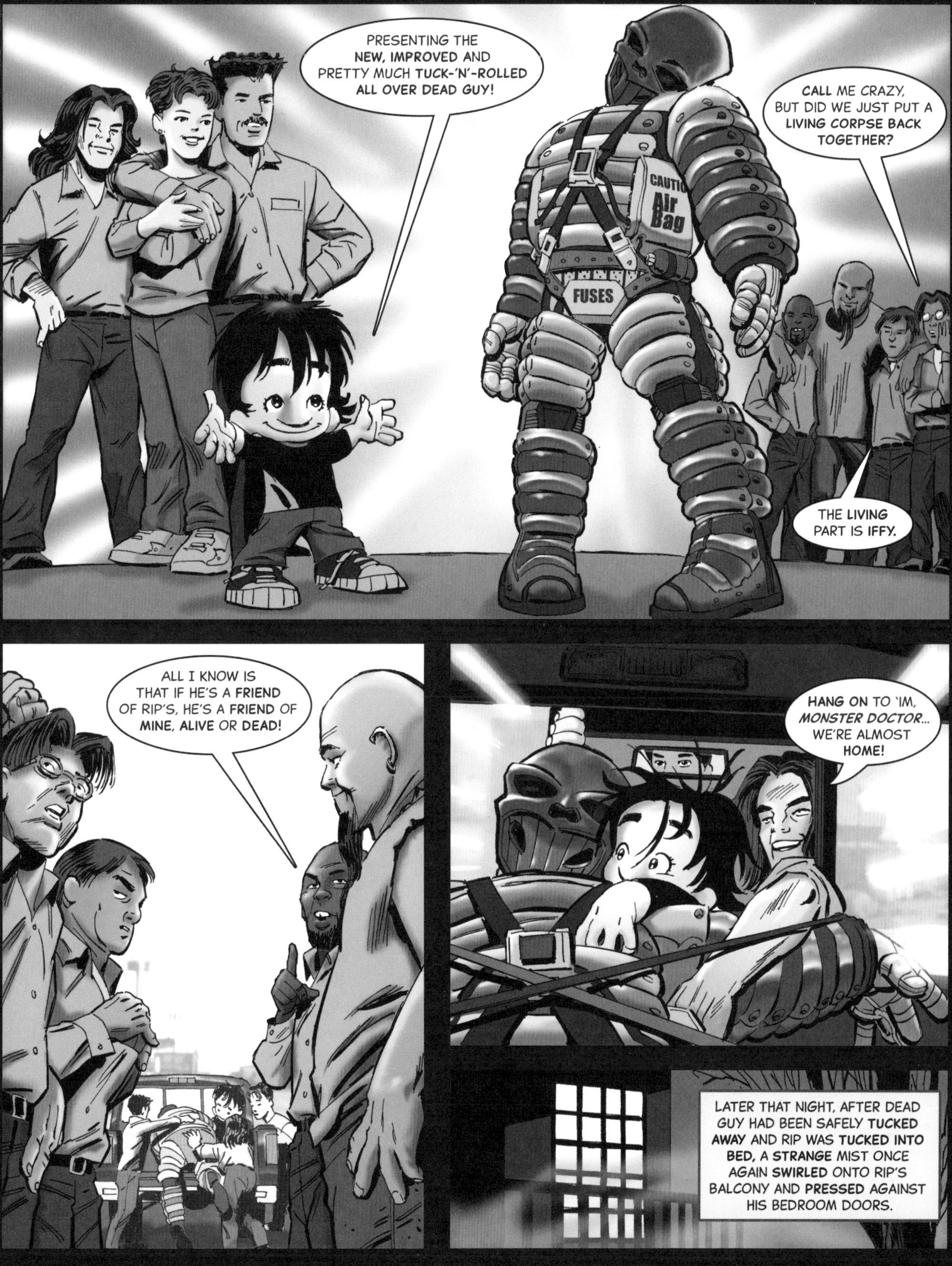
PRESENTING THE NEW, IMPROVED AND PRETTY MUCH TUCK-'N'-ROLLED ALL OVER DEAD GUY!
CAUTION Air Bag
FUSES
CALL ME CRAZY, BUT DID WE JUST PUT A LIVING CORPSE BACK TOGETHER?
THE LIVING PART IS IFFY.
ALL I KNOW IS THAT IF HE'S A FRIEND OF RIP'S, HE'S A FRIEND OF MINE, ALIVE OR DEAD!
HANG ON TO 'IM, MONSTER DOCTOR... WE'RE ALMOST HOME!
LATER THAT NIGHT, AFTER DEAD GUY HAD BEEN SAFELY TUCKED AWAY AND RIP WAS TUCKED INTO BED, A STRANGE MIST ONCE AGAIN SWIRLED ONTO RIP'S BALCONY AND PRESSED AGAINST HIS BEDROOM DOORS.

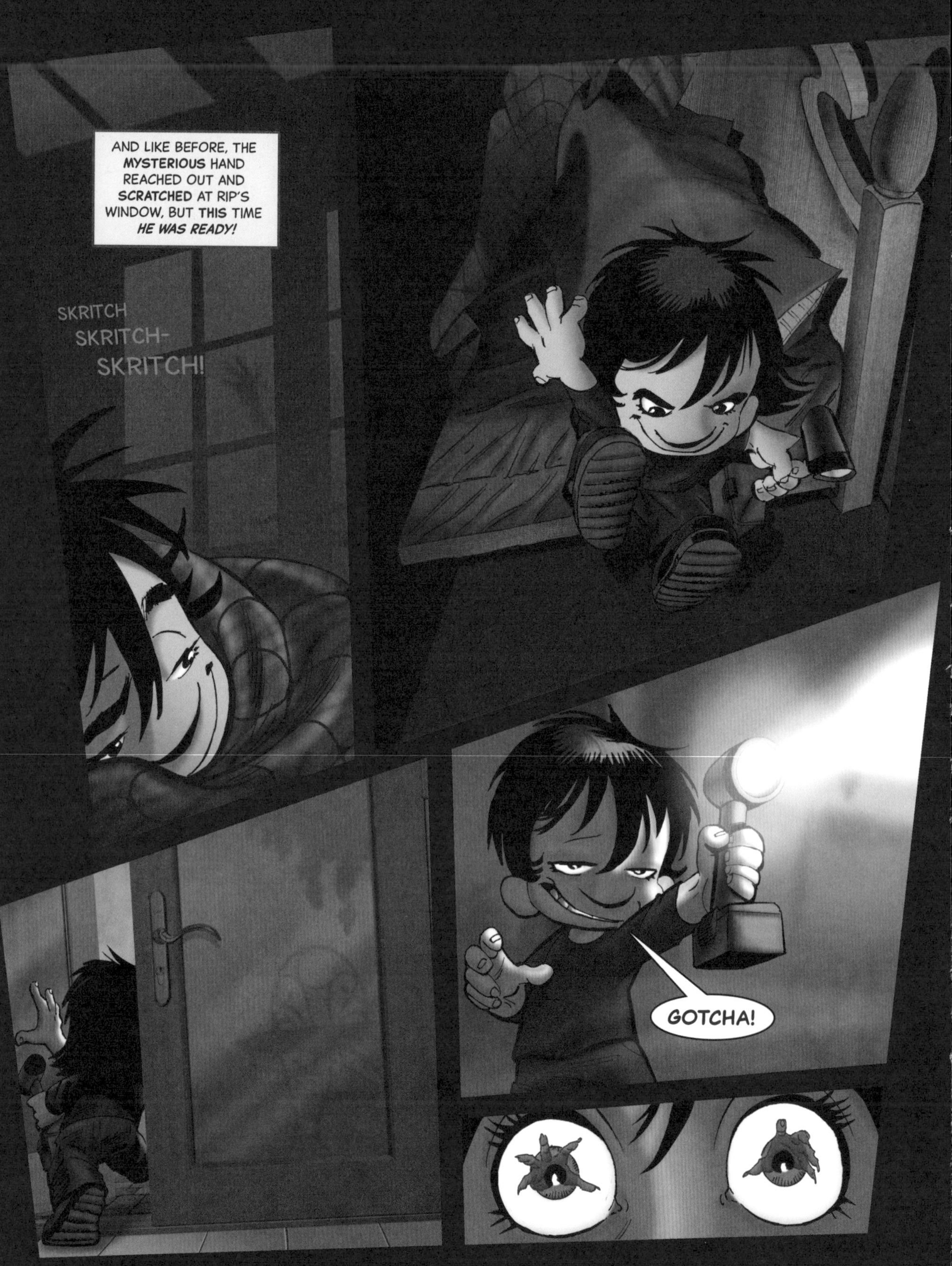
AND LIKE BEFORE, THE MYSTERIOUS HAND REACHED OUT AND SCRATCHED AT RIP'S WINDOW, BUT THIS TIME HE WAS READY!
SKRITCH SKRITCH-SKRITCH!
GOTCHA!

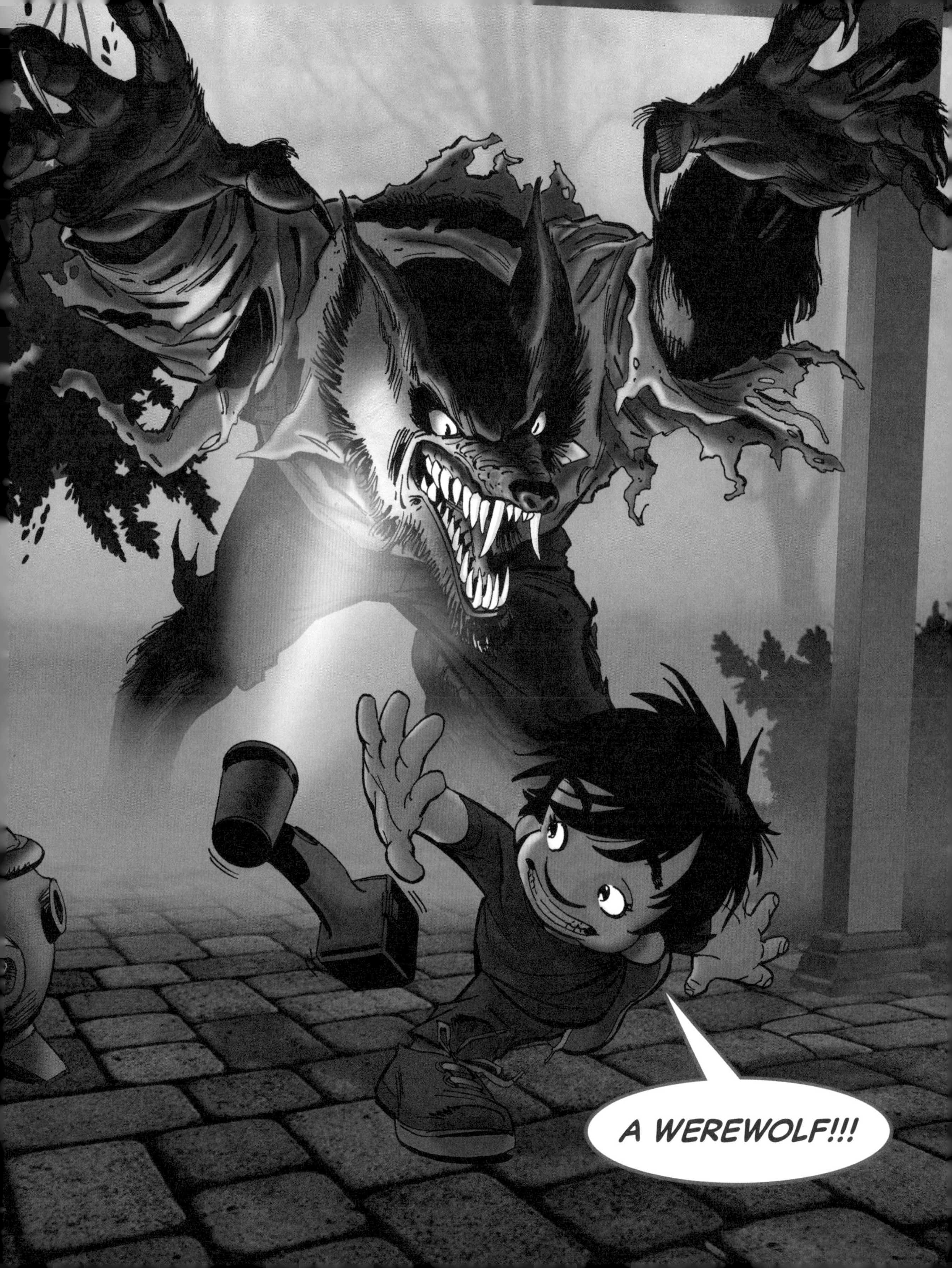
A WEREWOLF!!!

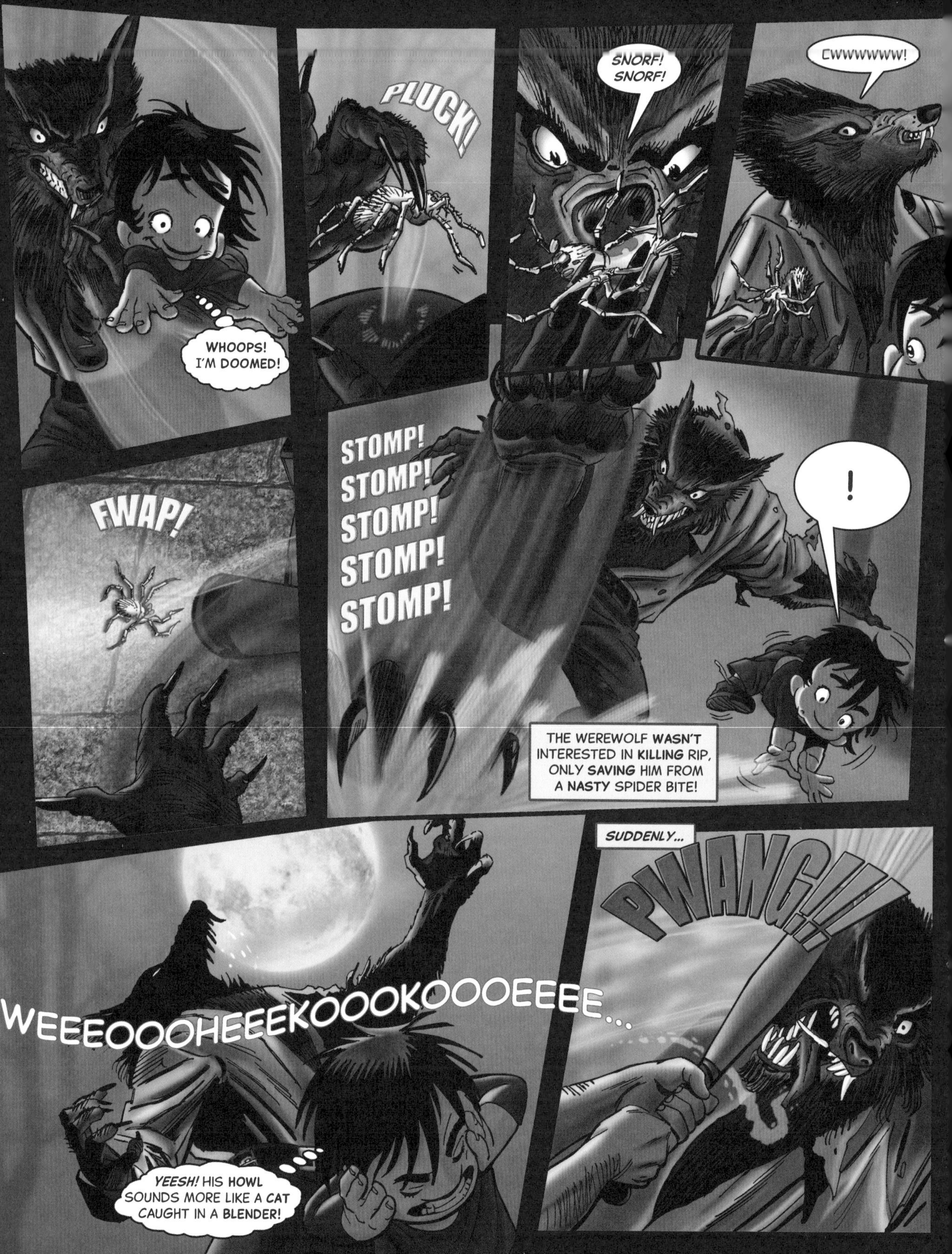
WHOOPS! I'M DOOMED!
PLUCK!
SNORF! SNORF!
CWWWWWWW!
FWAP!
STOMP! STOMP! STOMP! STOMP! STOMP!
!
THE WEREWOLF WASN'T INTERESTED IN KILLING RIP, ONLY SAVING HIM FROM A NASTY SPIDER BITE!
WEEEOOOHEEEKOOOKOOOEEEE...
YEESH! HIS HOWL SOUNDS MORE LIKE A CAT CAUGHT IN A BLENDER!
SUDDENLY...
PWANG!!!

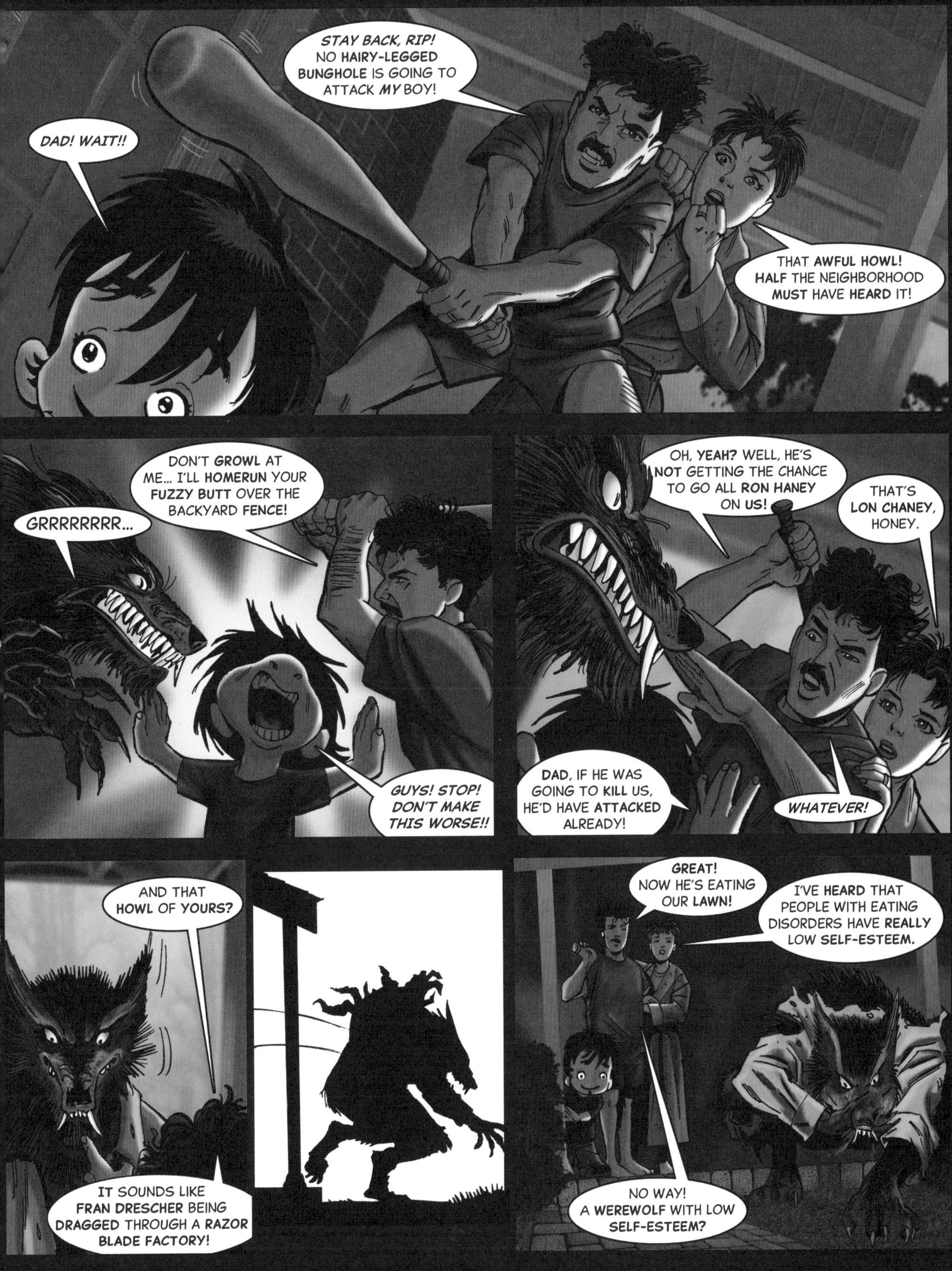
DAD! WAIT!!
STAY BACK, RIP! NO HAIRY-LEGGED BUNGHOLE IS GOING TO ATTACK MY BOY!
THAT AWFUL HOWL! HALF THE NEIGHBORHOOD MUST HAVE HEARD IT!
GRRRRRRRR...
DON'T GROWL AT ME... I'LL HOMERUN YOUR FUZZY BUTT OVER THE BACKYARD FENCE!
GUYS! STOP! DON'T MAKE THIS WORSE!!
OH, YEAH? WELL, HE'S NOT GETTING THE CHANCE TO GO ALL RON HANEY ON US!
THAT'S LON CHANEY, HONEY.
DAD, IF HE WAS GOING TO KILL US, HE'D HAVE ATTACKED ALREADY!
WHATEVER!
AND THAT HOWL OF YOURS?
IT SOUNDS LIKE FRAN DRESCHER BEING DRAGGED THROUGH A RAZOR BLADE FACTORY!
GREAT! NOW HE'S EATING OUR LAWN!
I'VE HEARD THAT PEOPLE WITH EATING DISORDERS HAVE REALLY LOW SELF-ESTEEM.
NO WAY! A WEREWOLF WITH LOW SELF-ESTEEM?

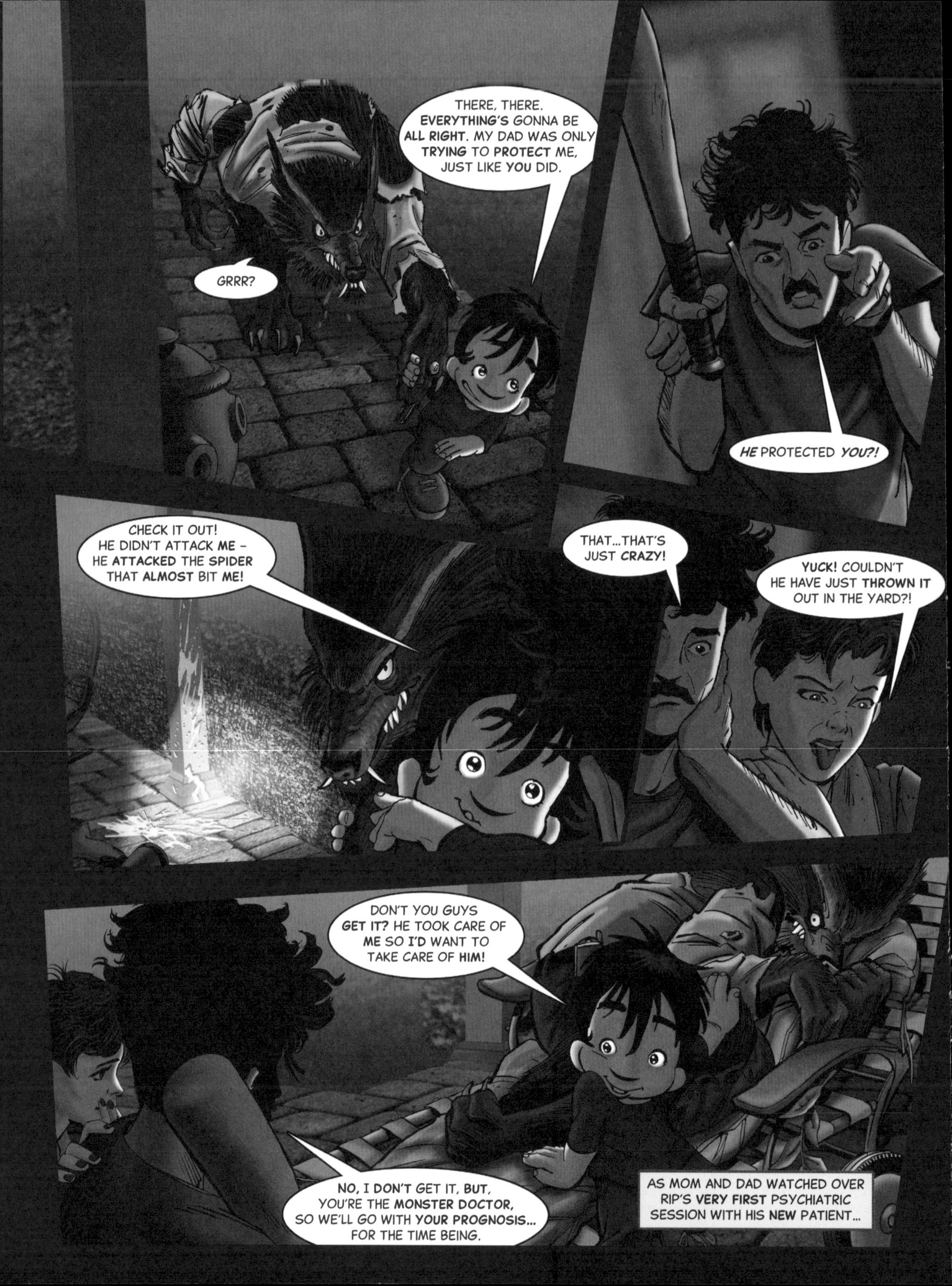
THERE, THERE. EVERYTHING'S GONNA BE ALL RIGHT. MY DAD WAS ONLY TRYING TO PROTECT ME, JUST LIKE YOU DID.
GRRR?
HE PROTECTED YOU?!
CHECK IT OUT! HE DIDN'T ATTACK ME – HE ATTACKED THE SPIDER THAT ALMOST BIT ME!
THAT...THAT'S JUST CRAZY!
YUCK! COULDN'T HE HAVE JUST THROWN IT OUT IN THE YARD?!
DON'T YOU GUYS GET IT? HE TOOK CARE OF ME SO I'D WANT TO TAKE CARE OF HIM!
NO, I DON'T GET IT, BUT, YOU'RE THE MONSTER DOCTOR, SO WE'LL GO WITH YOUR PROGNOSIS... FOR THE TIME BEING.
AS MOM AND DAD WATCHED OVER RIP'S VERY FIRST PSYCHIATRIC SESSION WITH HIS NEW PATIENT...

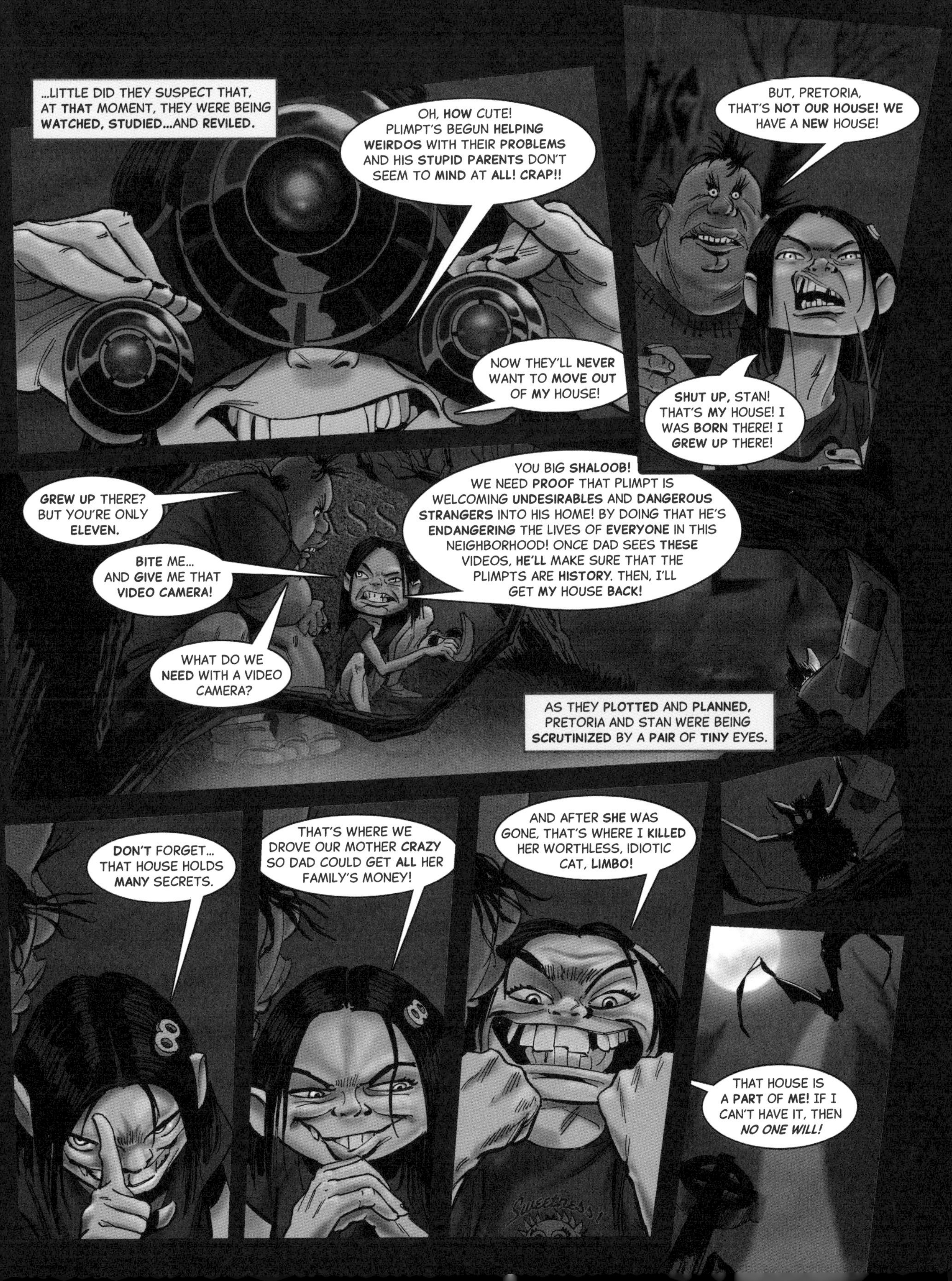
...LITTLE DID THEY SUSPECT THAT, AT THAT MOMENT, THEY WERE BEING WATCHED, STUDIED...AND REVILED.
OH, HOW CUTE! PLIMPT'S BEGUN HELPING WEIRDOS WITH THEIR PROBLEMS AND HIS STUPID PARENTS DON'T SEEM TO MIND AT ALL! CRAP!!
NOW THEY'LL NEVER WANT TO MOVE OUT OF MY HOUSE!
BUT, PRETORIA, THAT'S NOT OUR HOUSE! WE HAVE A NEW HOUSE!
SHUT UP, STAN! THAT'S MY HOUSE! I WAS BORN THERE! I GREW UP THERE!
GREW UP THERE? BUT YOU'RE ONLY ELEVEN.
BITE ME... AND GIVE ME THAT VIDEO CAMERA!
WHAT DO WE NEED WITH A VIDEO CAMERA?
YOU BIG SHALOOB! WE NEED PROOF THAT PLIMPT IS WELCOMING UNDESIRABLES AND DANGEROUS STRANGERS INTO HIS HOME! BY DOING THAT HE'S ENDANGERING THE LIVES OF EVERYONE IN THIS NEIGHBORHOOD! ONCE DAD SEES THESE VIDEOS, HE'LL MAKE SURE THAT THE PLIMPTS ARE HISTORY. THEN, I'LL GET MY HOUSE BACK!
AS THEY PLOTTED AND PLANNED, PRETORIA AND STAN WERE BEING SCRUTINIZED BY A PAIR OF TINY EYES.
DON'T FORGET... THAT HOUSE HOLDS MANY SECRETS.
THAT'S WHERE WE DROVE OUR MOTHER CRAZY SO DAD COULD GET ALL HER FAMILY'S MONEY!
AND AFTER SHE WAS GONE, THAT'S WHERE I KILLED HER WORTHLESS, IDIOTIC CAT, LIMBO!
SWEETNESS!
THAT HOUSE IS A PART OF ME! IF I CAN'T HAVE IT, THEN NO ONE WILL!

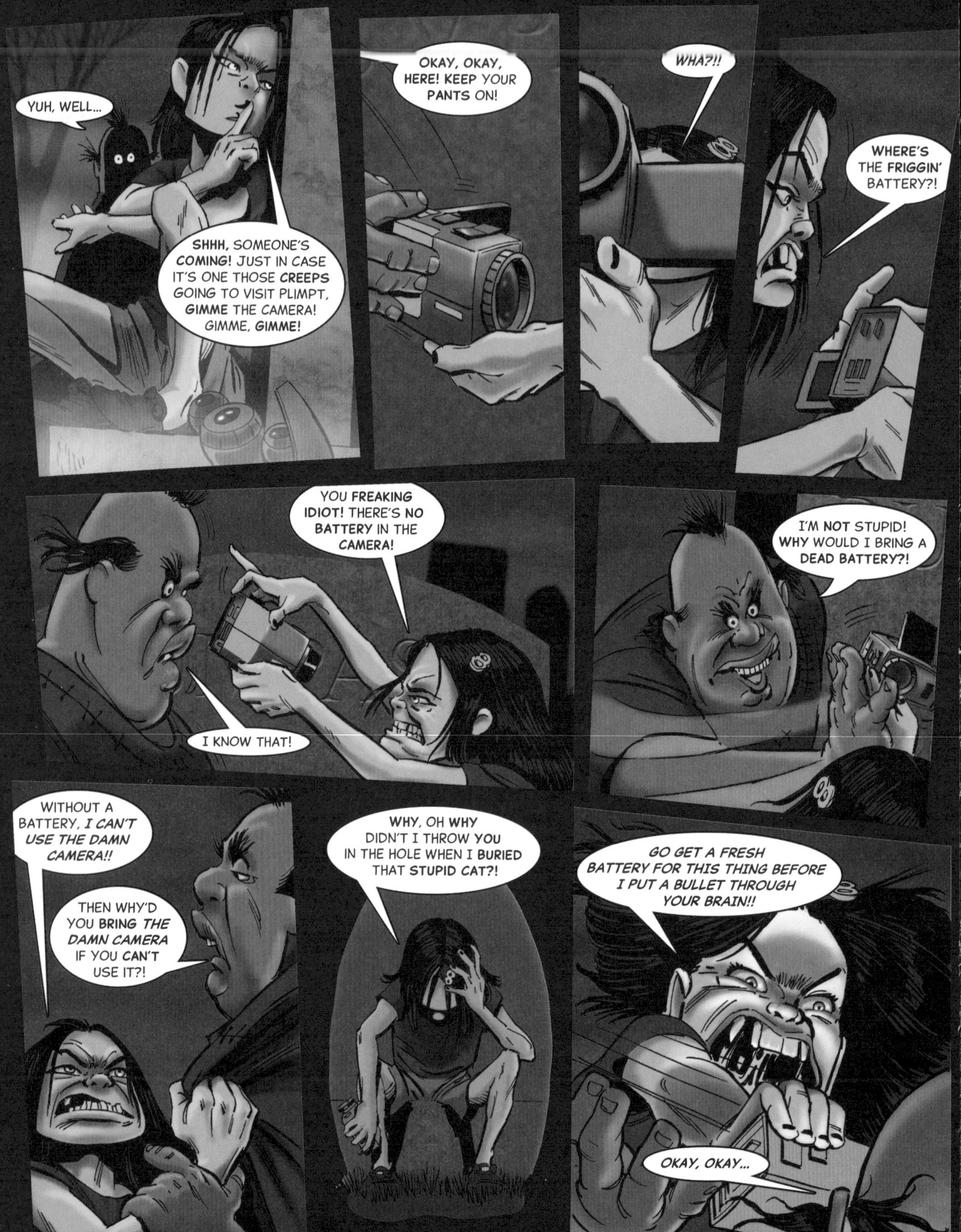
YUH, WELL...
SHHH, SOMEONE'S COMING! JUST IN CASE IT'S ONE THOSE CREEPS GOING TO VISIT PLIMPT, GIMME THE CAMERA! GIMME, GIMME!
OKAY, OKAY, HERE! KEEP YOUR PANTS ON!
WHA?!!
WHERE'S THE FRIGGIN' BATTERY?!
YOU FREAKING IDIOT! THERE'S NO BATTERY IN THE CAMERA!
I KNOW THAT!
I'M NOT STUPID! WHY WOULD I BRING A DEAD BATTERY?!
WITHOUT A BATTERY, I CAN'T USE THE DAMN CAMERA!!
THEN WHY'D YOU BRING THE DAMN CAMERA IF YOU CAN'T USE IT?!
WHY, OH WHY DIDN'T I THROW YOU IN THE HOLE WHEN I BURIED THAT STUPID CAT?!
GO GET A FRESH BATTERY FOR THIS THING BEFORE I PUT A BULLET THROUGH YOUR BRAIN!!
OKAY, OKAY...

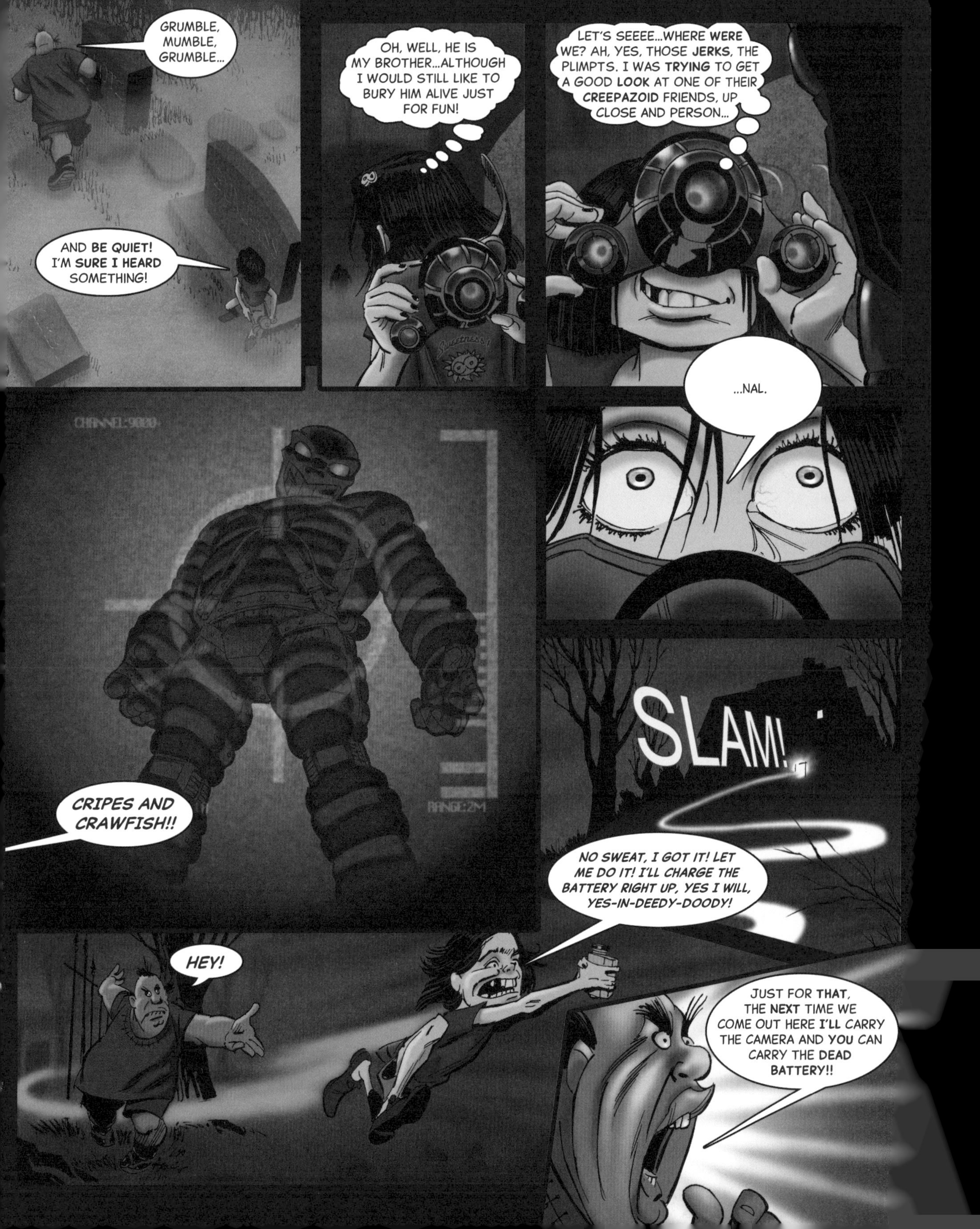
GRUMBLE, MUMBLE, GRUMBLE...
AND BE QUIET! I'M SURE I HEARD SOMETHING!
OH, WELL, HE IS MY BROTHER...ALTHOUGH I WOULD STILL LIKE TO BURY HIM ALIVE JUST FOR FUN!
LET'S SEEEE...WHERE WERE WE? AH, YES, THOSE JERKS, THE PLIMPTS. I WAS TRYING TO GET A GOOD LOOK AT ONE OF THEIR CREEPAZOID FRIENDS, UP CLOSE AND PERSON...
CHANNEL:9000
RANGE:2M
CRIPES AND CRAWFISH!!
...NAL.
SLAM!
NO SWEAT, I GOT IT! LET ME DO IT! I'LL CHARGE THE BATTERY RIGHT UP, YES I WILL, YES-IN-DEEDY-DOODY!
HEY!
JUST FOR THAT, THE NEXT TIME WE COME OUT HERE I'LL CARRY THE CAMERA AND YOU CAN CARRY THE DEAD BATTERY!!

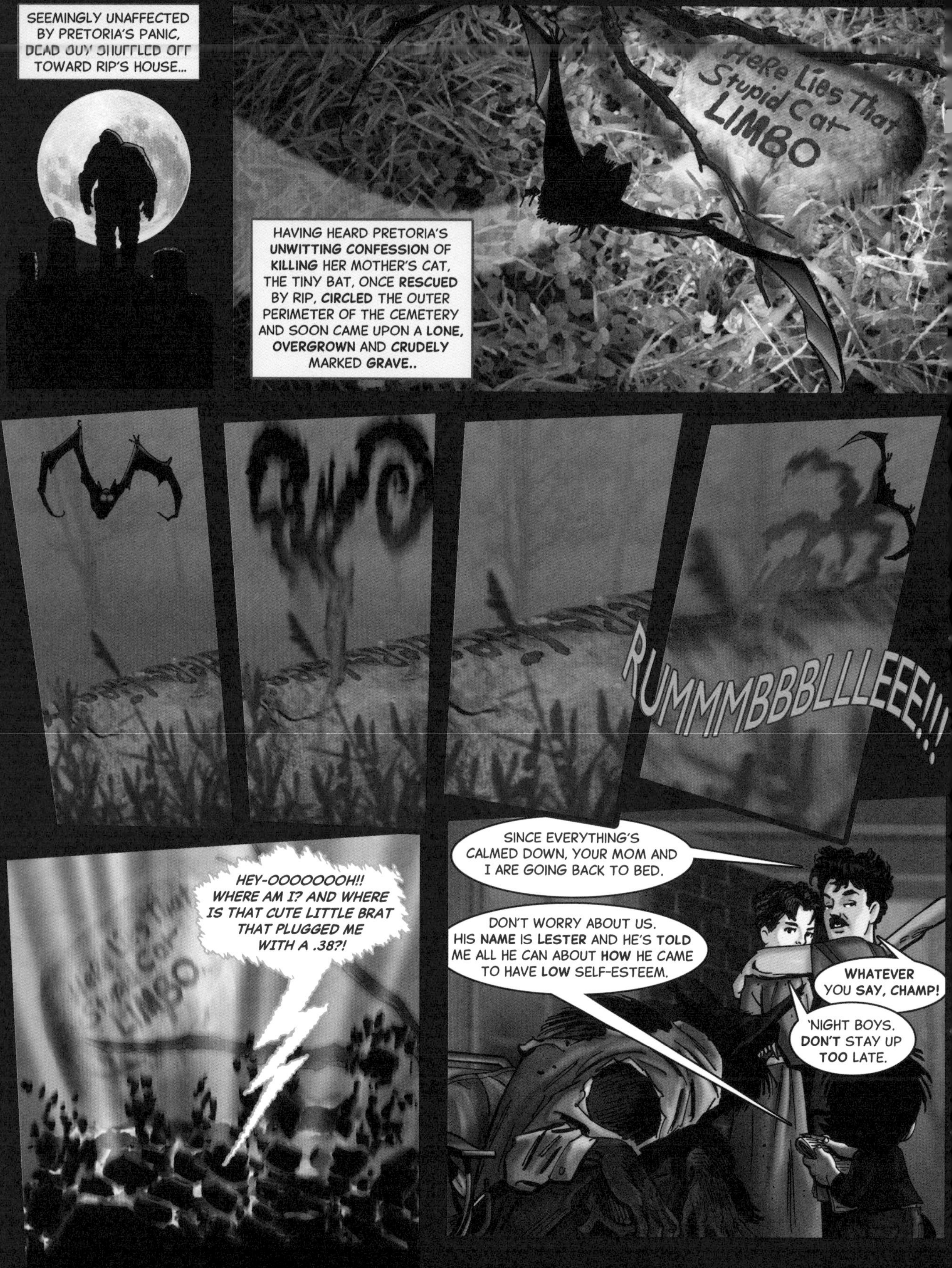

SEEMINGLY UNAFFECTED BY PRETORIA'S PANIC, DEAD GUY SHUFFLED OFF TOWARD RIP'S HOUSE...
HAVING HEARD PRETORIA'S UNWITTING CONFESSION OF KILLING HER MOTHER'S CAT, THE TINY BAT, ONCE RESCUED BY RIP, CIRCLED THE OUTER PERIMETER OF THE CEMETERY AND SOON CAME UPON A LONE, OVERGROWN AND CRUDELY MARKED GRAVE..
Here Lies That Stupid Cat LIMBO
RUMMMBBBLLLEEE!!!
HEY-OOOOOOOH!! WHERE AM I? AND WHERE IS THAT CUTE LITTLE BRAT THAT PLUGGED ME WITH A .38?!
SINCE EVERYTHING'S CALMED DOWN, YOUR MOM AND I ARE GOING BACK TO BED.
DON'T WORRY ABOUT US. HIS NAME IS LESTER AND HE'S TOLD ME ALL HE CAN ABOUT HOW HE CAME TO HAVE LOW SELF-ESTEEM.
WHATEVER YOU SAY, CHAMP!
'NIGHT BOYS. DON'T STAY UP TOO LATE.

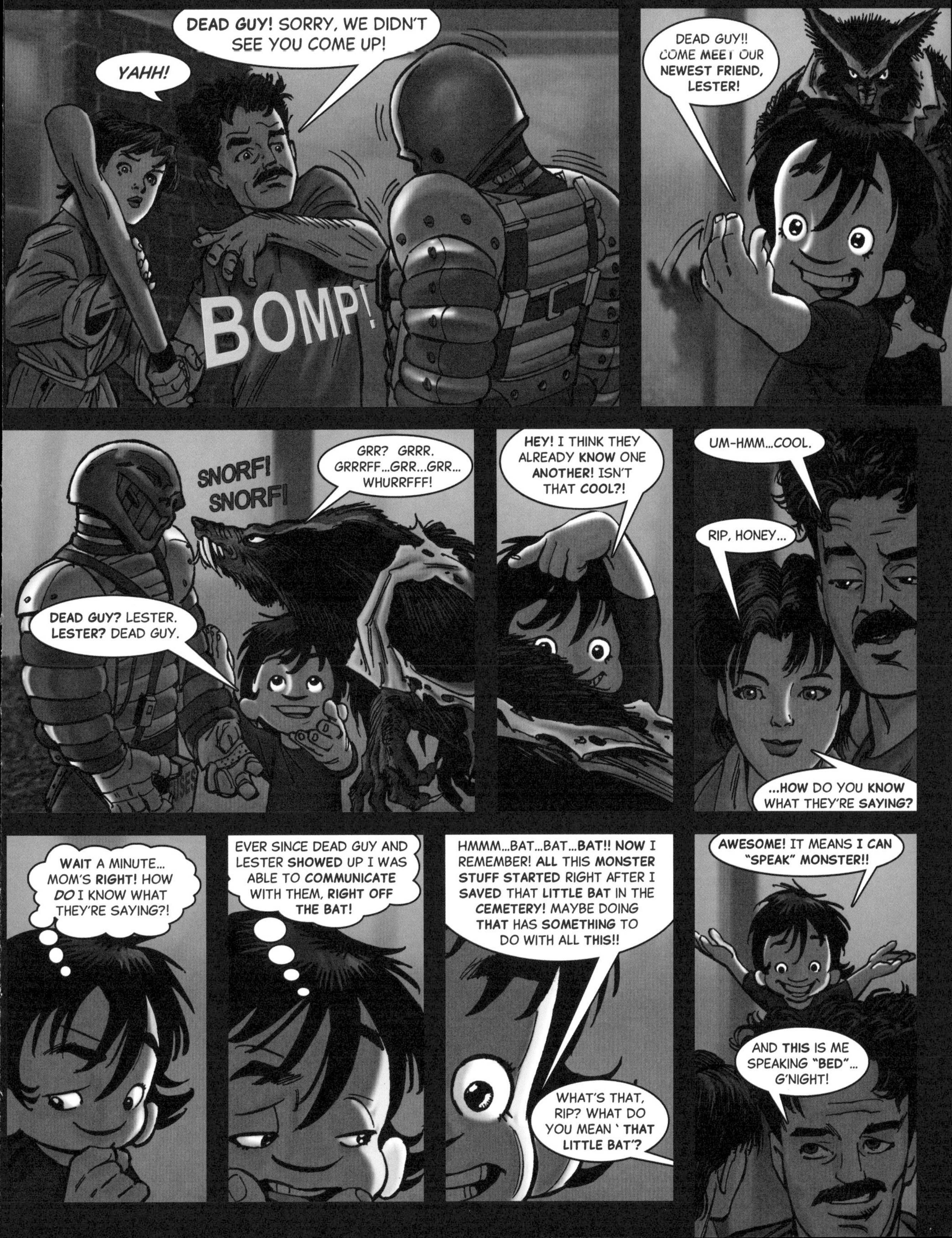
YAHH!
DEAD GUY! SORRY, WE DIDN'T SEE YOU COME UP!
BOMP!
DEAD GUY!! COME MEET OUR NEWEST FRIEND, LESTER!
SNORF! SNORF!
GRR? GRRR. GRRRFF...GRR...GRR... WHURRFFF!
DEAD GUY? LESTER. LESTER? DEAD GUY.
HEY! I THINK THEY ALREADY KNOW ONE ANOTHER! ISN'T THAT COOL?!
UM-HMM...COOL.
RIP, HONEY...
...HOW DO YOU KNOW WHAT THEY'RE SAYING?
WAIT A MINUTE... MOM'S RIGHT! HOW DO I KNOW WHAT THEY'RE SAYING?!
EVER SINCE DEAD GUY AND LESTER SHOWED UP I WAS ABLE TO COMMUNICATE WITH THEM, RIGHT OFF THE BAT!
HMMM...BAT...BAT...BAT!! NOW I REMEMBER! ALL THIS MONSTER STUFF STARTED RIGHT AFTER I SAVED THAT LITTLE BAT IN THE CEMETERY! MAYBE DOING THAT HAS SOMETHING TO DO WITH ALL THIS!!
WHAT'S THAT, RIP? WHAT DO YOU MEAN ' THAT LITTLE BAT'?
AWESOME! IT MEANS I CAN "SPEAK" MONSTER!!
AND THIS IS ME SPEAKING "BED"... G'NIGHT!

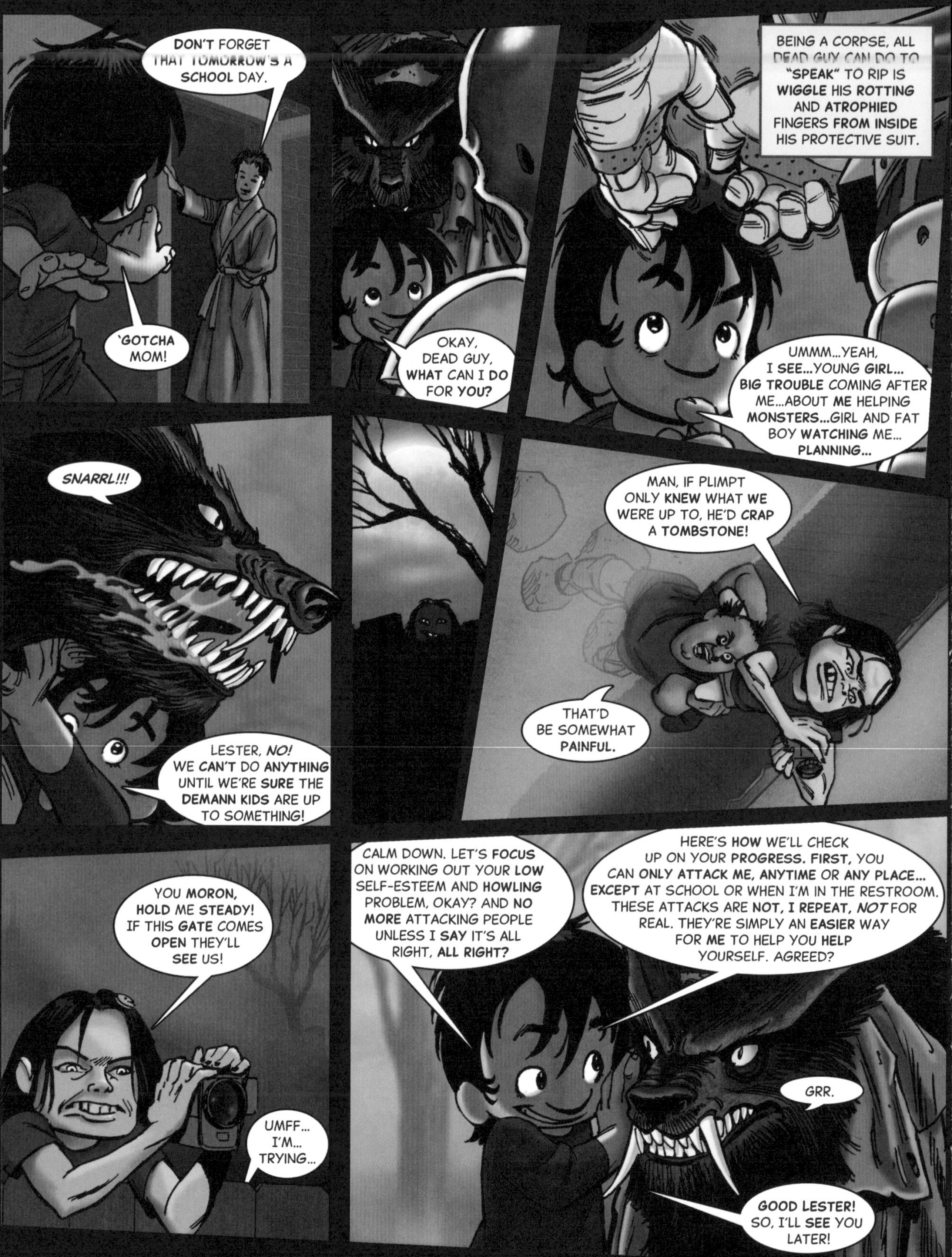
DON'T FORGET THAT TOMORROW'S A SCHOOL DAY.
'GOTCHA MOM!
OKAY, DEAD GUY, WHAT CAN I DO FOR YOU?
BEING A CORPSE, ALL DEAD GUY CAN DO TO "SPEAK" TO RIP IS WIGGLE HIS ROTTING AND ATROPHIED FINGERS FROM INSIDE HIS PROTECTIVE SUIT.
UMMM...YEAH, I SEE...YOUNG GIRL... BIG TROUBLE COMING AFTER ME...ABOUT ME HELPING MONSTERS...GIRL AND FAT BOY WATCHING ME... PLANNING...
SNARRL!!!
LESTER, NO! WE CAN'T DO ANYTHING UNTIL WE'RE SURE THE DEMANN KIDS ARE UP TO SOMETHING!
MAN, IF PLIMPT ONLY KNEW WHAT WE WERE UP TO, HE'D CRAP A TOMBSTONE!
THAT'D BE SOMEWHAT PAINFUL.
YOU MORON, HOLD ME STEADY! IF THIS GATE COMES OPEN THEY'LL SEE US!
UMFF... I'M... TRYING...
CALM DOWN. LET'S FOCUS ON WORKING OUT YOUR LOW SELF-ESTEEM AND HOWLING PROBLEM, OKAY? AND NO MORE ATTACKING PEOPLE UNLESS I SAY IT'S ALL RIGHT, ALL RIGHT?
HERE'S HOW WE'LL CHECK UP ON YOUR PROGRESS. FIRST, YOU CAN ONLY ATTACK ME, ANYTIME OR ANY PLACE... EXCEPT AT SCHOOL OR WHEN I'M IN THE RESTROOM. THESE ATTACKS ARE NOT, I REPEAT, NOT FOR REAL. THEY'RE SIMPLY AN EASIER WAY FOR ME TO HELP YOU HELP YOURSELF. AGREED?
GRR.
GOOD LESTER! SO, I'LL SEE YOU LATER!

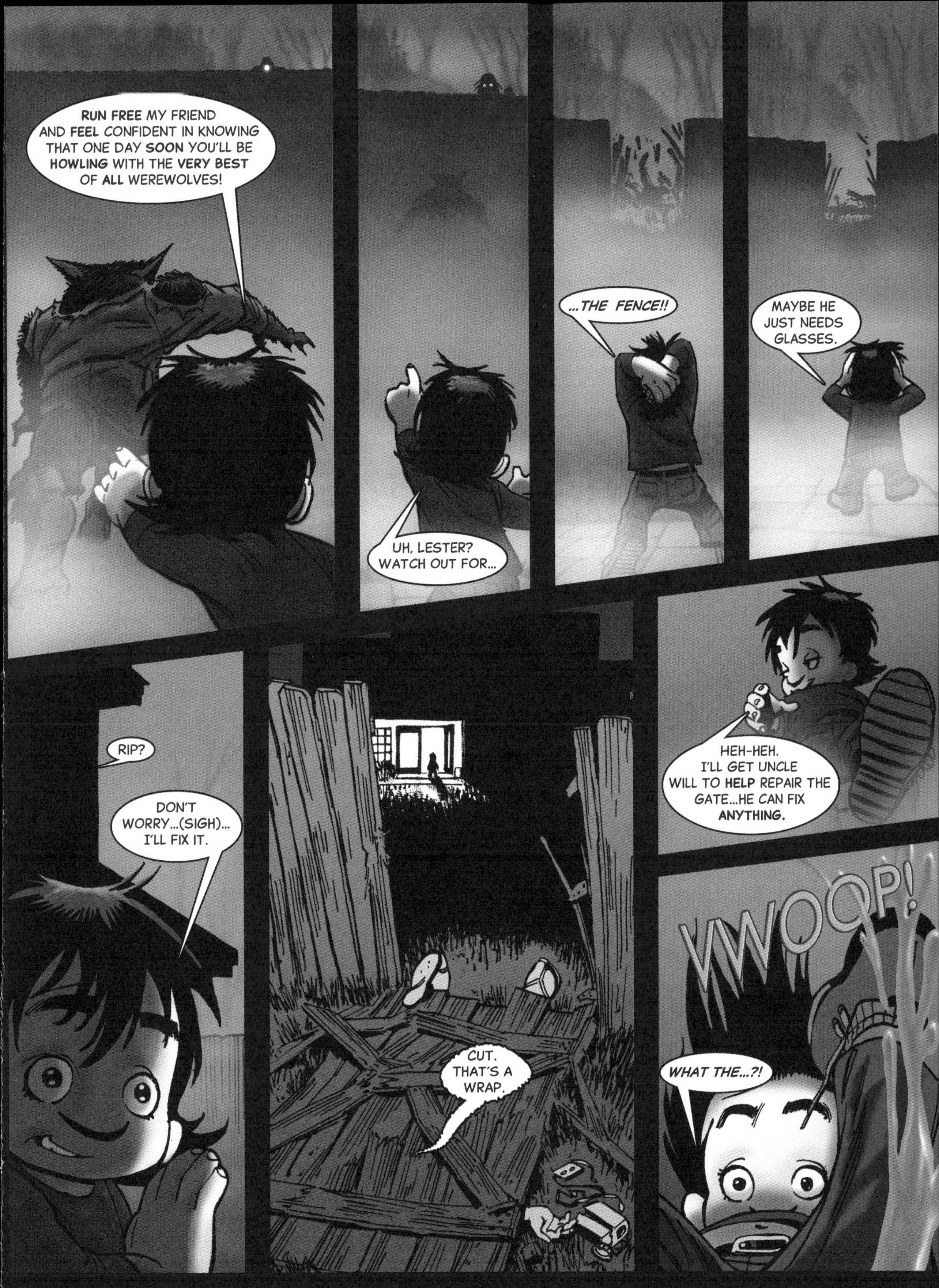
RUN FREE MY FRIEND AND FEEL CONFIDENT IN KNOWING THAT ONE DAY SOON YOU'LL BE HOWLING WITH THE VERY BEST OF ALL WEREWOLVES!
UH, LESTER? WATCH OUT FOR...
...THE FENCE!!
MAYBE HE JUST NEEDS GLASSES.
RIP?
DON'T WORRY...(SIGH)... I'LL FIX IT.
CUT. THAT'S A WRAP.
HEH-HEH. I'LL GET UNCLE WILL TO HELP REPAIR THE GATE...HE CAN FIX ANYTHING.
VWOOP!
WHAT THE...?!

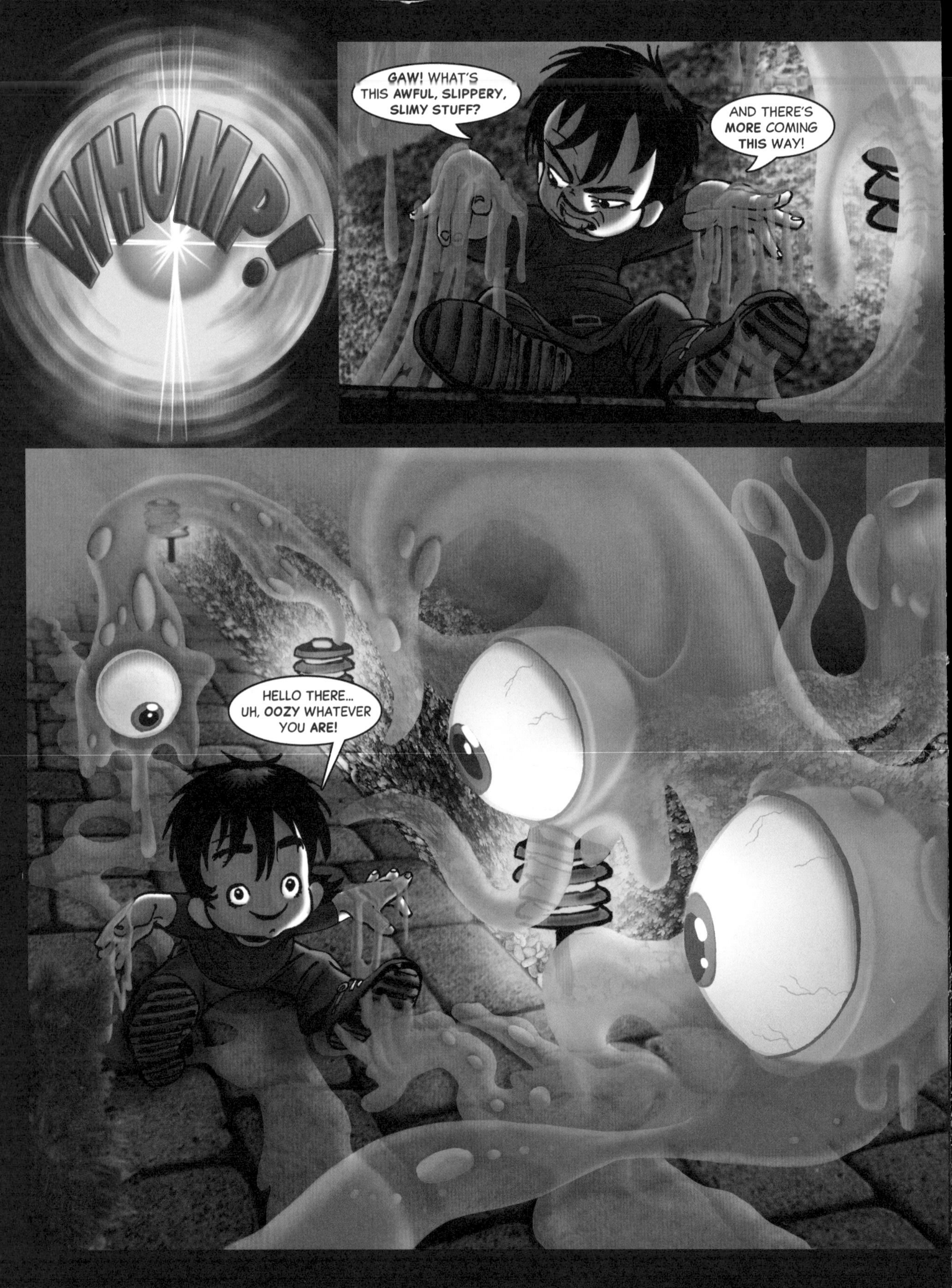
WHOMP!
GAW! WHAT'S THIS AWFUL, SLIPPERY, SLIMY STUFF?
AND THERE'S MORE COMING THIS WAY!
HELLO THERE... UH, OOZY WHATEVER YOU ARE!

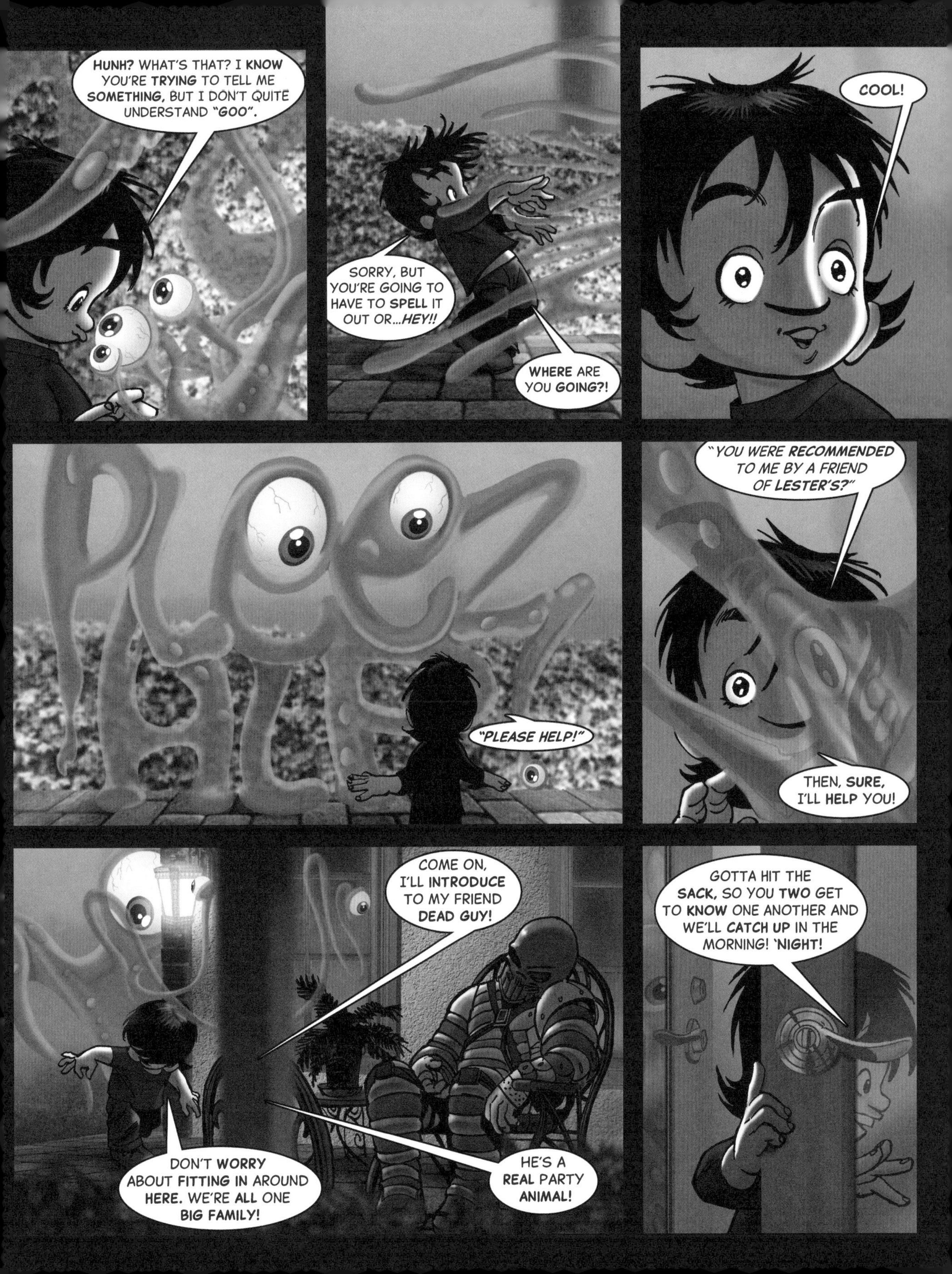
HUNH? WHAT'S THAT? I KNOW YOU'RE TRYING TO TELL ME SOMETHING, BUT I DON'T QUITE UNDERSTAND "GOO".
SORRY, BUT YOU'RE GOING TO HAVE TO SPELL IT OUT OR...HEY!!
WHERE ARE YOU GOING?!
COOL!
"PLEASE HELP!"
"YOU WERE RECOMMENDED TO ME BY A FRIEND OF LESTER'S?"
THEN, SURE, I'LL HELP YOU!
COME ON, I'LL INTRODUCE TO MY FRIEND DEAD GUY!
DON'T WORRY ABOUT FITTING IN AROUND HERE. WE'RE ALL ONE BIG FAMILY!
HE'S A REAL PARTY ANIMAL!
GOTTA HIT THE SACK, SO YOU TWO GET TO KNOW ONE ANOTHER AND WE'LL CATCH UP IN THE MORNING! 'NIGHT!

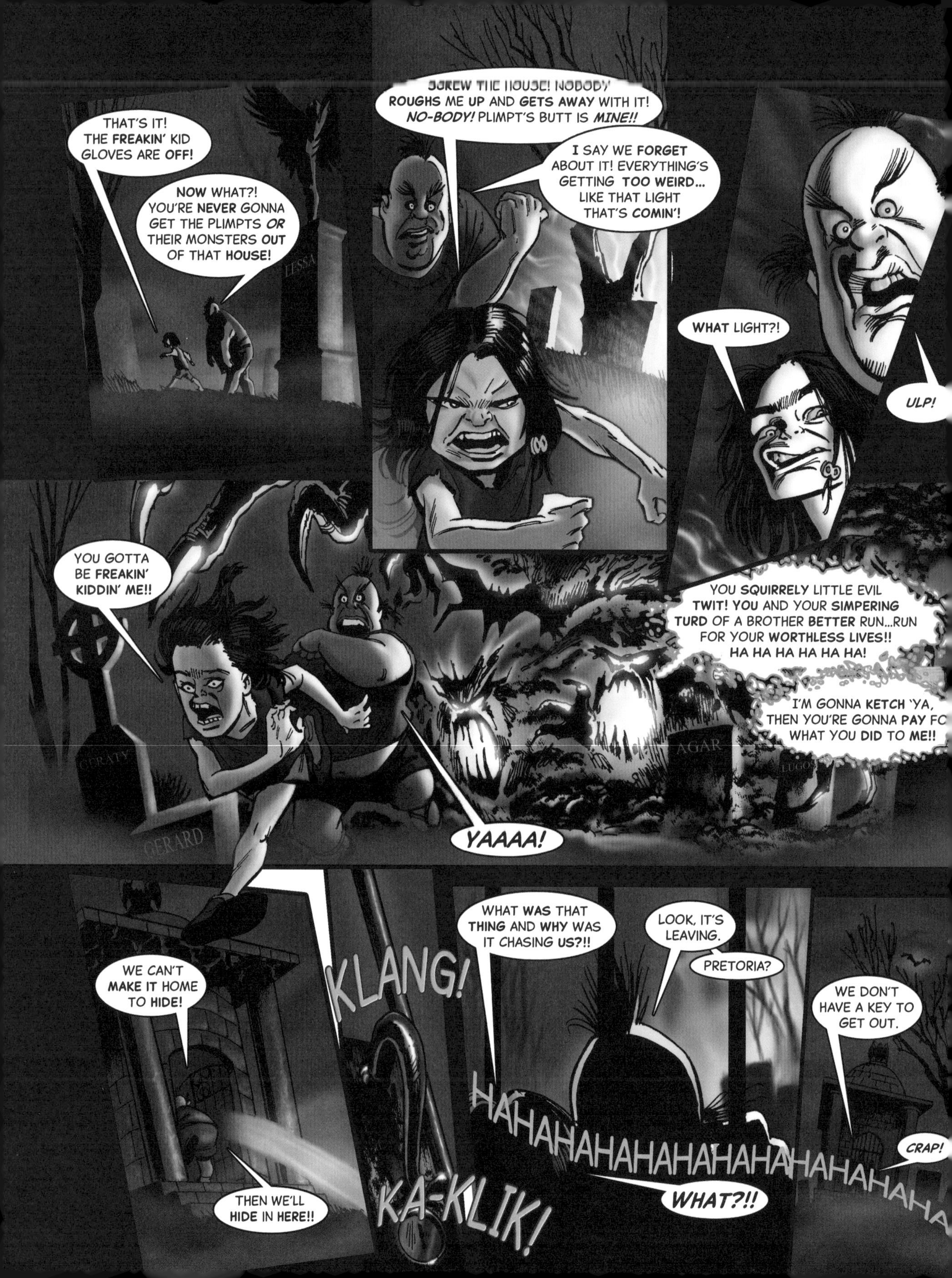
THAT'S IT! THE FREAKIN' KID GLOVES ARE OFF!
NOW WHAT?! YOU'RE NEVER GONNA GET THE PLIMPTS OR THEIR MONSTERS OUT OF THAT HOUSE!
LESSA
SCREW THE HOUSE! NOBODY ROUGHS ME UP AND GETS AWAY WITH IT! NO-BODY! PLIMPT'S BUTT IS MINE!!
I SAY WE FORGET ABOUT IT! EVERYTHING'S GETTING TOO WEIRD... LIKE THAT LIGHT THAT'S COMIN'!
WHAT LIGHT?!
ULP!
YOU GOTTA BE FREAKIN' KIDDIN' ME!!
YOU SQUIRRELY LITTLE EVIL TWIT! YOU AND YOUR SIMPERING TURD OF A BROTHER BETTER RUN...RUN FOR YOUR WORTHLESS LIVES!! HA HA HA HA HA HA!
I'M GONNA KETCH 'YA, THEN YOU'RE GONNA PAY FO WHAT YOU DID TO ME!!
GERATY
AGAR
GERARD
YAAAA!
WE CAN'T MAKE IT HOME TO HIDE!
THEN WE'LL HIDE IN HERE!!
KLANG!
KA-KLIK!
WHAT WAS THAT THING AND WHY WAS IT CHASING US?!!
LOOK, IT'S LEAVING.
PRETORIA?
HAHAHAHAHAHAHAHAHAHAHAHAHAHA
WHAT?!!
WE DON'T HAVE A KEY TO GET OUT.
CRAP!

WHAT A **NIGHT!** RIP WAS BEAT. HE'D ALWAYS WANTED TO MEET A **REAL** MONSTER AND HIS WISH HAD COME TRUE...IN **SPADES!** NOW THAT HE WAS JUGGLING **THREE,** THIS MONSTER-DOCTOR GIG WAS **CLOSE** TO BECOMING **OVERWHELMING!**

HE'D **IMAGINED** THAT IF HE REALLY **DID** MEET A MONSTER ALL HE'D WANT IS A LITTLE **FRIENDSHIP** OR **UNDERSTANDING.** INSTEAD, HE DISCOVERED, QUITE SURPRISINGLY, THAT **REAL MONSTERS** HAVE **BIGGER** HANG UPS THAN REAL PEOPLE! A WEREWOLF WITH LOW **SELF-ESTEEM** WHO DOESN'T REALIZE THAT IT'S A BIG ENOUGH PROBLEM JUST **BEING A WEREWOLF?!** OR A **LONELY** OLD GUY WHO ONLY WANTS A LITTLE FAMILY **ATTENTION...**AFTER HE'S BEEN DEAD FOR **YEARS!**

AND NOW THAT OOZY BLOB THING HANGING AROUND OUT BACK AND ASKING "PLEEZ HLP" – WHAT WAS THAT ALL ABOUT? RIP WAS GOING TO TRY AS HARD AS HE COULD TO MAKE SENSE OF IT ALL WHILE TRYING TO FIT THIS NEW CAREER AS MONSTER-DOCTOR INTO HIS ALL-TOO-NORMAL LIFE.

...HE **HOPED** THAT HE WAS UP TO THE **CHALLENGE...**BUT WHAT HE REALLY HOPED FOR WAS THAT HIS PARENTS WERE UP TO IT, TOO.

YEP, HE'S **ALWAYS** WISHED TO MEET A REAL MONSTER AND **NOW** THAT HE HAD...

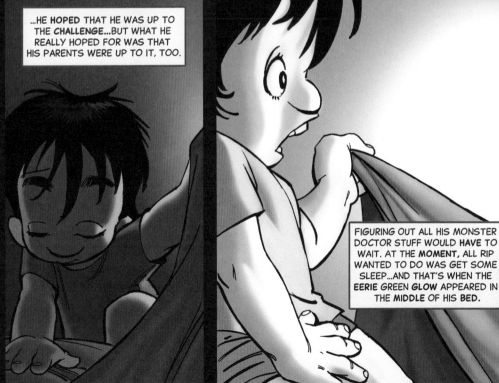

FIGURING OUT ALL HIS MONSTER DOCTOR STUFF WOULD **HAVE** TO WAIT. AT THE **MOMENT,** ALL RIP WANTED TO DO WAS GET SOME SLEEP...AND THAT'S WHEN THE **EERIE** GREEN **GLOW** APPEARED IN THE **MIDDLE** OF HIS BED.

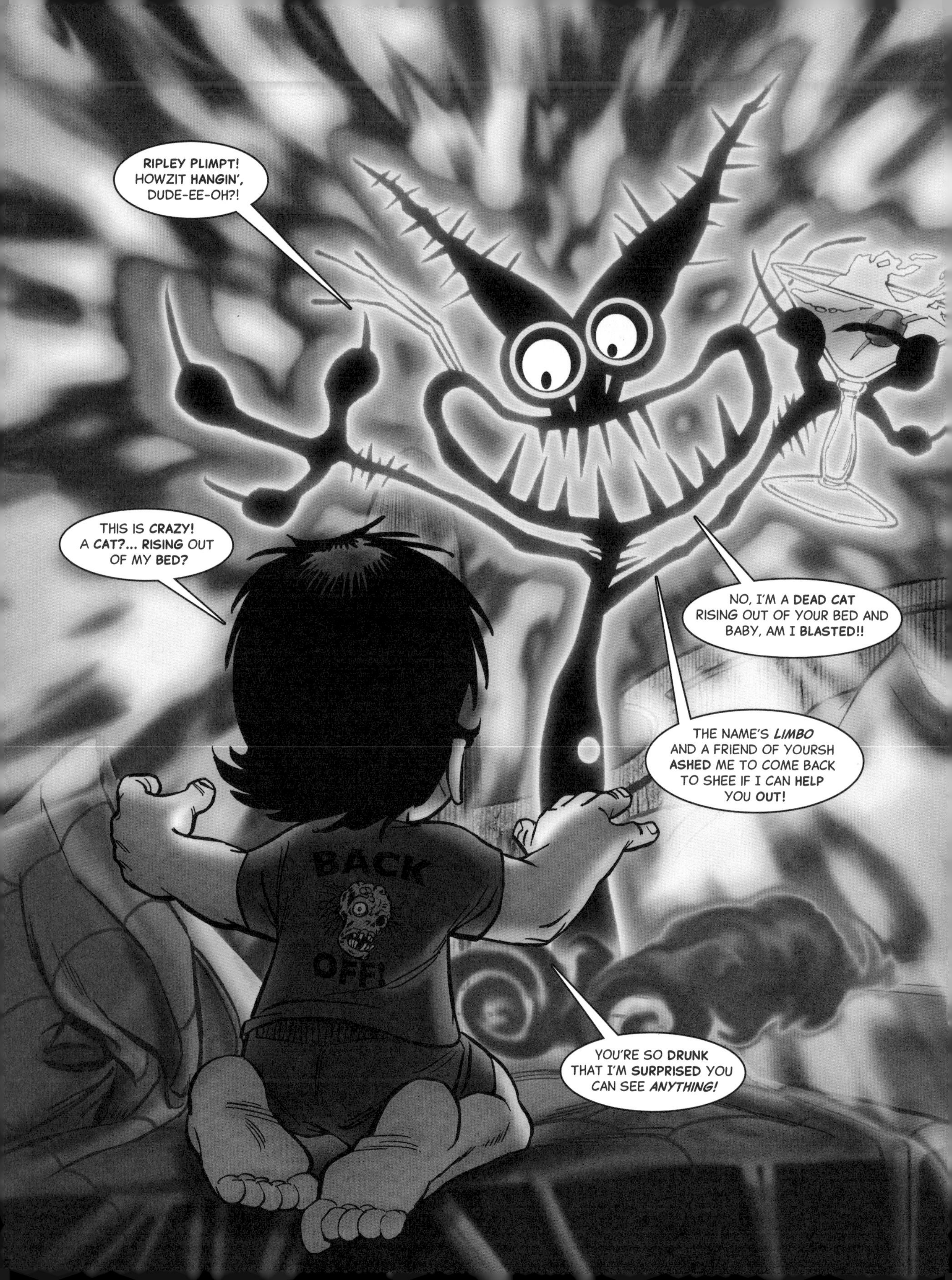
RIPLEY PLIMPT! HOWZIT HANGIN', DUDE-EE-OH?!
THIS IS CRAZY! A CAT?... RISING OUT OF MY BED?
NO, I'M A DEAD CAT RISING OUT OF YOUR BED AND BABY, AM I BLASTED!!
THE NAME'S LIMBO AND A FRIEND OF YOURSH ASHED ME TO COME BACK TO SHEE IF I CAN HELP YOU OUT!
YOU'RE SO DRUNK THAT I'M SURPRISED YOU CAN SEE ANYTHING!
BACK OFF!

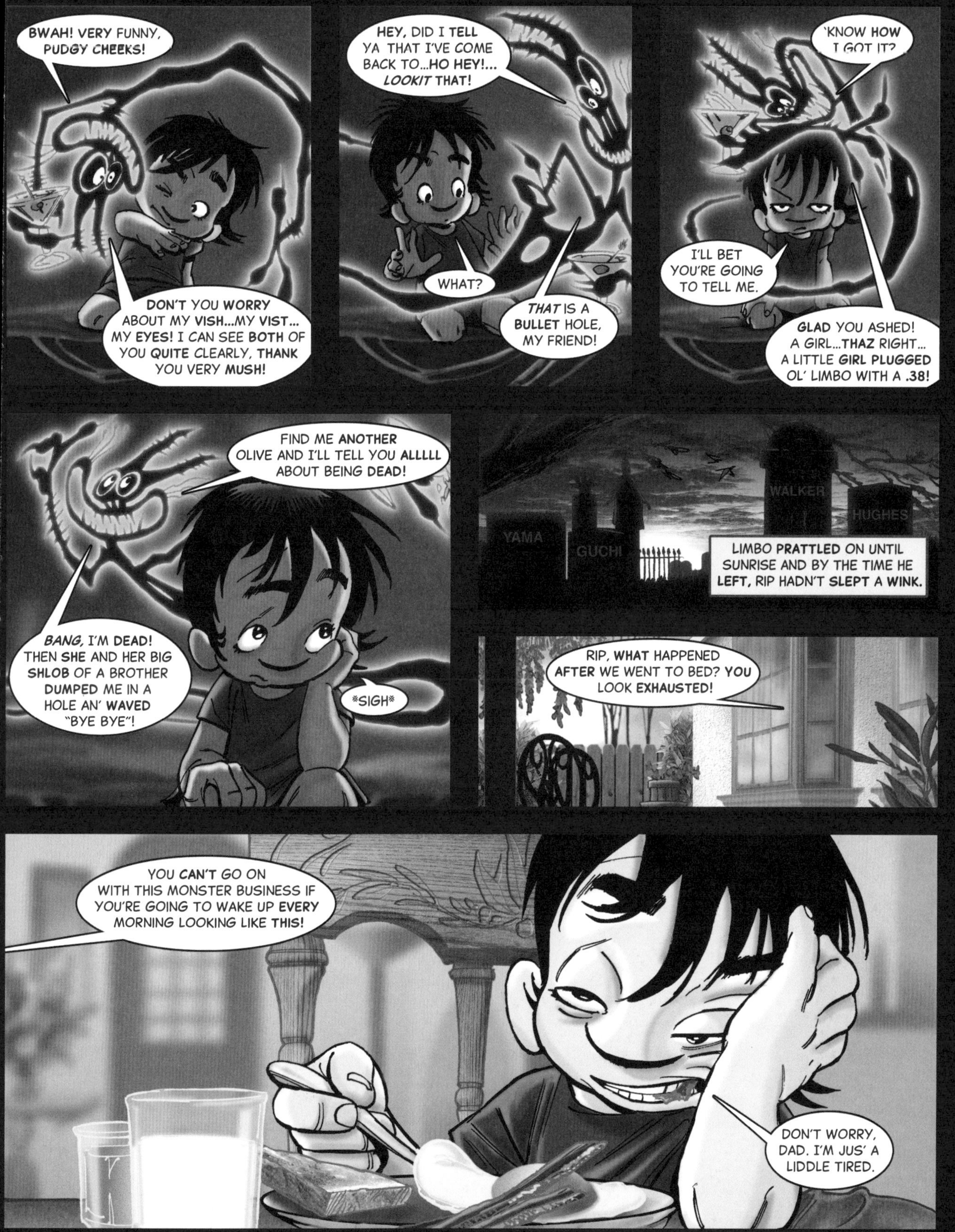

BWAH! VERY FUNNY, PUDGY CHEEKS!
DON'T YOU WORRY ABOUT MY VISH...MY VIST... MY EYES! I CAN SEE BOTH OF YOU QUITE CLEARLY, THANK YOU VERY MUSH!
HEY, DID I TELL YA THAT I'VE COME BACK TO...HO HEY!... LOOKIT THAT!
WHAT?
THAT IS A BULLET HOLE, MY FRIEND!
'KNOW HOW I GOT IT?
I'LL BET YOU'RE GOING TO TELL ME.
GLAD YOU ASHED! A GIRL...THAZ RIGHT... A LITTLE GIRL PLUGGED OL' LIMBO WITH A .38!
FIND ME ANOTHER OLIVE AND I'LL TELL YOU ALLLLL ABOUT BEING DEAD!
BANG, I'M DEAD! THEN SHE AND HER BIG SHLOB OF A BROTHER DUMPED ME IN A HOLE AN' WAVED "BYE BYE"!
SIGH
WALKER
HUGHES
YAMA
GUCHI
LIMBO PRATTLED ON UNTIL SUNRISE AND BY THE TIME HE LEFT, RIP HADN'T SLEPT A WINK.
RIP, WHAT HAPPENED AFTER WE WENT TO BED? YOU LOOK EXHAUSTED!
YOU CAN'T GO ON WITH THIS MONSTER BUSINESS IF YOU'RE GOING TO WAKE UP EVERY MORNING LOOKING LIKE THIS!
DON'T WORRY, DAD. I'M JUS' A LIDDLE TIRED.

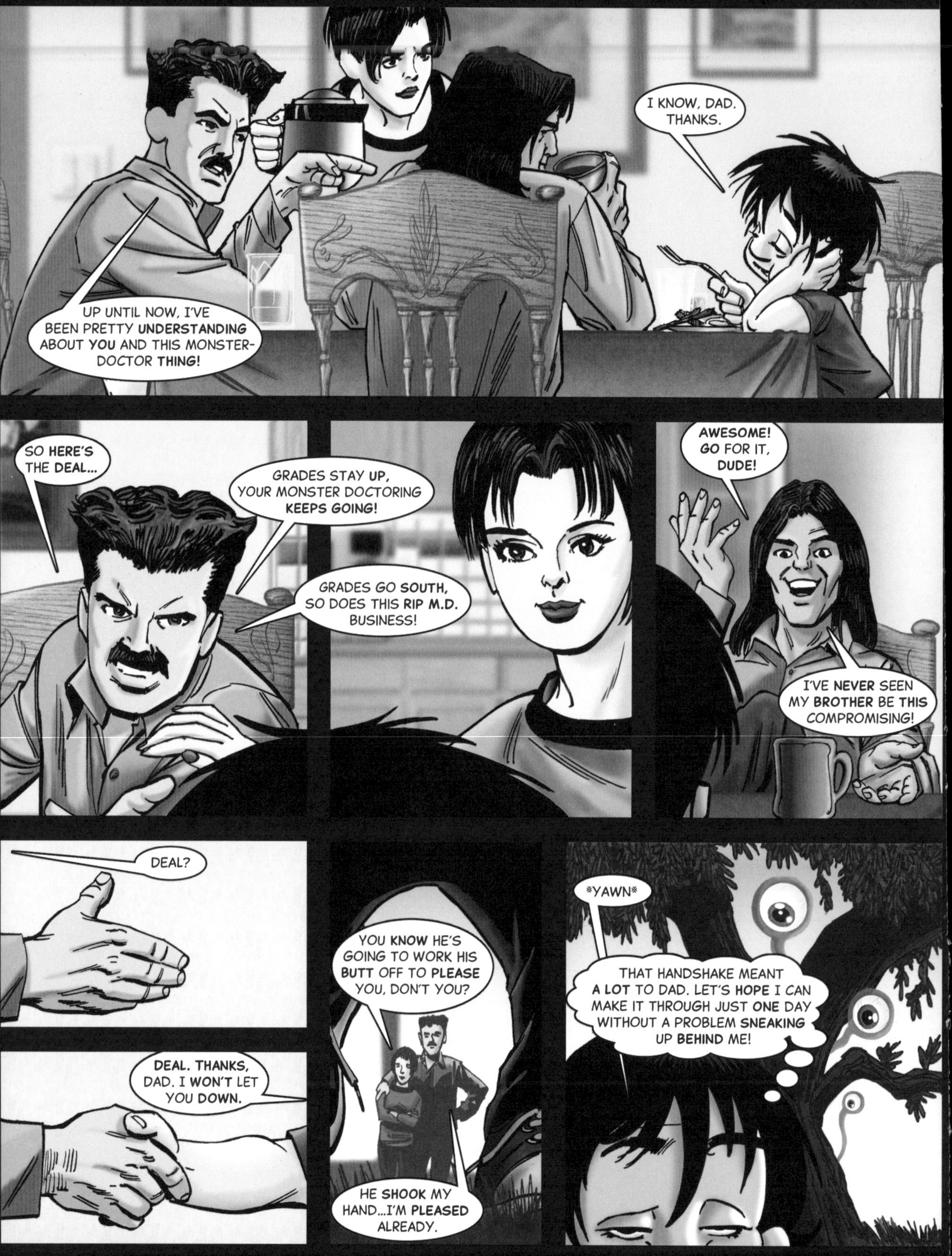
I KNOW, DAD. THANKS.
UP UNTIL NOW, I'VE BEEN PRETTY UNDERSTANDING ABOUT YOU AND THIS MONSTER-DOCTOR THING!
SO HERE'S THE DEAL...
GRADES STAY UP, YOUR MONSTER DOCTORING KEEPS GOING!
GRADES GO SOUTH, SO DOES THIS RIP M.D. BUSINESS!
AWESOME! GO FOR IT, DUDE!
I'VE NEVER SEEN MY BROTHER BE THIS COMPROMISING!
DEAL?
DEAL. THANKS, DAD. I WON'T LET YOU DOWN.
YOU KNOW HE'S GOING TO WORK HIS BUTT OFF TO PLEASE YOU, DON'T YOU?
HE SHOOK MY HAND...I'M PLEASED ALREADY.
YAWN
THAT HANDSHAKE MEANT A LOT TO DAD. LET'S HOPE I CAN MAKE IT THROUGH JUST ONE DAY WITHOUT A PROBLEM SNEAKING UP BEHIND ME!

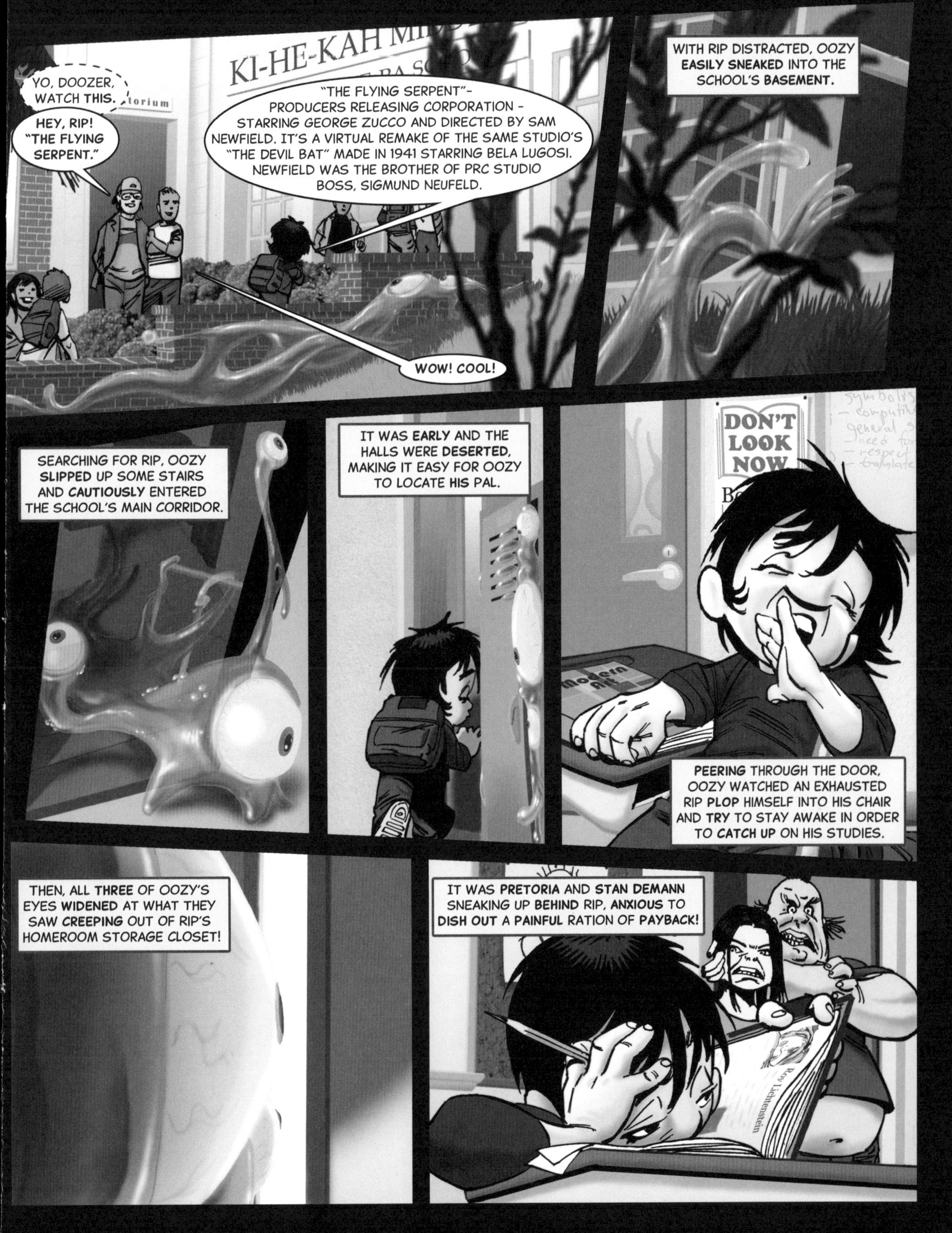
YO, DOOZER, WATCH THIS.
HEY, RIP! "THE FLYING SERPENT."
"THE FLYING SERPENT"– PRODUCERS RELEASING CORPORATION – STARRING GEORGE ZUCCO AND DIRECTED BY SAM NEWFIELD. IT'S A VIRTUAL REMAKE OF THE SAME STUDIO'S "THE DEVIL BAT" MADE IN 1941 STARRING BELA LUGOSI. NEWFIELD WAS THE BROTHER OF PRC STUDIO BOSS, SIGMUND NEUFELD.
WOW! COOL!
WITH RIP DISTRACTED, OOZY EASILY SNEAKED INTO THE SCHOOL'S BASEMENT.
SEARCHING FOR RIP, OOZY SLIPPED UP SOME STAIRS AND CAUTIOUSLY ENTERED THE SCHOOL'S MAIN CORRIDOR.
IT WAS EARLY AND THE HALLS WERE DESERTED, MAKING IT EASY FOR OOZY TO LOCATE HIS PAL.
DON'T LOOK NOW
Modern Art
PEERING THROUGH THE DOOR, OOZY WATCHED AN EXHAUSTED RIP PLOP HIMSELF INTO HIS CHAIR AND TRY TO STAY AWAKE IN ORDER TO CATCH UP ON HIS STUDIES.
THEN, ALL THREE OF OOZY'S EYES WIDENED AT WHAT THEY SAW CREEPING OUT OF RIP'S HOMEROOM STORAGE CLOSET!
IT WAS PRETORIA AND STAN DEMANN SNEAKING UP BEHIND RIP, ANXIOUS TO DISH OUT A PAINFUL RATION OF PAYBACK!
Roy Lichtenstein

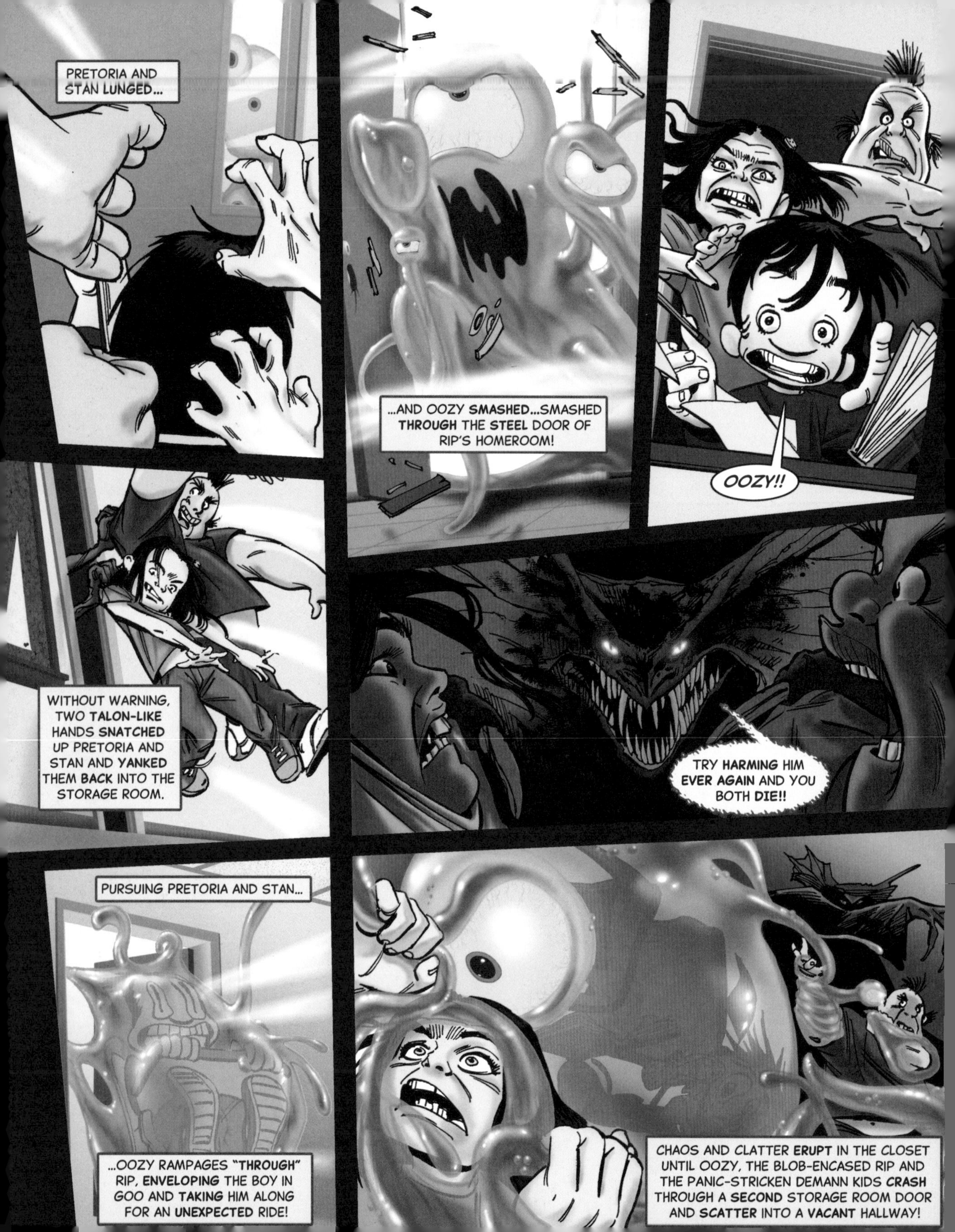
PRETORIA AND STAN LUNGED...
...AND OOZY SMASHED...SMASHED THROUGH THE STEEL DOOR OF RIP'S HOMEROOM!
OOZY!!
WITHOUT WARNING, TWO TALON-LIKE HANDS SNATCHED UP PRETORIA AND STAN AND YANKED THEM BACK INTO THE STORAGE ROOM.
TRY HARMING HIM EVER AGAIN AND YOU BOTH DIE!!
PURSUING PRETORIA AND STAN...
...OOZY RAMPAGES "THROUGH" RIP, ENVELOPING THE BOY IN GOO AND TAKING HIM ALONG FOR AN UNEXPECTED RIDE!
CHAOS AND CLATTER ERUPT IN THE CLOSET UNTIL OOZY, THE BLOB-ENCASED RIP AND THE PANIC-STRICKEN DEMANN KIDS CRASH THROUGH A SECOND STORAGE ROOM DOOR AND SCATTER INTO A VACANT HALLWAY!

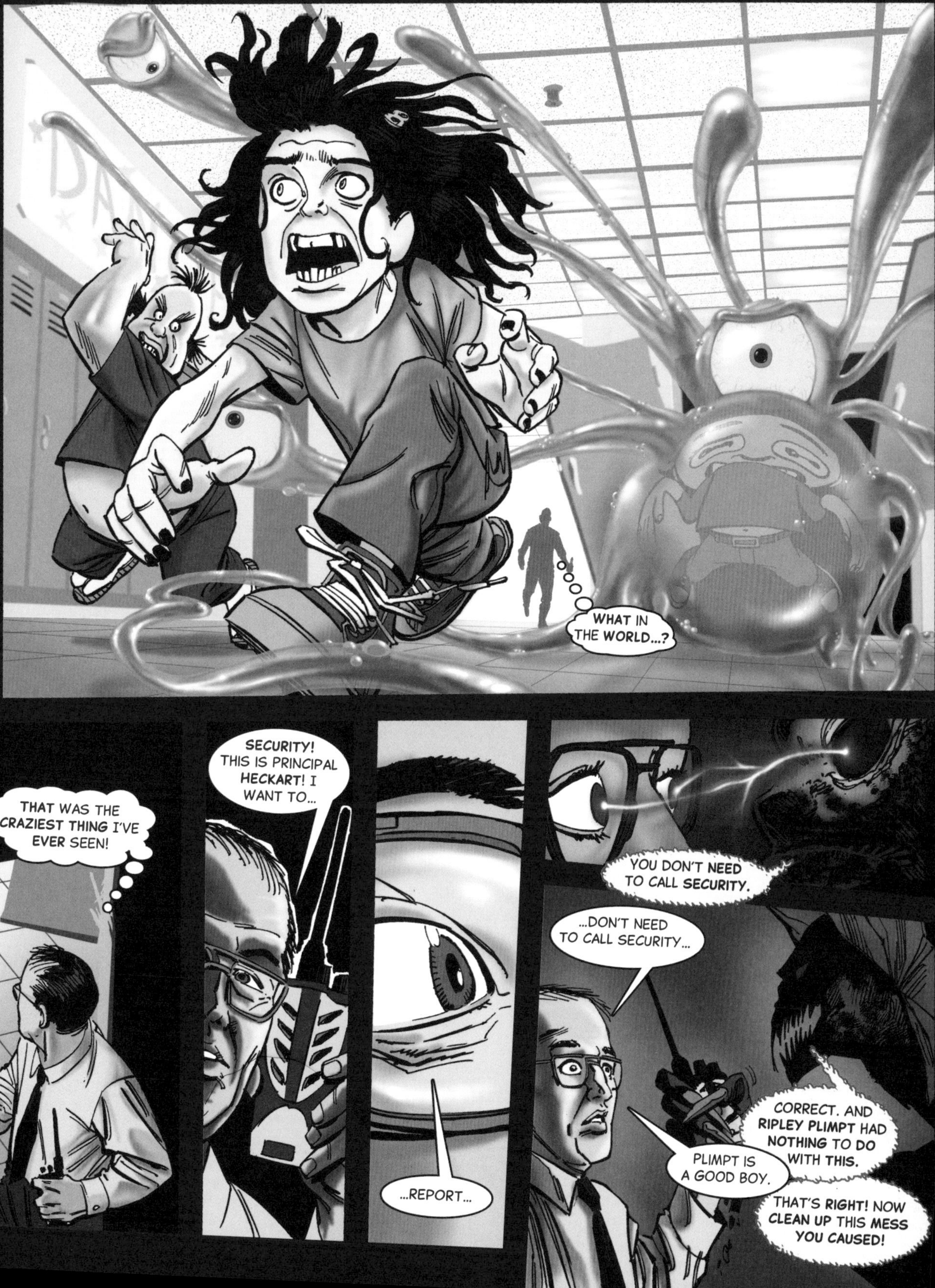
WHAT IN THE WORLD...?
THAT WAS THE CRAZIEST THING I'VE EVER SEEN!
SECURITY! THIS IS PRINCIPAL HECKART! I WANT TO...
...REPORT...
YOU DON'T NEED TO CALL SECURITY.
...DON'T NEED TO CALL SECURITY...
CORRECT. AND RIPLEY PLIMPT HAD NOTHING TO DO WITH THIS.
PLIMPT IS A GOOD BOY.
THAT'S RIGHT! NOW CLEAN UP THIS MESS YOU CAUSED!

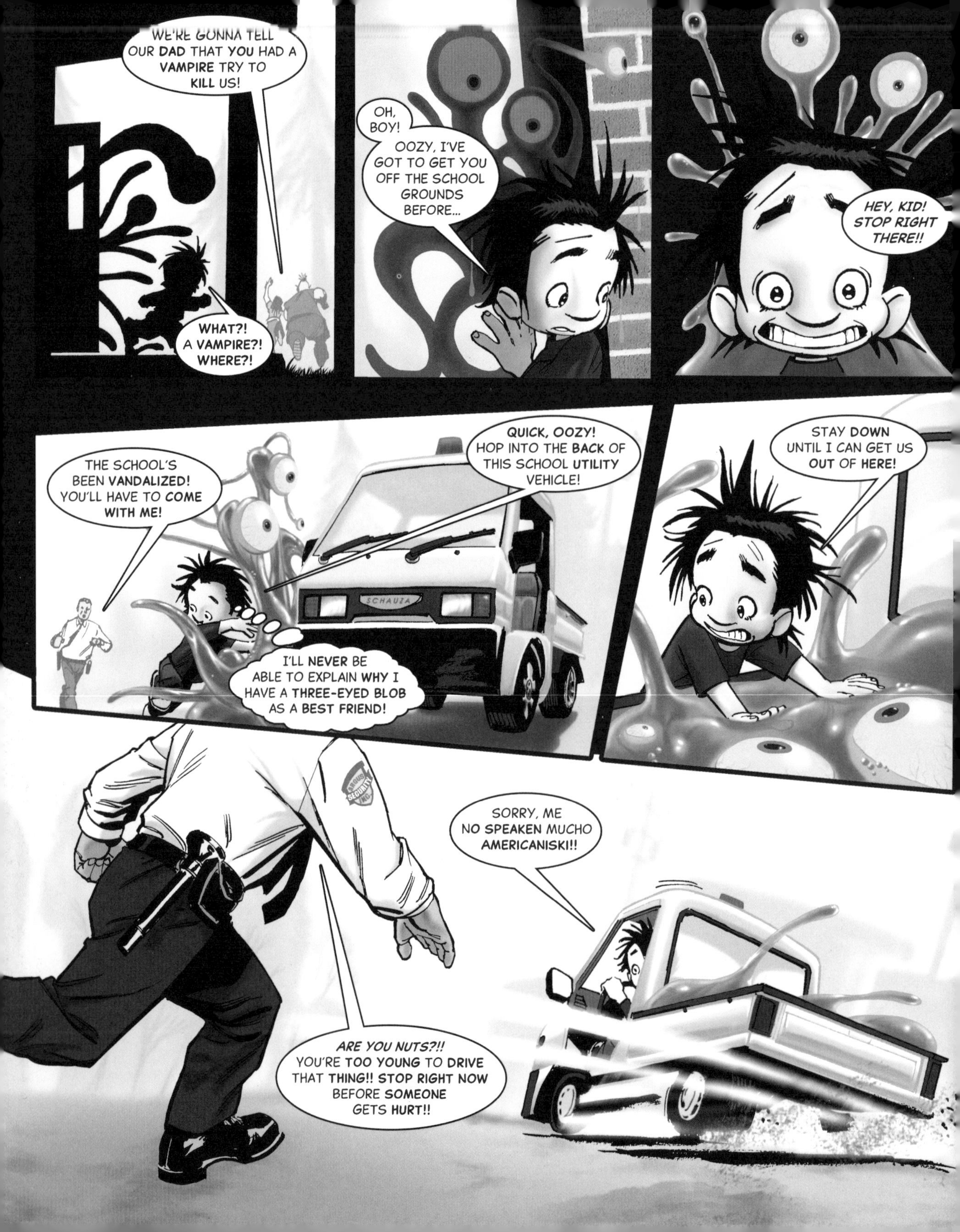
WE'RE GONNA TELL OUR DAD THAT YOU HAD A VAMPIRE TRY TO KILL US!
WHAT?! A VAMPIRE?! WHERE?!
OH, BOY!
OOZY, I'VE GOT TO GET YOU OFF THE SCHOOL GROUNDS BEFORE...
HEY, KID! STOP RIGHT THERE!!
THE SCHOOL'S BEEN VANDALIZED! YOU'LL HAVE TO COME WITH ME!
QUICK, OOZY! HOP INTO THE BACK OF THIS SCHOOL UTILITY VEHICLE!
SCHAUZA
I'LL NEVER BE ABLE TO EXPLAIN WHY I HAVE A THREE-EYED BLOB AS A BEST FRIEND!
STAY DOWN UNTIL I CAN GET US OUT OF HERE!
SORRY, ME NO SPEAKEN MUCHO AMERICANISKI!!
ARE YOU NUTS?!! YOU'RE TOO YOUNG TO DRIVE THAT THING!! STOP RIGHT NOW BEFORE SOMEONE GETS HURT!!

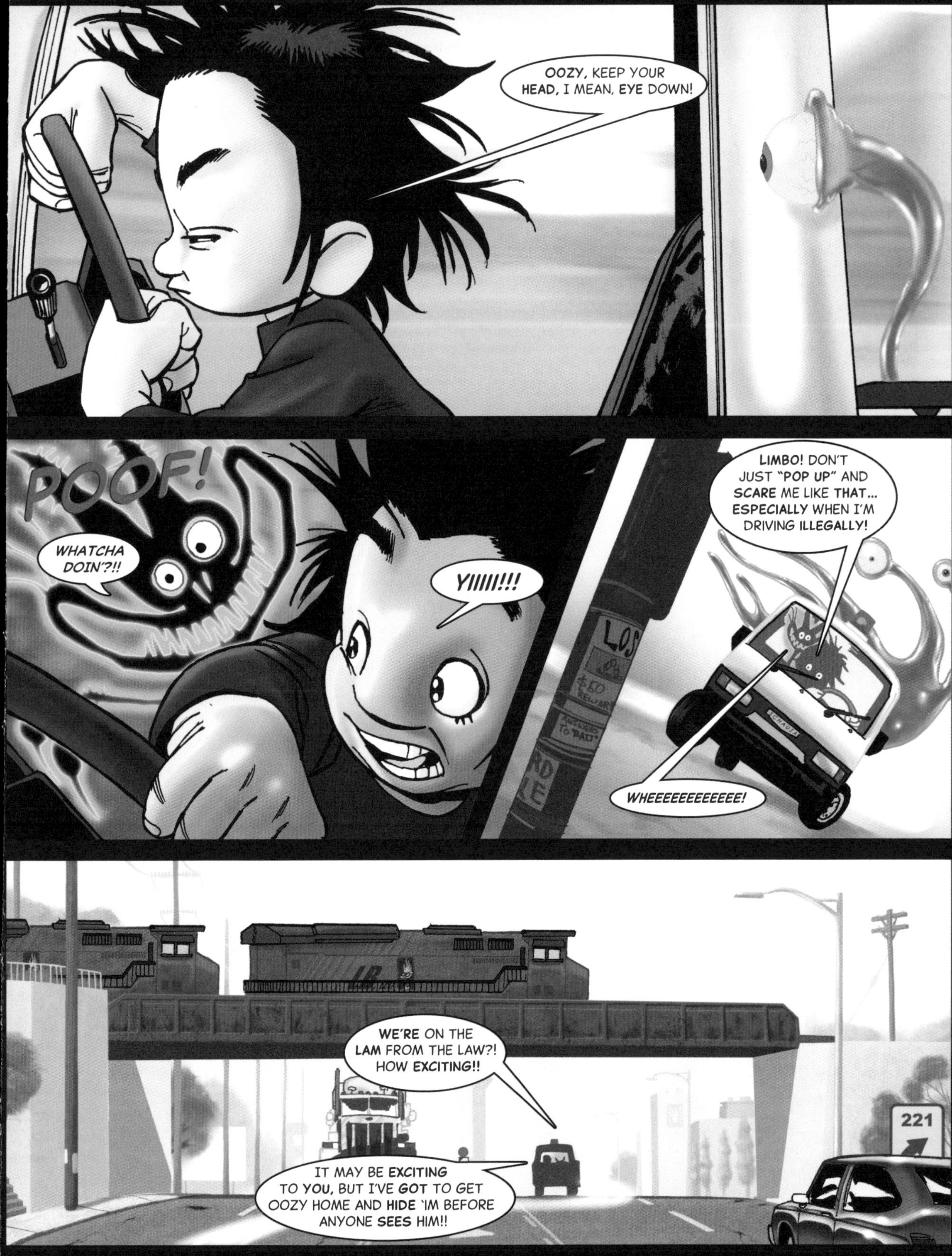
OOZY, KEEP YOUR HEAD, I MEAN, EYE DOWN!
POOF!
WHATCHA DOIN'?!!
YIIIII!!!
LIMBO! DON'T JUST "POP UP" AND SCARE ME LIKE THAT... ESPECIALLY WHEN I'M DRIVING ILLEGALLY!
WHEEEEEEEEEEEE!
WE'RE ON THE LAM FROM THE LAW?! HOW EXCITING!!
IT MAY BE EXCITING TO YOU, BUT I'VE GOT TO GET OOZY HOME AND HIDE 'IM BEFORE ANYONE SEES HIM!!
221

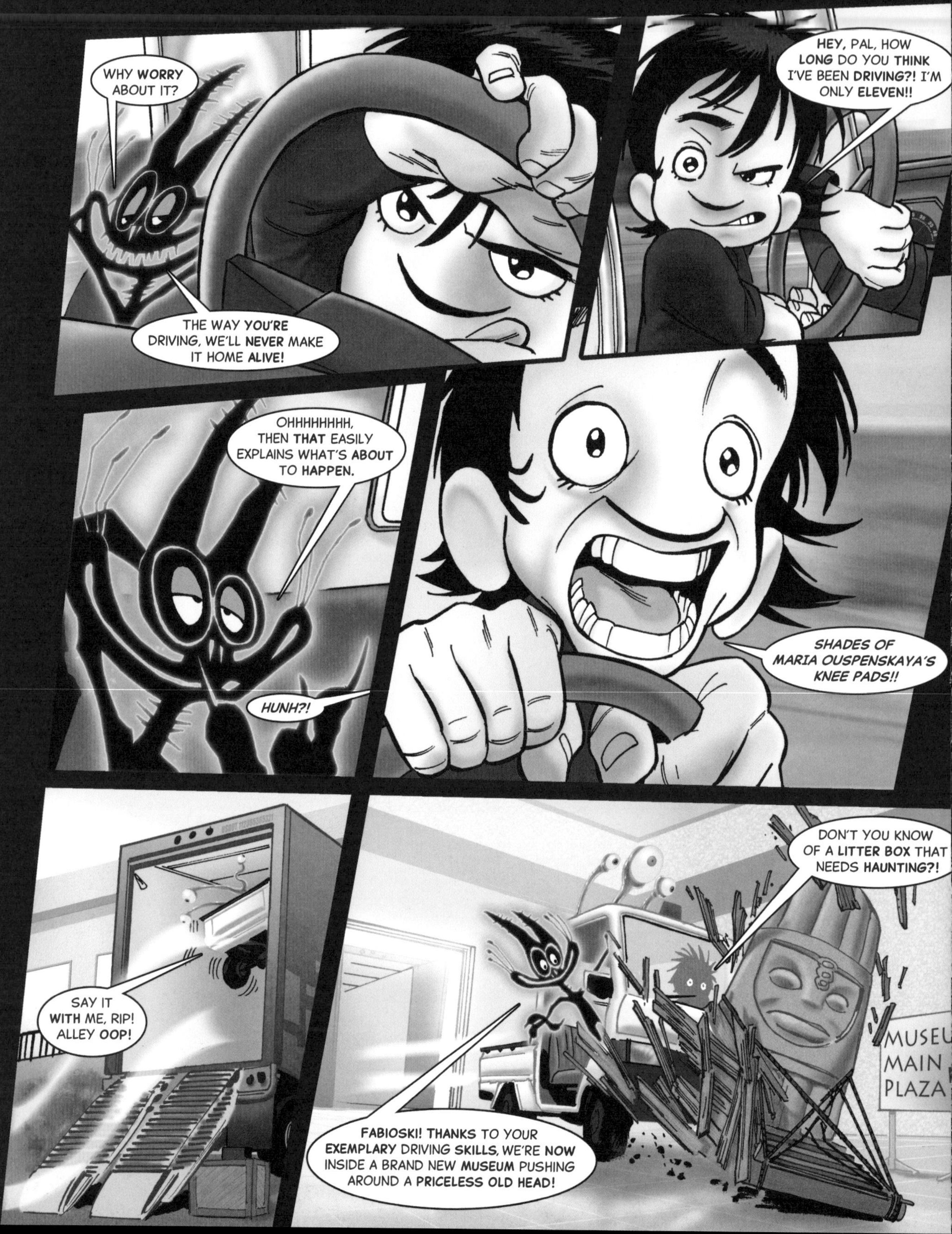
WHY WORRY ABOUT IT?
THE WAY YOU'RE DRIVING, WE'LL NEVER MAKE IT HOME ALIVE!
HEY, PAL, HOW LONG DO YOU THINK I'VE BEEN DRIVING?! I'M ONLY ELEVEN!!
OHHHHHHHH, THEN THAT EASILY EXPLAINS WHAT'S ABOUT TO HAPPEN.
HUNH?!
SHADES OF MARIA OUSPENSKAYA'S KNEE PADS!!
SAY IT WITH ME, RIP! ALLEY OOP!
DON'T YOU KNOW OF A LITTER BOX THAT NEEDS HAUNTING?!
FABIOSKI! THANKS TO YOUR EXEMPLARY DRIVING SKILLS, WE'RE NOW INSIDE A BRAND NEW MUSEUM PUSHING AROUND A PRICELESS OLD HEAD!
MUSEU
MAIN
PLAZA

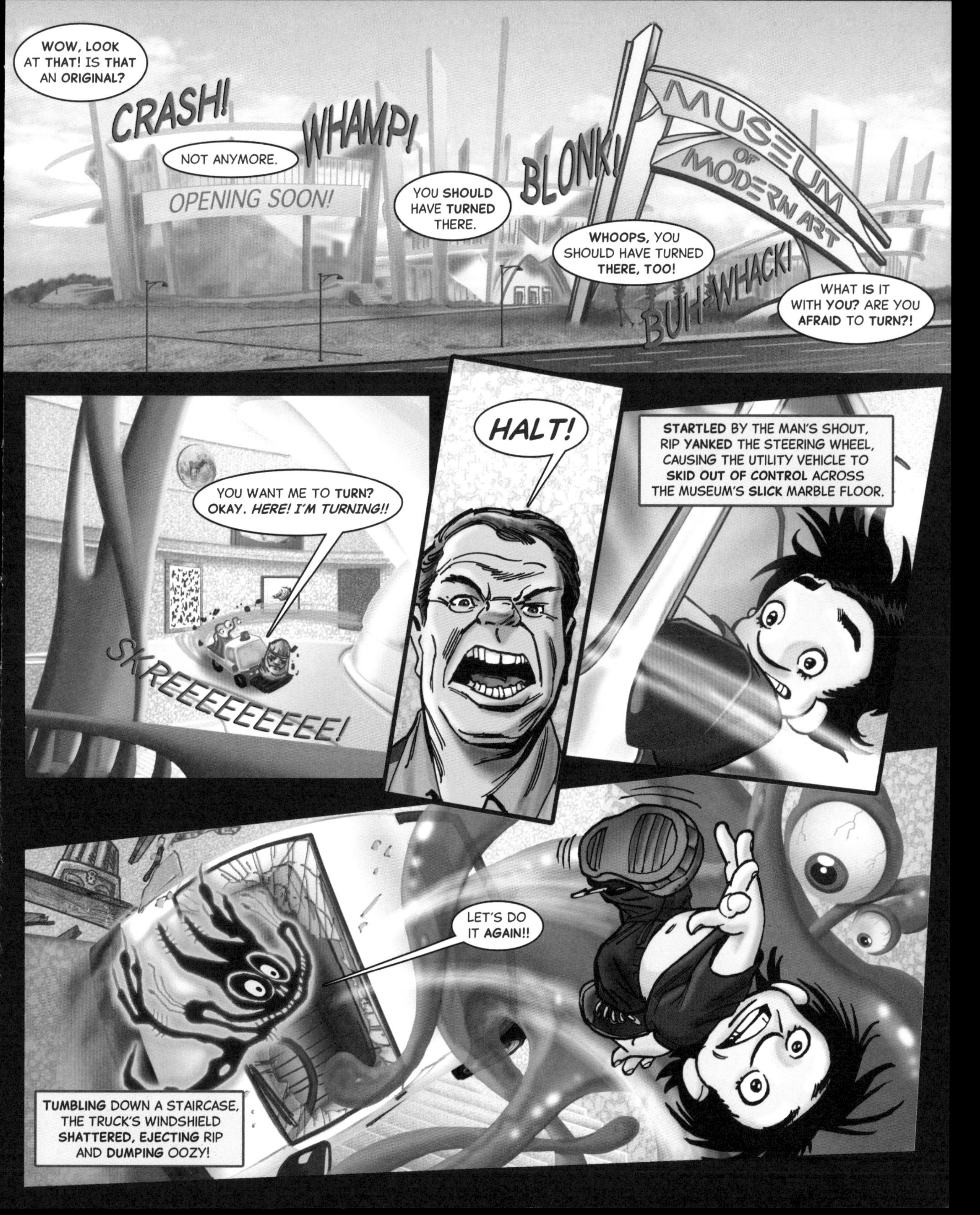
WOW, LOOK AT THAT! IS THAT AN ORIGINAL?
CRASH!
NOT ANYMORE.
OPENING SOON!
WHAMP!
YOU SHOULD HAVE TURNED THERE.
BLONK!
MUSEUM OF MODERN ART
WHOOPS, YOU SHOULD HAVE TURNED THERE, TOO!
BUH-WHACK!
WHAT IS IT WITH YOU? ARE YOU AFRAID TO TURN?!
YOU WANT ME TO TURN? OKAY. HERE! I'M TURNING!!
SKREEEEEEEEEEE!
HALT!
STARTLED BY THE MAN'S SHOUT, RIP YANKED THE STEERING WHEEL, CAUSING THE UTILITY VEHICLE TO SKID OUT OF CONTROL ACROSS THE MUSEUM'S SLICK MARBLE FLOOR.
LET'S DO IT AGAIN!!
TUMBLING DOWN A STAIRCASE, THE TRUCK'S WINDSHIELD SHATTERED, EJECTING RIP AND DUMPING OOZY!

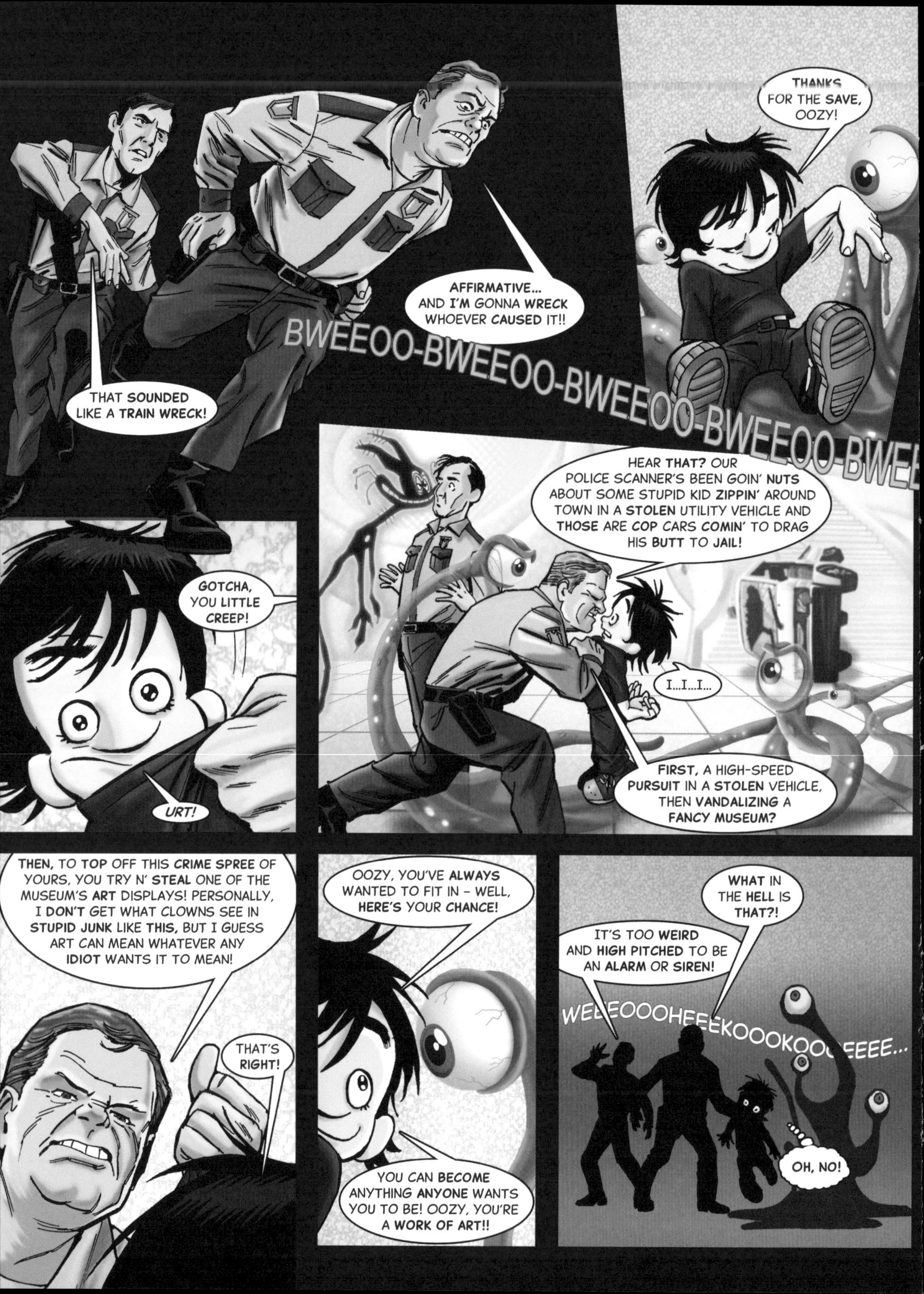
THAT SOUNDED LIKE A TRAIN WRECK!
AFFIRMATIVE... AND I'M GONNA WRECK WHOEVER CAUSED IT!!
BWEEOO-BWEEOO-BWEEOO-BWEEOO-BWEE
THANKS FOR THE SAVE, OOZY!
GOTCHA, YOU LITTLE CREEP!
URT!
HEAR THAT? OUR POLICE SCANNER'S BEEN GOIN' NUTS ABOUT SOME STUPID KID ZIPPIN' AROUND TOWN IN A STOLEN UTILITY VEHICLE AND THOSE ARE COP CARS COMIN' TO DRAG HIS BUTT TO JAIL!
I...I...I...
FIRST, A HIGH-SPEED PURSUIT IN A STOLEN VEHICLE, THEN VANDALIZING A FANCY MUSEUM?
THEN, TO TOP OFF THIS CRIME SPREE OF YOURS, YOU TRY N' STEAL ONE OF THE MUSEUM'S ART DISPLAYS! PERSONALLY, I DON'T GET WHAT CLOWNS SEE IN STUPID JUNK LIKE THIS, BUT I GUESS ART CAN MEAN WHATEVER ANY IDIOT WANTS IT TO MEAN!
THAT'S RIGHT!
OOZY, YOU'VE ALWAYS WANTED TO FIT IN – WELL, HERE'S YOUR CHANCE!
YOU CAN BECOME ANYTHING ANYONE WANTS YOU TO BE! OOZY, YOU'RE A WORK OF ART!!
WHAT IN THE HELL IS THAT?!
IT'S TOO WEIRD AND HIGH PITCHED TO BE AN ALARM OR SIREN!
WEEEOOOHEEEKOOOKOOOEEEE...
OH, NO!

WEEEOOOHEEEKOOOKOOOEEEE...
CRIPES! IT'S A WEREWOLF!! A VERY GAY LOOKING WEREWOLF!!!
IT'S ATTACKING THE KID!
LESTER, NO! THIS ISN'T THE TIME TO PRACTICE AN ATTACK!!
NO ONE'S GETTING ATTACKED ON MY WATCH, NOT EVEN A THIEVING LITTLE KID!
FULLY CHARGED! LET 'IM HAVE IT!!
BROTAZE
FWOWFF!

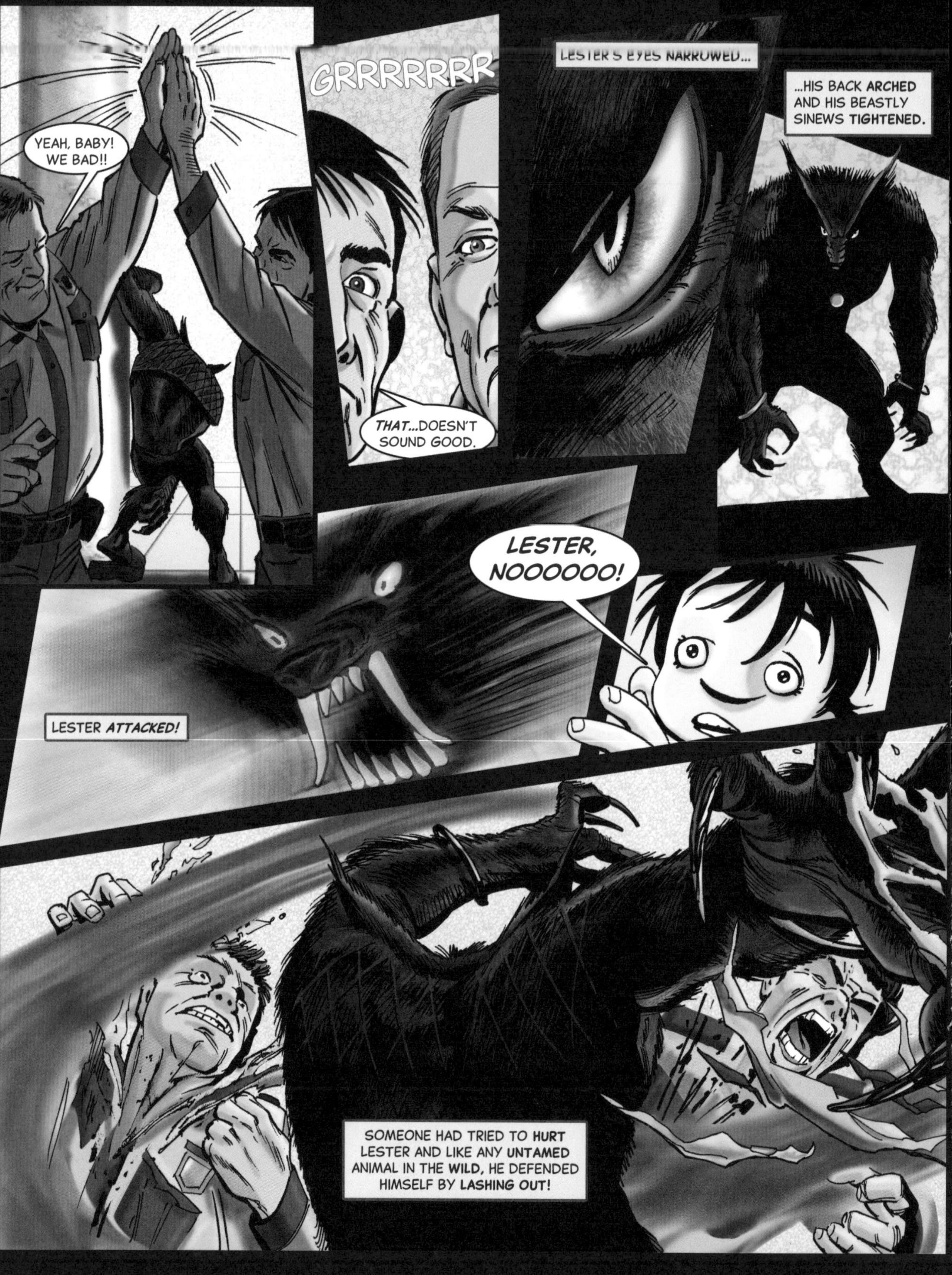
YEAH, BABY! WE BAD!!
GRRRRRRR
THAT...DOESN'T SOUND GOOD.
LESTER'S EYES NARROWED...
...HIS BACK ARCHED AND HIS BEASTLY SINEWS TIGHTENED.
LESTER ATTACKED!
LESTER, NOOOOOO!
SOMEONE HAD TRIED TO HURT LESTER AND LIKE ANY UNTAMED ANIMAL IN THE WILD, HE DEFENDED HIMSELF BY LASHING OUT!

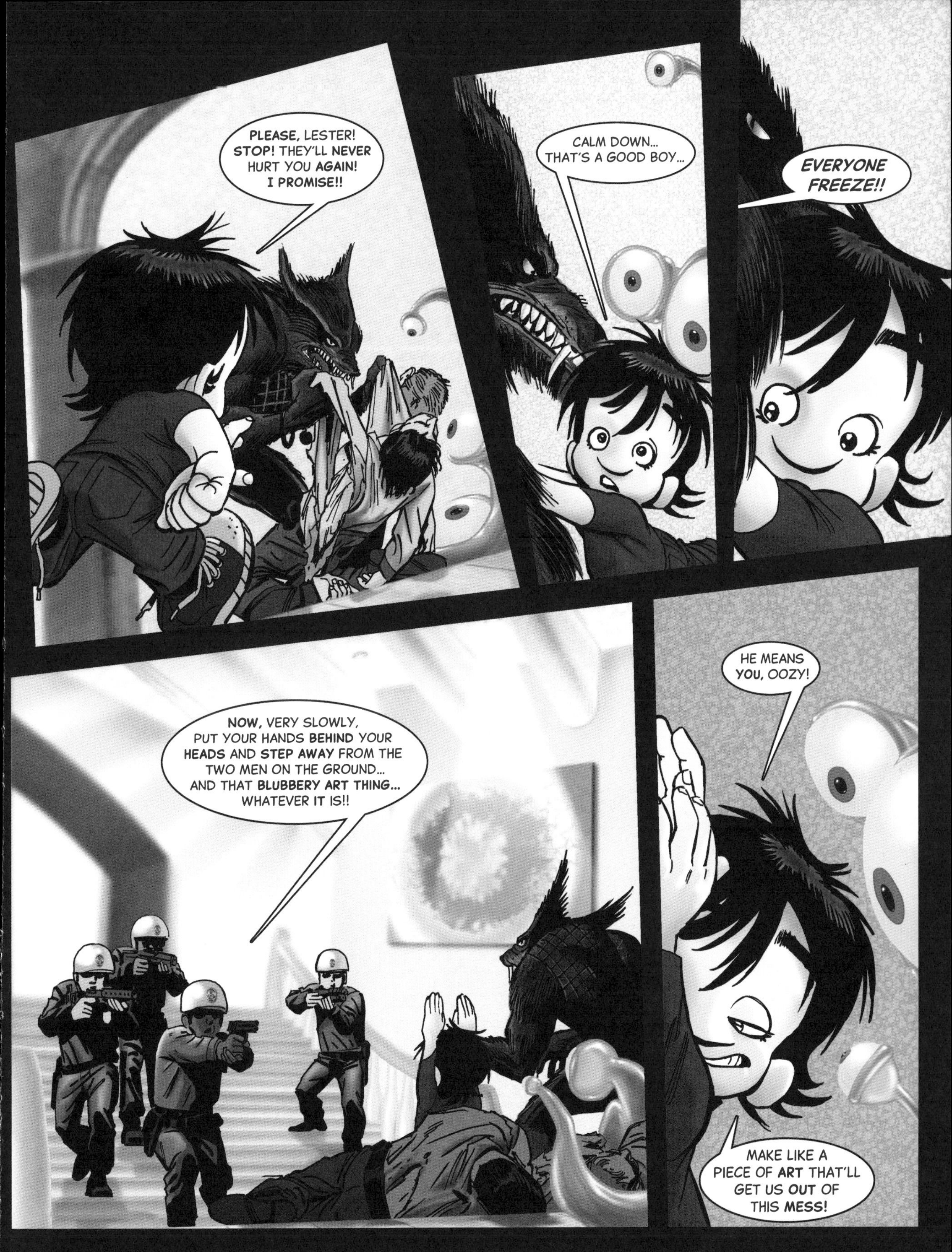
PLEASE, LESTER! STOP! THEY'LL NEVER HURT YOU AGAIN! I PROMISE!!
CALM DOWN... THAT'S A GOOD BOY...
EVERYONE FREEZE!!
NOW, VERY SLOWLY, PUT YOUR HANDS BEHIND YOUR HEADS AND STEP AWAY FROM THE TWO MEN ON THE GROUND... AND THAT BLUBBERY ART THING... WHATEVER IT IS!!
HE MEANS YOU, OOZY!
MAKE LIKE A PIECE OF ART THAT'LL GET US OUT OF THIS MESS!

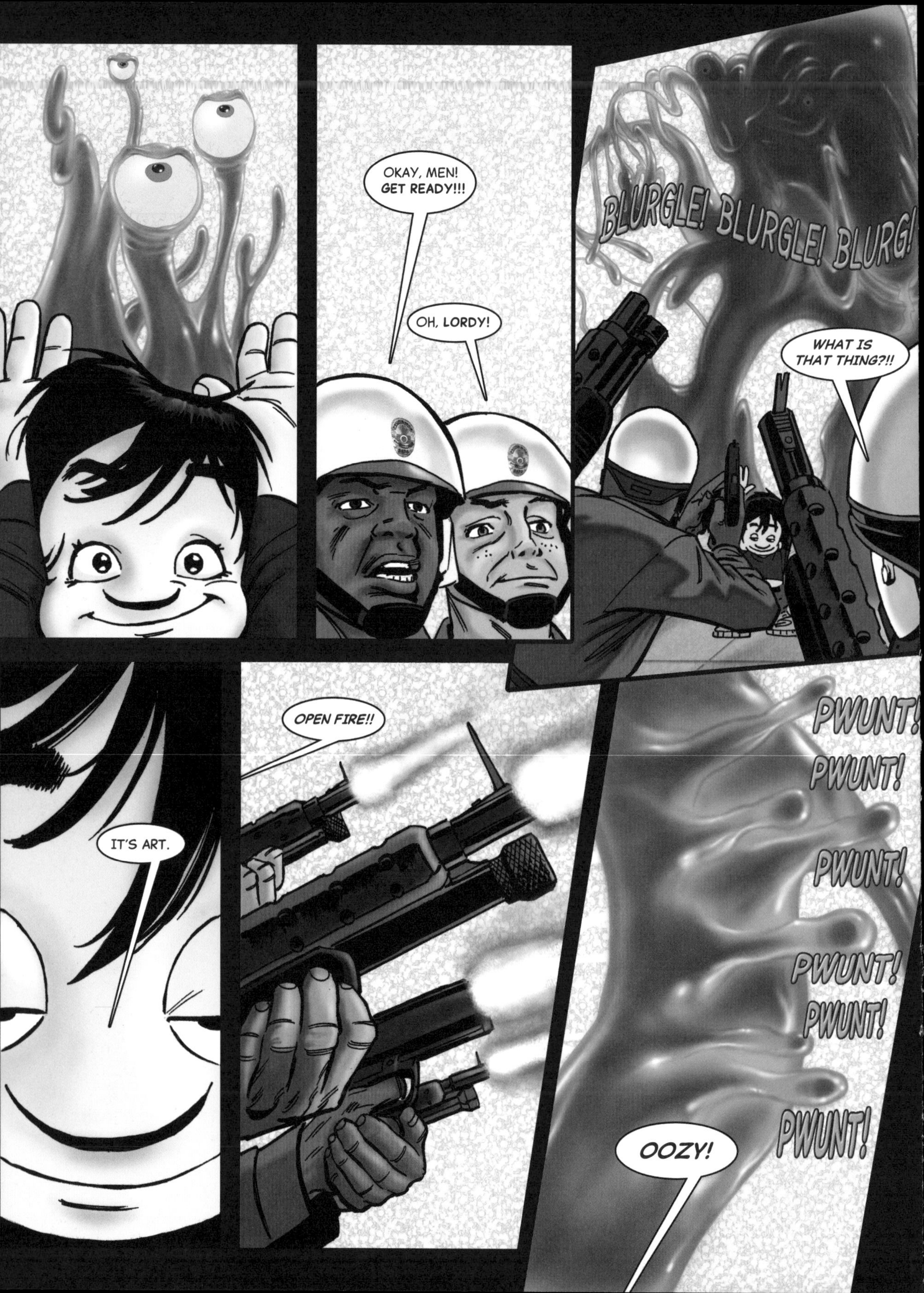

OKAY, MEN! GET READY!!!
OH, LORDY!
BLURGLE! BLURGLE! BLURG!
WHAT IS THAT THING?!!
IT'S ART.
OPEN FIRE!!
PWUNT!
PWUNT!
PWUNT!
PWUNT!
PWUNT!
PWUNT!
OOZY!

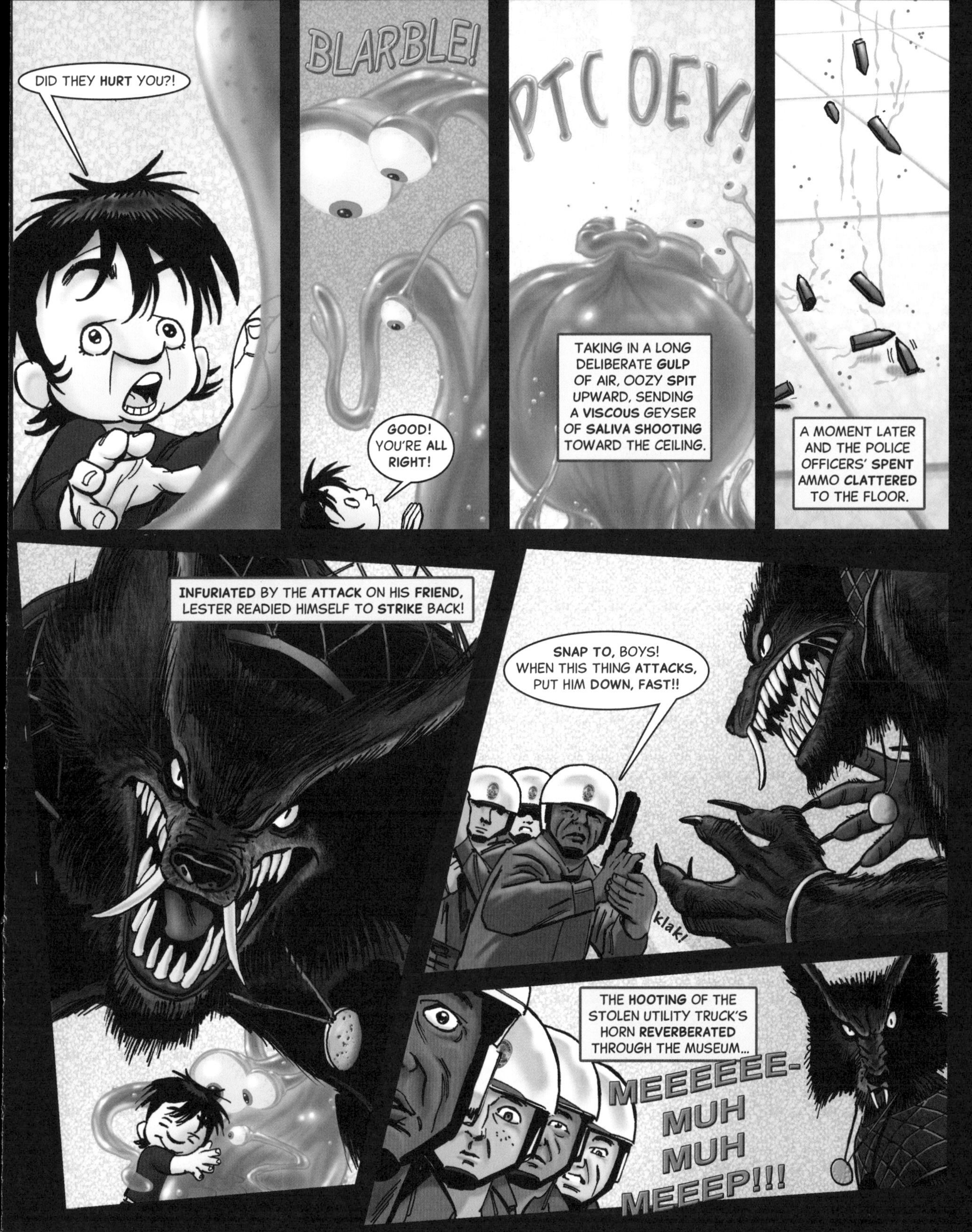
DID THEY **HURT** YOU?!
BLARBLE!
GOOD! YOU'RE **ALL RIGHT**!
PTC OEY!
TAKING IN A LONG DELIBERATE **GULP** OF AIR, OOZY **SPIT** UPWARD, SENDING A **VISCOUS** GEYSER OF **SALIVA SHOOTING** TOWARD THE CEILING.
A MOMENT LATER AND THE POLICE OFFICERS' **SPENT** AMMO **CLATTERED** TO THE FLOOR.
INFURIATED BY THE **ATTACK** ON HIS **FRIEND**, LESTER READIED HIMSELF TO **STRIKE** BACK!
SNAP TO, BOYS! WHEN THIS THING **ATTACKS**, PUT HIM **DOWN, FAST!!**
klak!
THE **HOOTING** OF THE STOLEN UTILITY TRUCK'S HORN **REVERBERATED** THROUGH THE MUSEUM...
MEEEEEE-MUH MUH MEEEP!!!

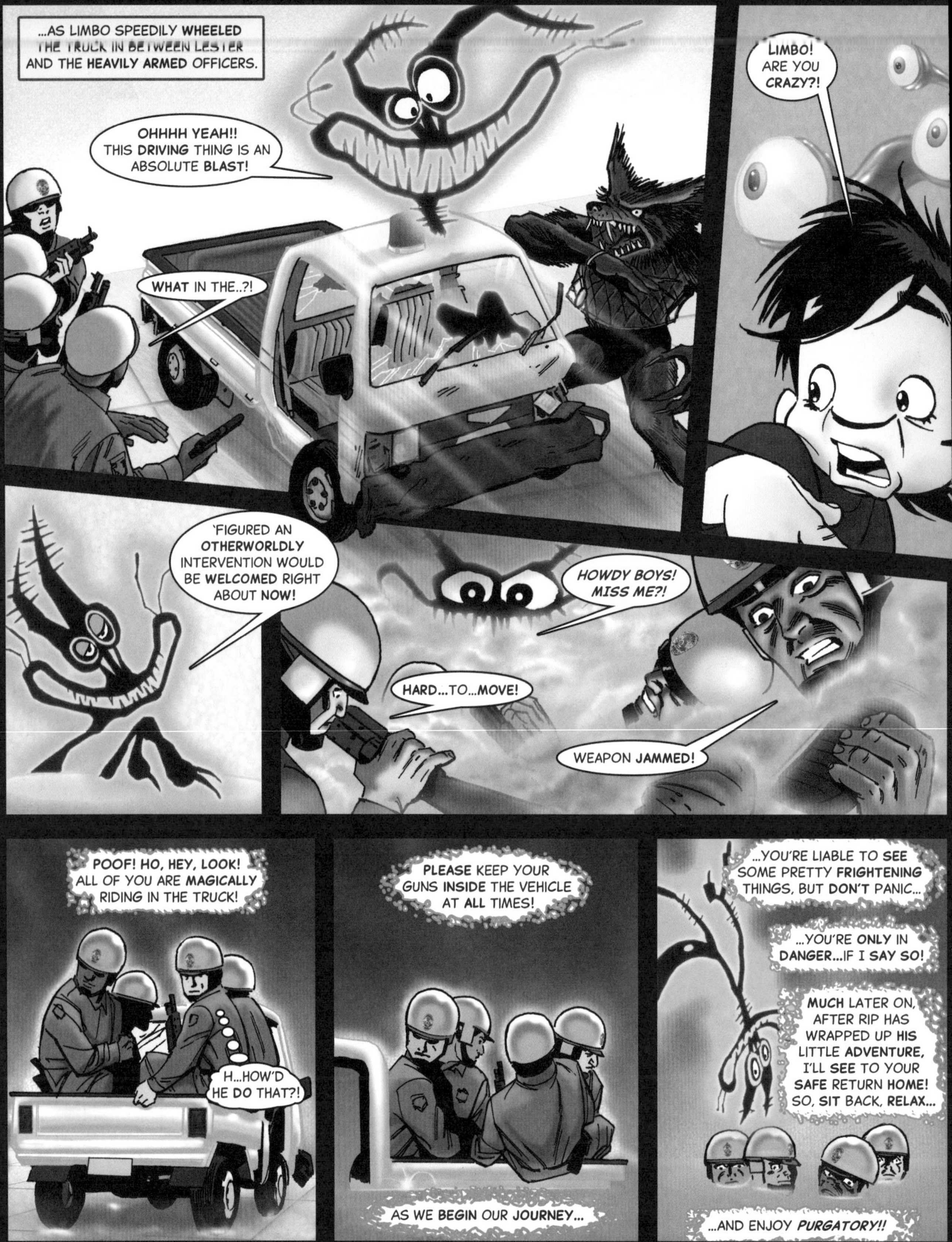
...AS LIMBO SPEEDILY WHEELED THE TRUCK IN BETWEEN LESTER AND THE HEAVILY ARMED OFFICERS.
OHHHH YEAH!! THIS DRIVING THING IS AN ABSOLUTE BLAST!
WHAT IN THE..?!
LIMBO! ARE YOU CRAZY?!
'FIGURED AN OTHERWORLDLY INTERVENTION WOULD BE WELCOMED RIGHT ABOUT NOW!
HOWDY BOYS! MISS ME?!
HARD...TO...MOVE!
WEAPON JAMMED!
POOF! HO, HEY, LOOK! ALL OF YOU ARE MAGICALLY RIDING IN THE TRUCK!
H...HOW'D HE DO THAT?!
PLEASE KEEP YOUR GUNS INSIDE THE VEHICLE AT ALL TIMES!
AS WE BEGIN OUR JOURNEY...
...YOU'RE LIABLE TO SEE SOME PRETTY FRIGHTENING THINGS, BUT DON'T PANIC...
...YOU'RE ONLY IN DANGER...IF I SAY SO!
MUCH LATER ON, AFTER RIP HAS WRAPPED UP HIS LITTLE ADVENTURE, I'LL SEE TO YOUR SAFE RETURN HOME! SO, SIT BACK, RELAX...
...AND ENJOY PURGATORY!!

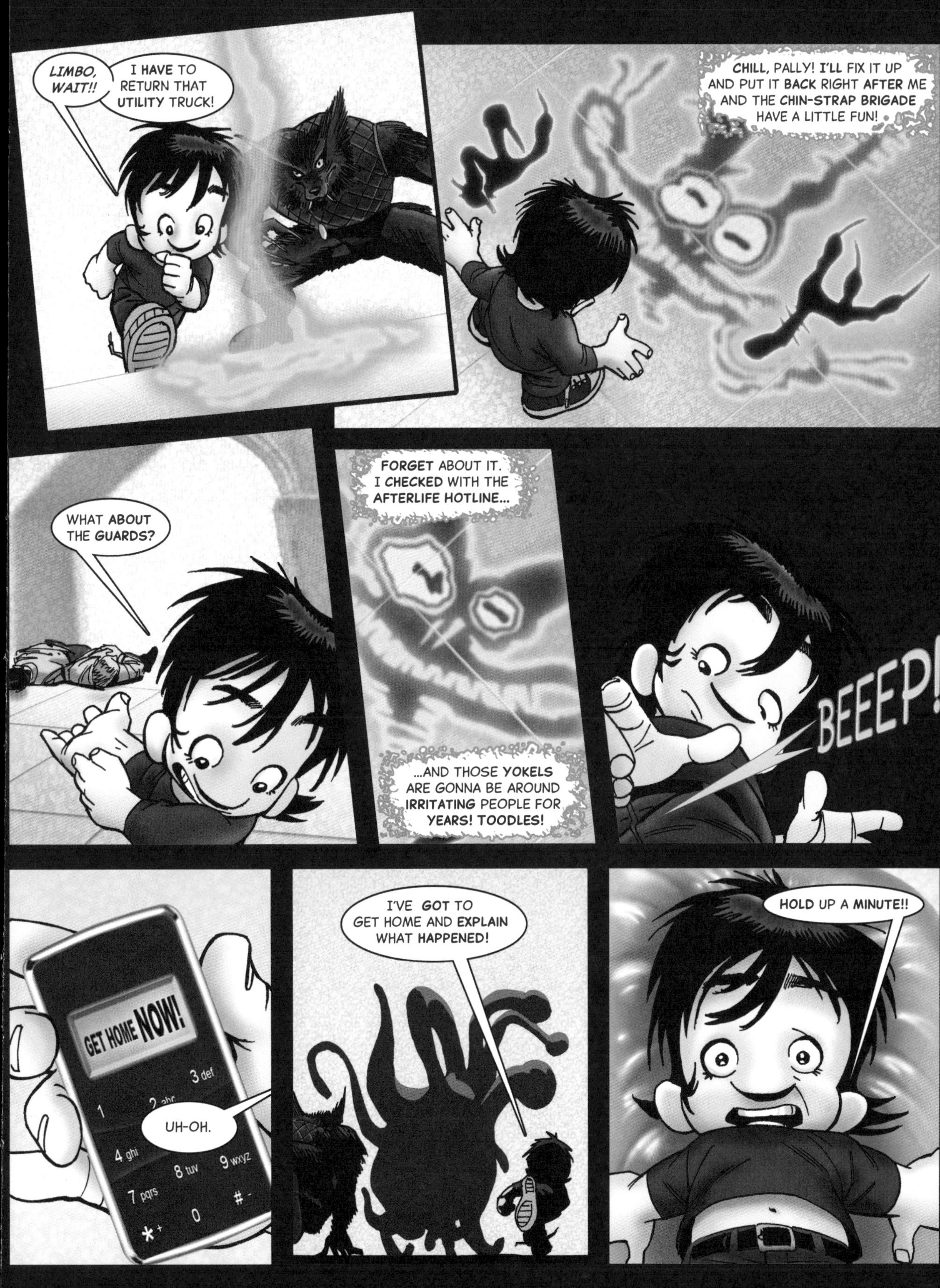
LIMBO, WAIT!!
I HAVE TO RETURN THAT UTILITY TRUCK!
CHILL, PALLY! I'LL FIX IT UP AND PUT IT BACK RIGHT AFTER ME AND THE CHIN-STRAP BRIGADE HAVE A LITTLE FUN!
WHAT ABOUT THE GUARDS?
FORGET ABOUT IT. I CHECKED WITH THE AFTERLIFE HOTLINE...
...AND THOSE YOKELS ARE GONNA BE AROUND IRRITATING PEOPLE FOR YEARS! TOODLES!
BEEEP!
GET HOME NOW!
3 def
2 abc
1
UH-OH.
4 ghi
8 tuv
9 wxyz
7 pqrs
0
#
*+
I'VE GOT TO GET HOME AND EXPLAIN WHAT HAPPENED!
HOLD UP A MINUTE!!

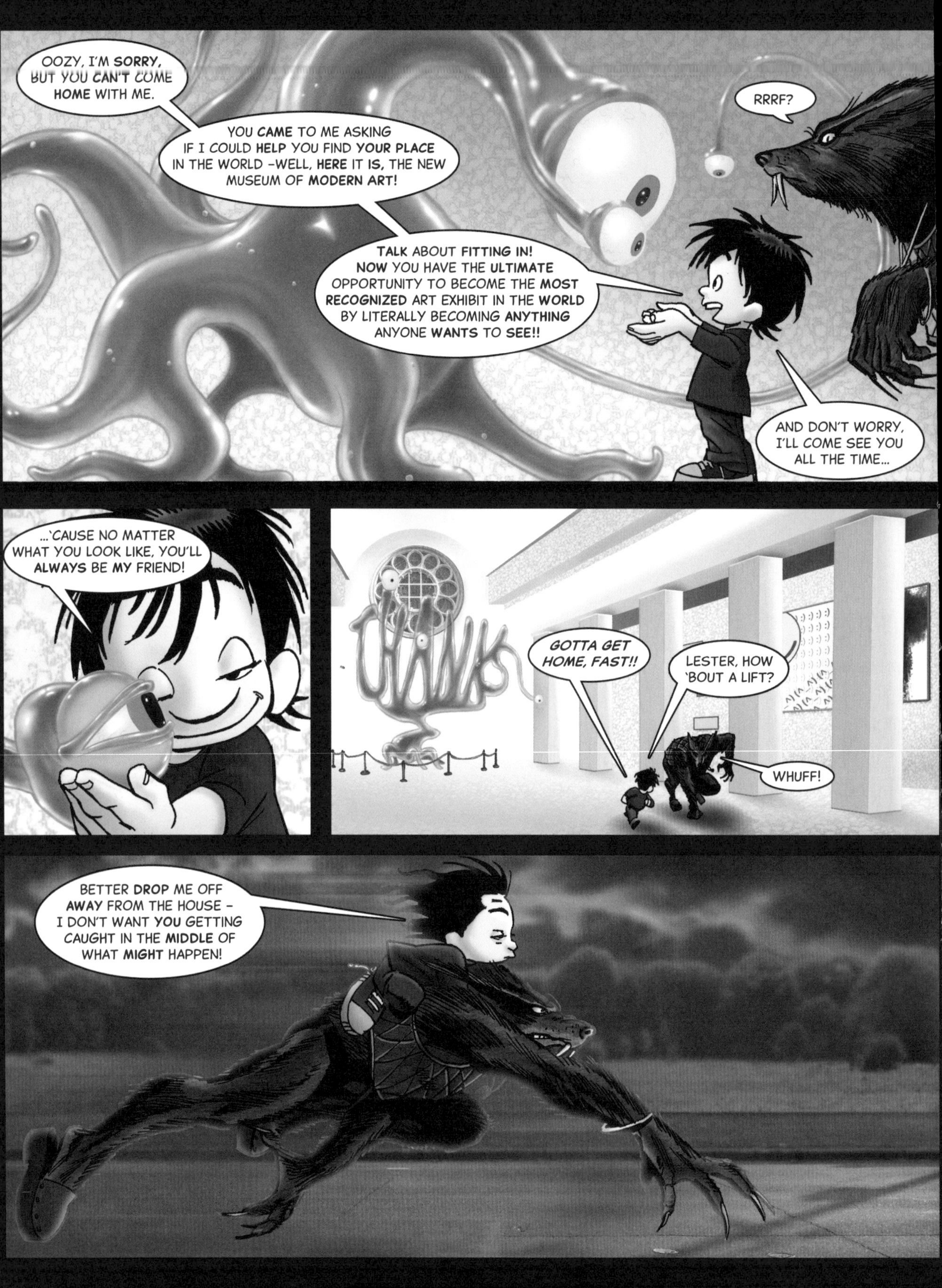
OOZY, I'M SORRY, BUT YOU CAN'T COME HOME WITH ME.
RRRF?
YOU CAME TO ME ASKING IF I COULD HELP YOU FIND YOUR PLACE IN THE WORLD –WELL, HERE IT IS, THE NEW MUSEUM OF MODERN ART!
TALK ABOUT FITTING IN! NOW YOU HAVE THE ULTIMATE OPPORTUNITY TO BECOME THE MOST RECOGNIZED ART EXHIBIT IN THE WORLD BY LITERALLY BECOMING ANYTHING ANYONE WANTS TO SEE!!
AND DON'T WORRY, I'LL COME SEE YOU ALL THE TIME...
...'CAUSE NO MATTER WHAT YOU LOOK LIKE, YOU'LL ALWAYS BE MY FRIEND!
GOTTA GET HOME, FAST!!
LESTER, HOW 'BOUT A LIFT?
WHUFF!
BETTER DROP ME OFF AWAY FROM THE HOUSE – I DON'T WANT YOU GETTING CAUGHT IN THE MIDDLE OF WHAT MIGHT HAPPEN!

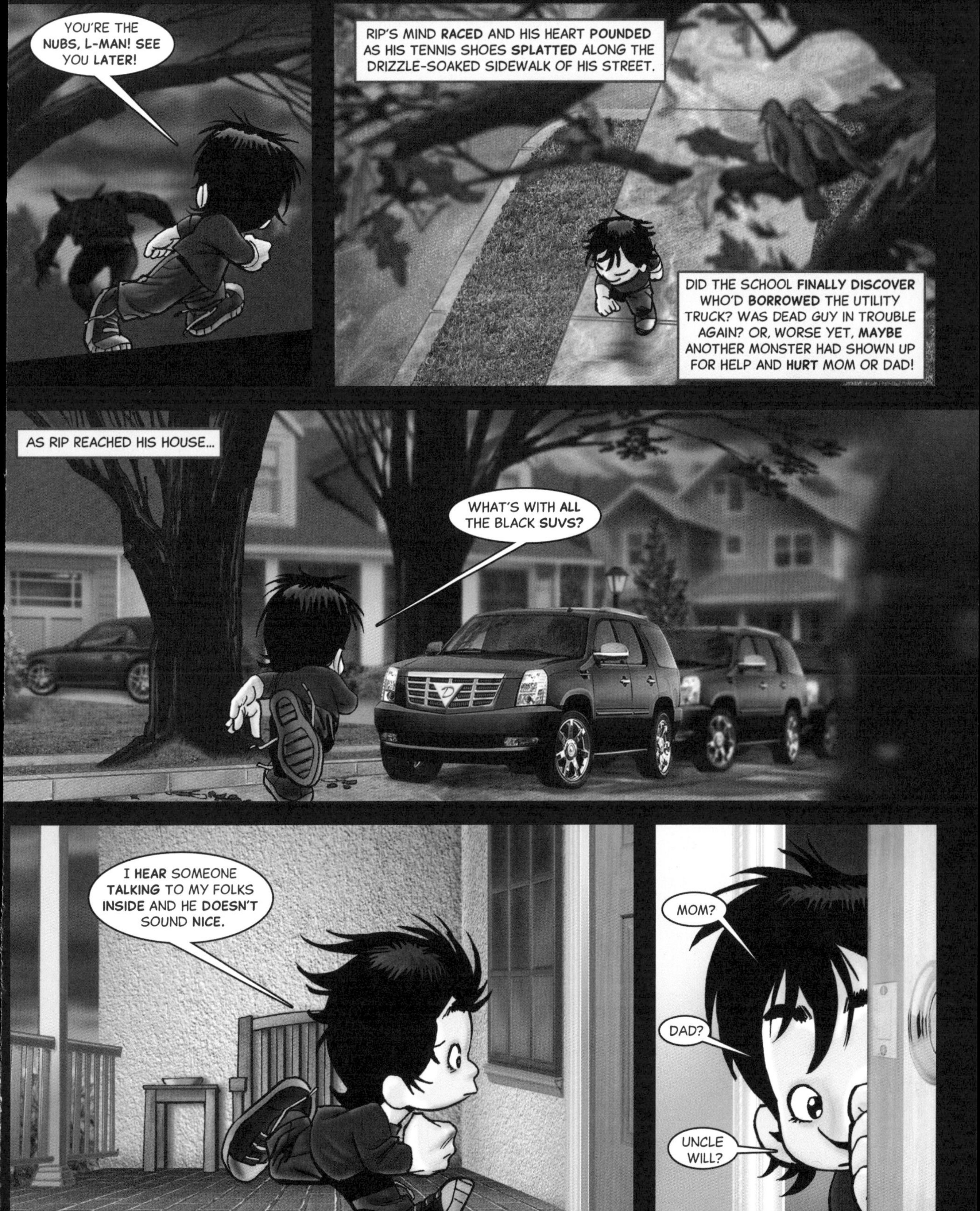
YOU'RE THE NUBS, L-MAN! SEE YOU LATER!
RIP'S MIND RACED AND HIS HEART POUNDED AS HIS TENNIS SHOES SPLATTED ALONG THE DRIZZLE-SOAKED SIDEWALK OF HIS STREET.
DID THE SCHOOL FINALLY DISCOVER WHO'D BORROWED THE UTILITY TRUCK? WAS DEAD GUY IN TROUBLE AGAIN? OR, WORSE YET, MAYBE ANOTHER MONSTER HAD SHOWN UP FOR HELP AND HURT MOM OR DAD!
AS RIP REACHED HIS HOUSE...
WHAT'S WITH ALL THE BLACK SUVS?
I HEAR SOMEONE TALKING TO MY FOLKS INSIDE AND HE DOESN'T SOUND NICE.
MOM?
DAD?
UNCLE WILL?

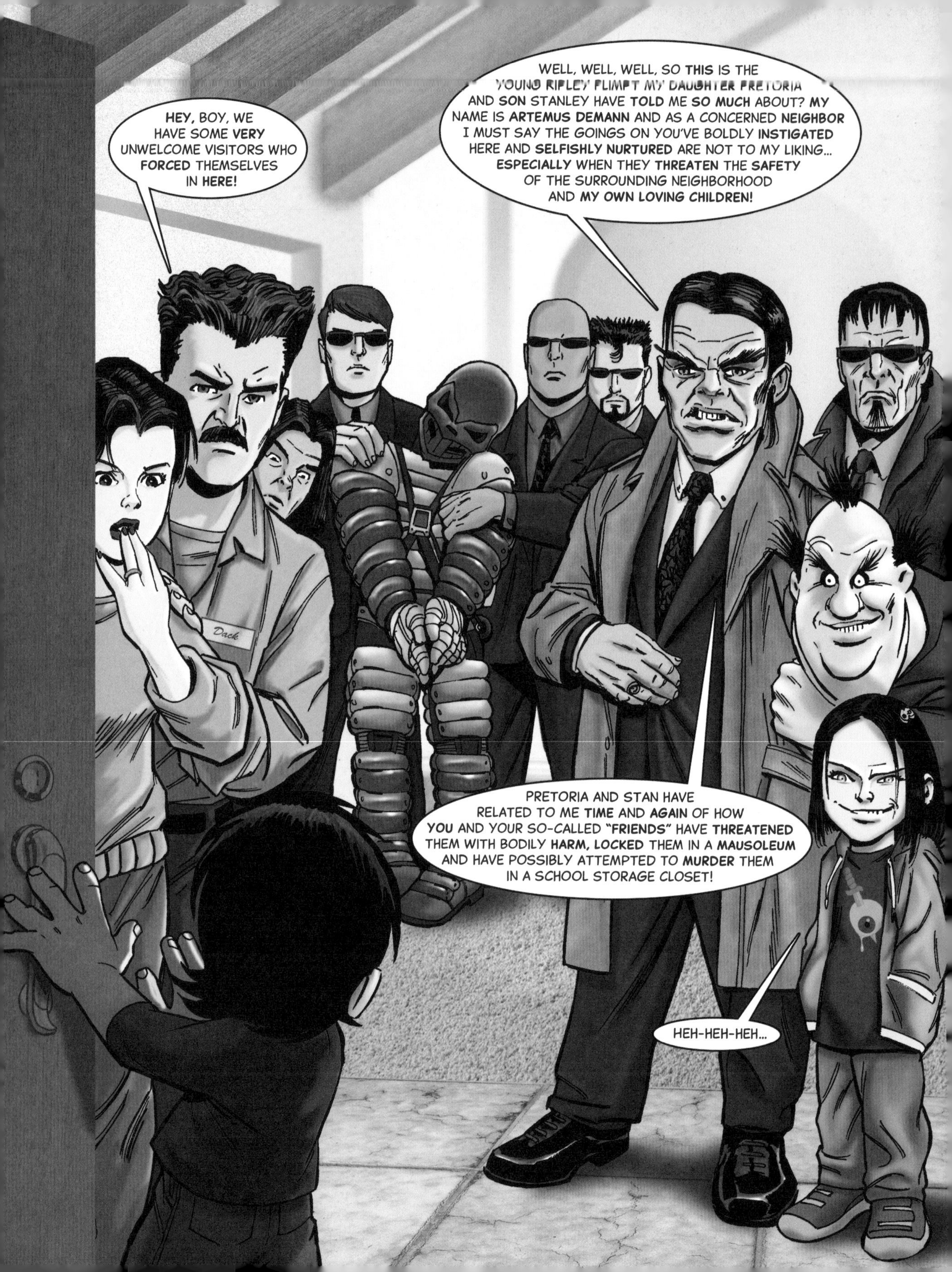
HEY, BOY, WE HAVE SOME VERY UNWELCOME VISITORS WHO FORCED THEMSELVES IN HERE!
WELL, WELL, WELL, SO THIS IS THE YOUNG RIPLEY FLIMPT MY DAUGHTER PRETORIA AND SON STANLEY HAVE TOLD ME SO MUCH ABOUT? MY NAME IS ARTEMUS DEMANN AND AS A CONCERNED NEIGHBOR I MUST SAY THE GOINGS ON YOU'VE BOLDLY INSTIGATED HERE AND SELFISHLY NURTURED ARE NOT TO MY LIKING... ESPECIALLY WHEN THEY THREATEN THE SAFETY OF THE SURROUNDING NEIGHBORHOOD AND MY OWN LOVING CHILDREN!
Dack
PRETORIA AND STAN HAVE RELATED TO ME TIME AND AGAIN OF HOW YOU AND YOUR SO-CALLED "FRIENDS" HAVE THREATENED THEM WITH BODILY HARM, LOCKED THEM IN A MAUSOLEUM AND HAVE POSSIBLY ATTEMPTED TO MURDER THEM IN A SCHOOL STORAGE CLOSET!
HEH-HEH-HEH...

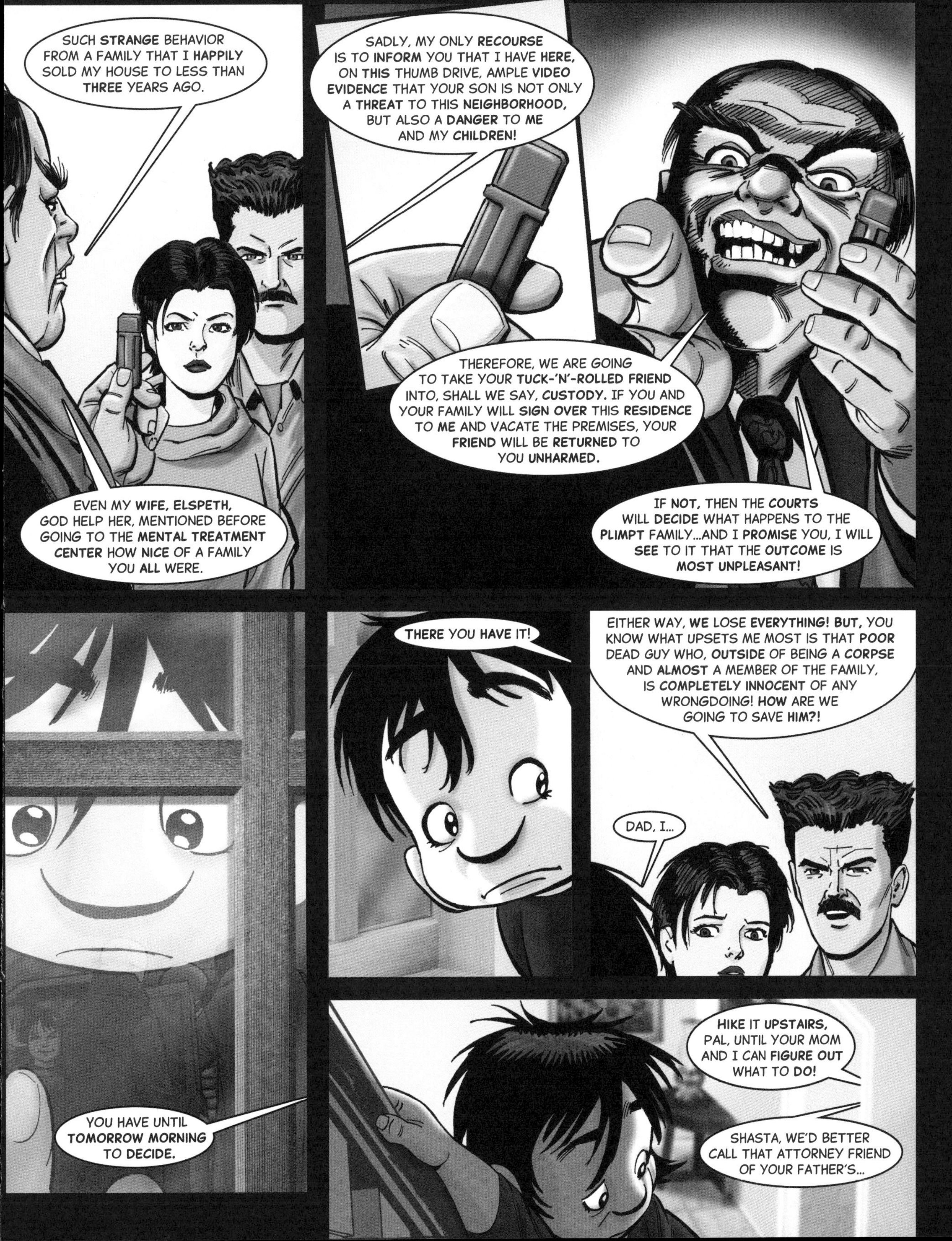
SUCH STRANGE BEHAVIOR FROM A FAMILY THAT I HAPPILY SOLD MY HOUSE TO LESS THAN THREE YEARS AGO.
EVEN MY WIFE, ELSPETH, GOD HELP HER, MENTIONED BEFORE GOING TO THE MENTAL TREATMENT CENTER HOW NICE OF A FAMILY YOU ALL WERE.
SADLY, MY ONLY RECOURSE IS TO INFORM YOU THAT I HAVE HERE, ON THIS THUMB DRIVE, AMPLE VIDEO EVIDENCE THAT YOUR SON IS NOT ONLY A THREAT TO THIS NEIGHBORHOOD, BUT ALSO A DANGER TO ME AND MY CHILDREN!
THEREFORE, WE ARE GOING TO TAKE YOUR TUCK-'N'-ROLLED FRIEND INTO, SHALL WE SAY, CUSTODY. IF YOU AND YOUR FAMILY WILL SIGN OVER THIS RESIDENCE TO ME AND VACATE THE PREMISES, YOUR FRIEND WILL BE RETURNED TO YOU UNHARMED.
IF NOT, THEN THE COURTS WILL DECIDE WHAT HAPPENS TO THE PLIMPT FAMILY...AND I PROMISE YOU, I WILL SEE TO IT THAT THE OUTCOME IS MOST UNPLEASANT!
YOU HAVE UNTIL TOMORROW MORNING TO DECIDE.
THERE YOU HAVE IT!
EITHER WAY, WE LOSE EVERYTHING! BUT, YOU KNOW WHAT UPSETS ME MOST IS THAT POOR DEAD GUY WHO, OUTSIDE OF BEING A CORPSE AND ALMOST A MEMBER OF THE FAMILY, IS COMPLETELY INNOCENT OF ANY WRONGDOING! HOW ARE WE GOING TO SAVE HIM?!
DAD, I...
HIKE IT UPSTAIRS, PAL, UNTIL YOUR MOM AND I CAN FIGURE OUT WHAT TO DO!
SHASTA, WE'D BETTER CALL THAT ATTORNEY FRIEND OF YOUR FATHER'S...

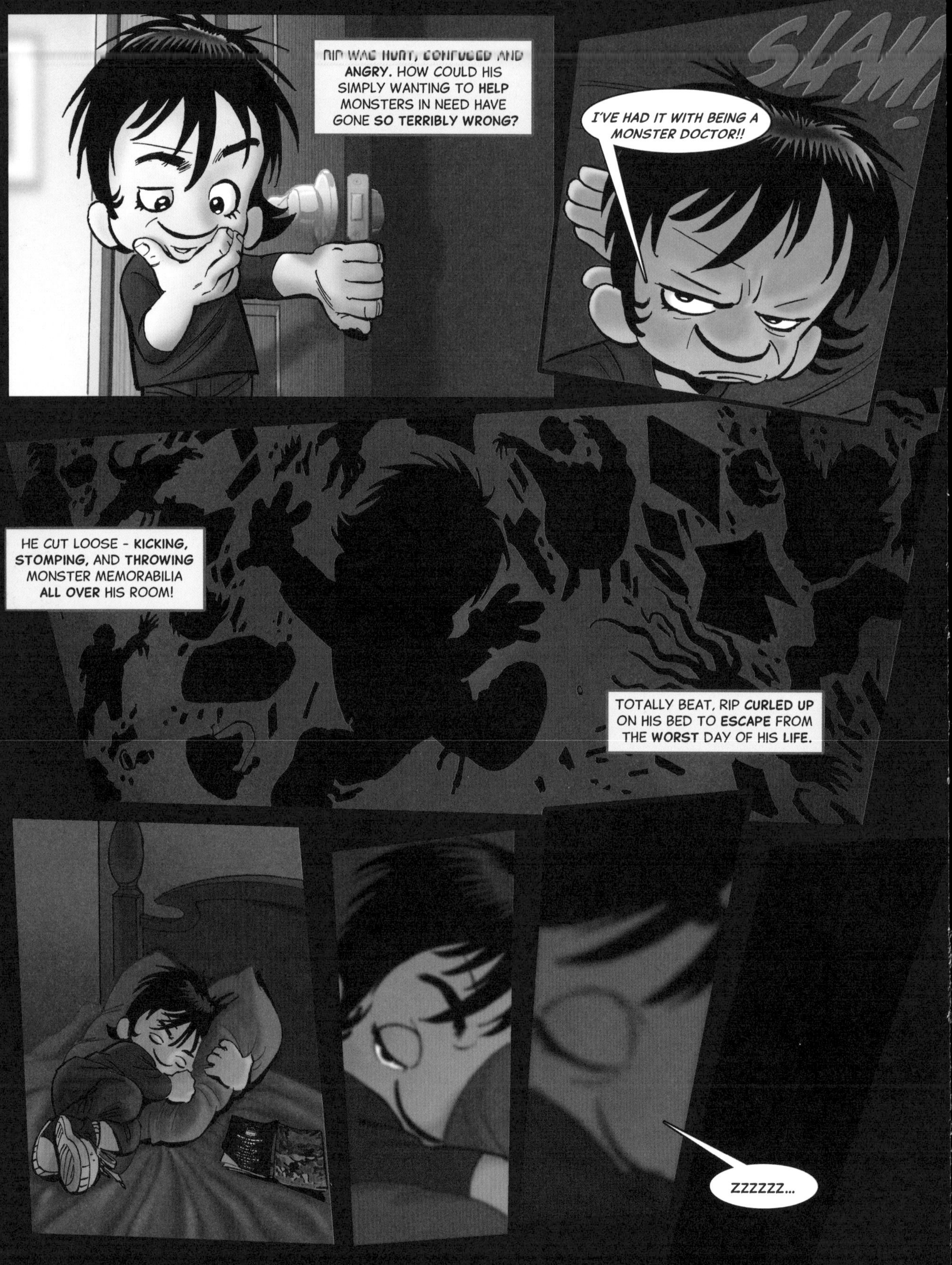

RIP WAS HURT, CONFUSED AND ANGRY. HOW COULD HIS SIMPLY WANTING TO HELP MONSTERS IN NEED HAVE GONE SO TERRIBLY WRONG?
SLAM!
I'VE HAD IT WITH BEING A MONSTER DOCTOR!!
HE CUT LOOSE - KICKING, STOMPING, AND THROWING MONSTER MEMORABILIA ALL OVER HIS ROOM!
TOTALLY BEAT, RIP CURLED UP ON HIS BED TO ESCAPE FROM THE WORST DAY OF HIS LIFE.
ZZZZZZ...

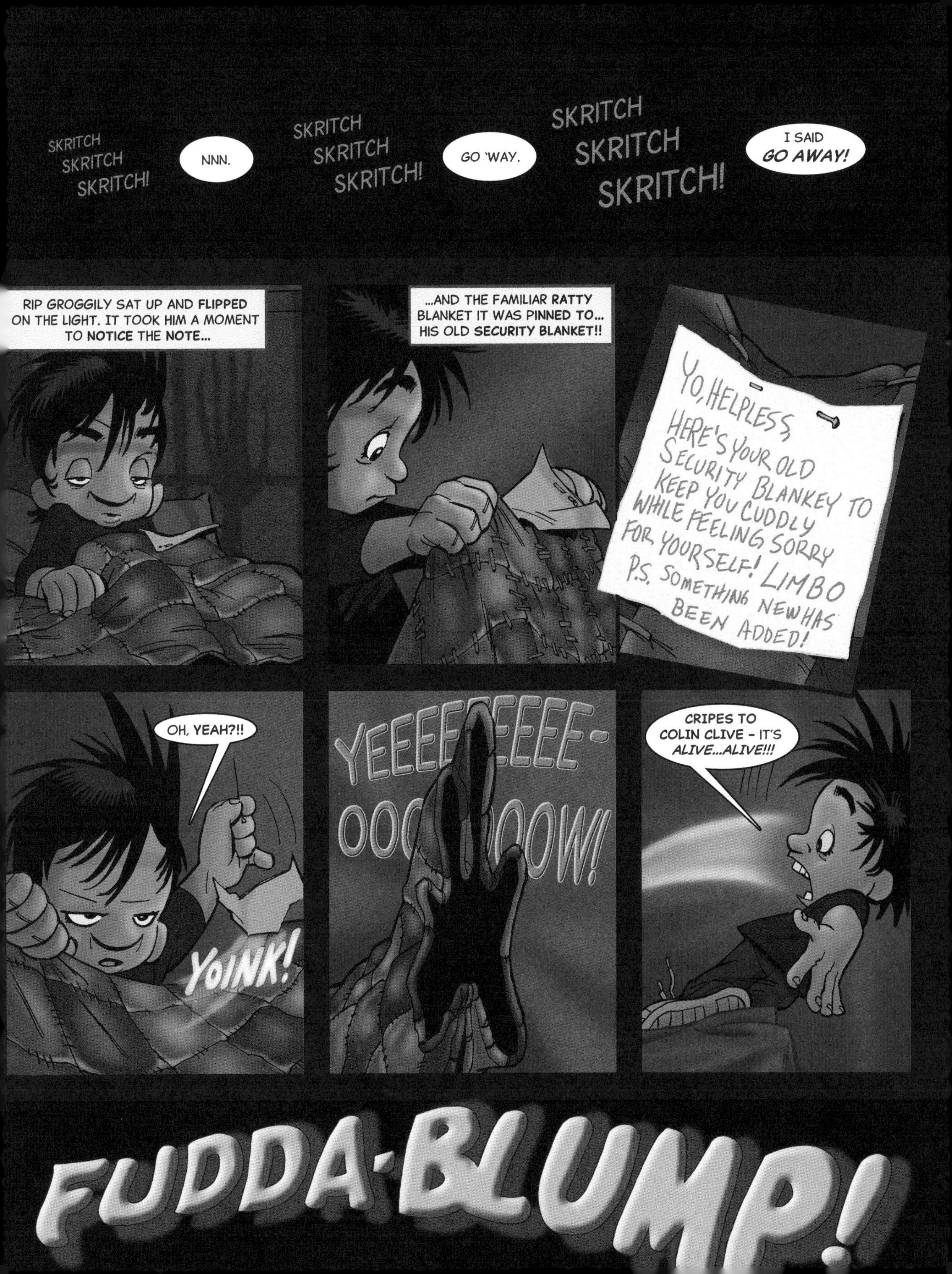
SKRITCH
SKRITCH
SKRITCH!
NNN.
SKRITCH
SKRITCH
SKRITCH!
GO 'WAY.
SKRITCH
SKRITCH
SKRITCH!
I SAID GO AWAY!
RIP GROGGILY SAT UP AND FLIPPED ON THE LIGHT. IT TOOK HIM A MOMENT TO NOTICE THE NOTE...
...AND THE FAMILIAR RATTY BLANKET IT WAS PINNED TO... HIS OLD SECURITY BLANKET!!
YO, HELPLESS, HERE'S YOUR OLD SECURITY BLANKEY TO KEEP YOU CUDDLY WHILE FEELING SORRY FOR YOURSELF! LIMBO
P.S. SOMETHING NEW HAS BEEN ADDED!
OH, YEAH?!!
YOINK!
CRIPES TO COLIN CLIVE – IT'S ALIVE...ALIVE!!!
FUDDA-BLUMP!

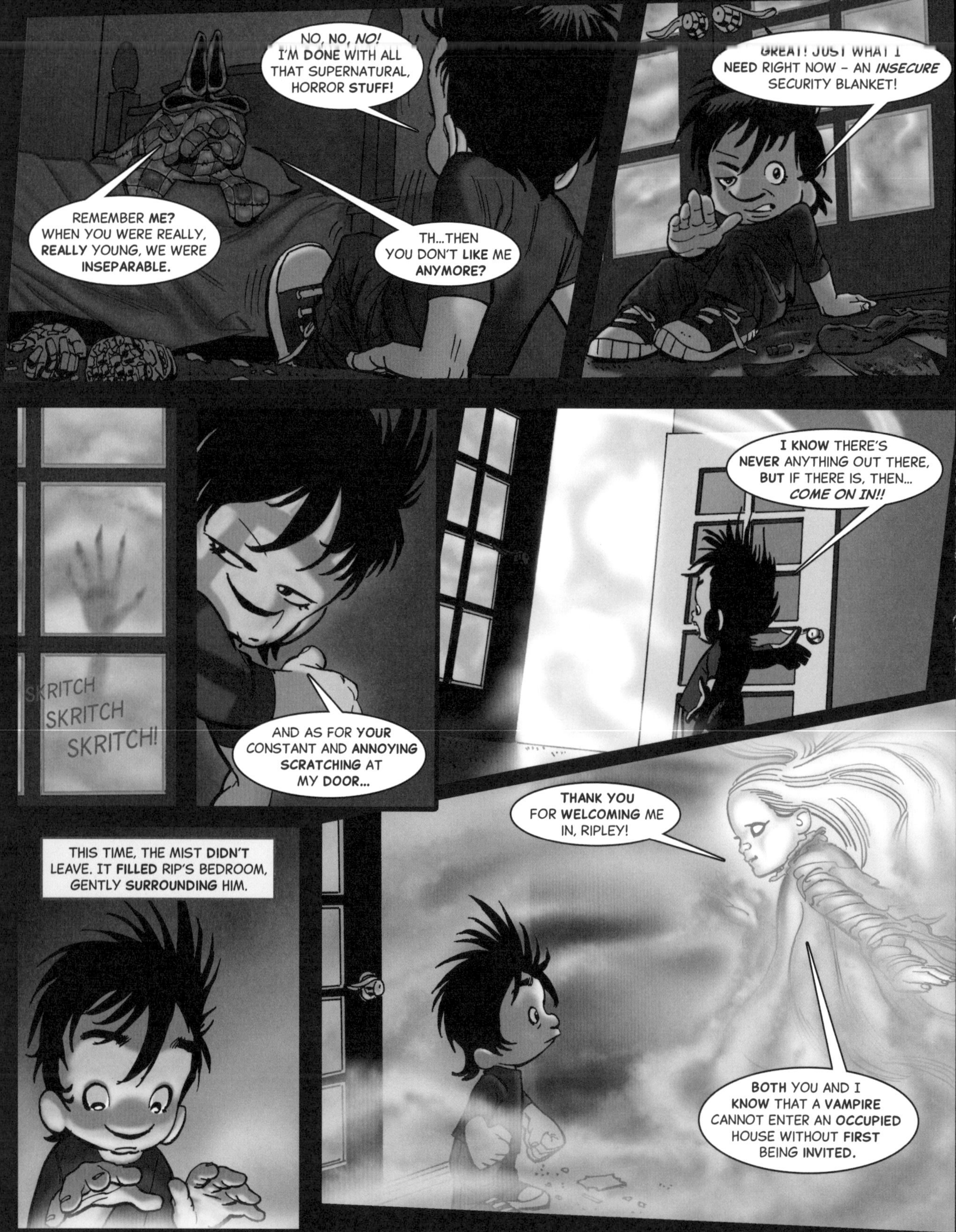
REMEMBER ME? WHEN YOU WERE REALLY, REALLY YOUNG, WE WERE INSEPARABLE.
NO, NO, NO! I'M DONE WITH ALL THAT SUPERNATURAL, HORROR STUFF!
TH...THEN YOU DON'T LIKE ME ANYMORE?
GREAT! JUST WHAT I NEED RIGHT NOW – AN INSECURE SECURITY BLANKET!
SKRITCH SKRITCH SKRITCH!
AND AS FOR YOUR CONSTANT AND ANNOYING SCRATCHING AT MY DOOR...
I KNOW THERE'S NEVER ANYTHING OUT THERE, BUT IF THERE IS, THEN... COME ON IN!!
THIS TIME, THE MIST DIDN'T LEAVE. IT FILLED RIP'S BEDROOM, GENTLY SURROUNDING HIM.
THANK YOU FOR WELCOMING ME IN, RIPLEY!
BOTH YOU AND I KNOW THAT A VAMPIRE CANNOT ENTER AN OCCUPIED HOUSE WITHOUT FIRST BEING INVITED.

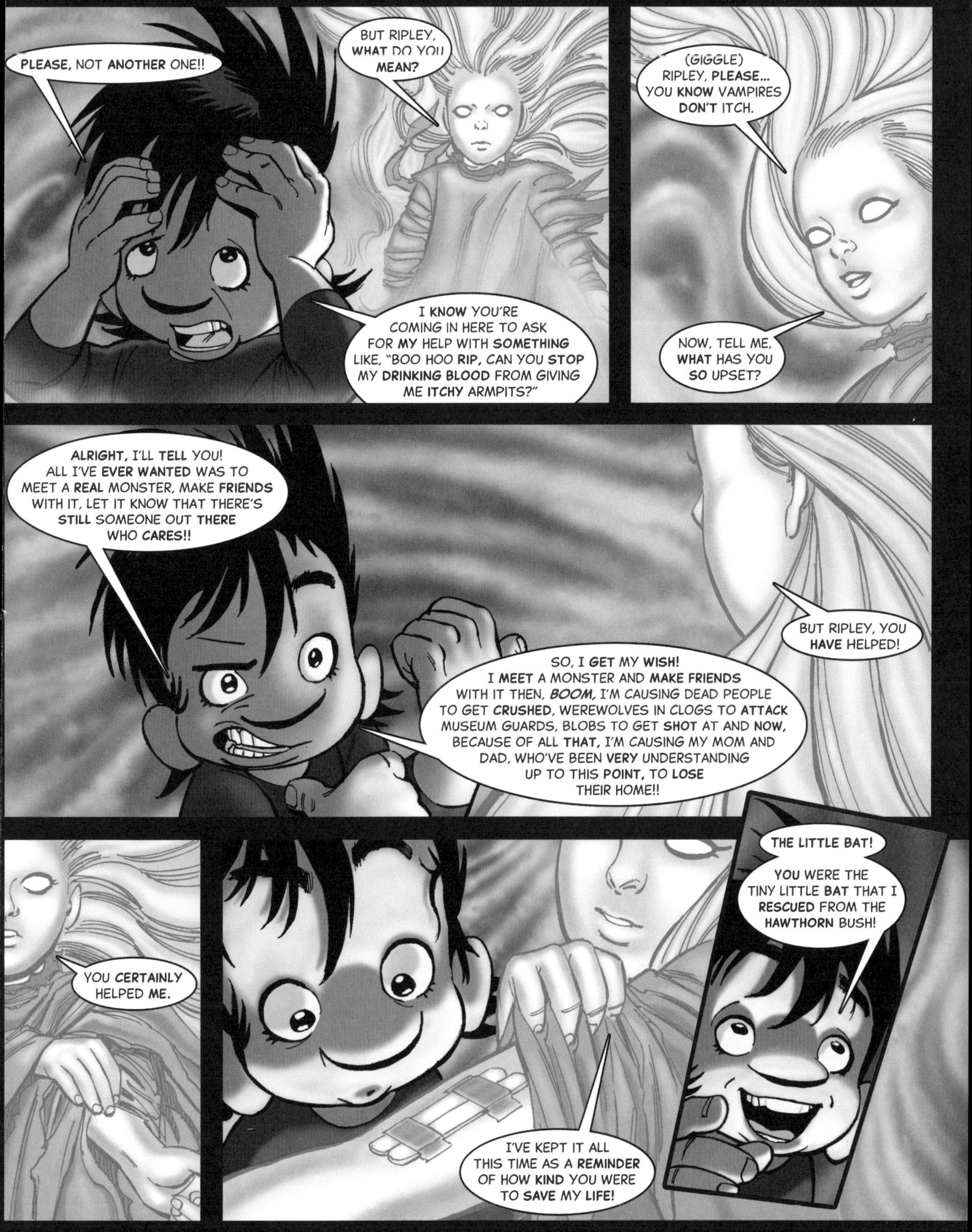
PLEASE, NOT ANOTHER ONE!!
BUT RIPLEY, WHAT DO YOU MEAN?
I KNOW YOU'RE COMING IN HERE TO ASK FOR MY HELP WITH SOMETHING LIKE, "BOO HOO RIP, CAN YOU STOP MY DRINKING BLOOD FROM GIVING ME ITCHY ARMPITS?"
(GIGGLE) RIPLEY, PLEASE... YOU KNOW VAMPIRES DON'T ITCH.
NOW, TELL ME, WHAT HAS YOU SO UPSET?
ALRIGHT, I'LL TELL YOU! ALL I'VE EVER WANTED WAS TO MEET A REAL MONSTER, MAKE FRIENDS WITH IT, LET IT KNOW THAT THERE'S STILL SOMEONE OUT THERE WHO CARES!!
SO, I GET MY WISH! I MEET A MONSTER AND MAKE FRIENDS WITH IT THEN, BOOM, I'M CAUSING DEAD PEOPLE TO GET CRUSHED, WEREWOLVES IN CLOGS TO ATTACK MUSEUM GUARDS, BLOBS TO GET SHOT AT AND NOW, BECAUSE OF ALL THAT, I'M CAUSING MY MOM AND DAD, WHO'VE BEEN VERY UNDERSTANDING UP TO THIS POINT, TO LOSE THEIR HOME!!
BUT RIPLEY, YOU HAVE HELPED!
YOU CERTAINLY HELPED ME.
I'VE KEPT IT ALL THIS TIME AS A REMINDER OF HOW KIND YOU WERE TO SAVE MY LIFE!
THE LITTLE BAT!
YOU WERE THE TINY LITTLE BAT THAT I RESCUED FROM THE HAWTHORN BUSH!

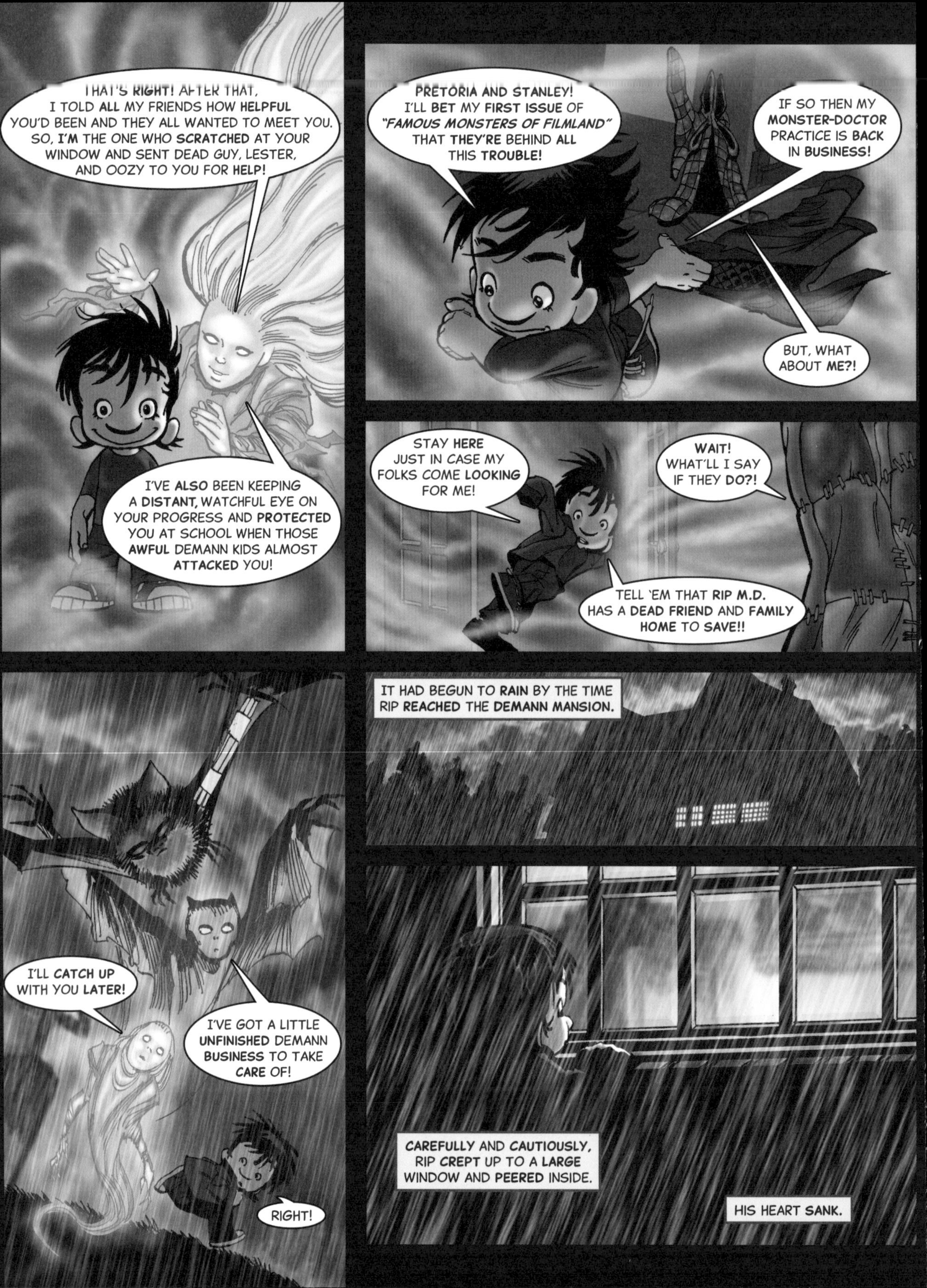
THAT'S RIGHT! AFTER THAT, I TOLD ALL MY FRIENDS HOW HELPFUL YOU'D BEEN AND THEY ALL WANTED TO MEET YOU. SO, I'M THE ONE WHO SCRATCHED AT YOUR WINDOW AND SENT DEAD GUY, LESTER, AND OOZY TO YOU FOR HELP!
I'VE ALSO BEEN KEEPING A DISTANT, WATCHFUL EYE ON YOUR PROGRESS AND PROTECTED YOU AT SCHOOL WHEN THOSE AWFUL DEMANN KIDS ALMOST ATTACKED YOU!
PRETORIA AND STANLEY! I'LL BET MY FIRST ISSUE OF "FAMOUS MONSTERS OF FILMLAND" THAT THEY'RE BEHIND ALL THIS TROUBLE!
IF SO THEN MY MONSTER-DOCTOR PRACTICE IS BACK IN BUSINESS!
BUT, WHAT ABOUT ME?!
STAY HERE JUST IN CASE MY FOLKS COME LOOKING FOR ME!
WAIT! WHAT'LL I SAY IF THEY DO?!
TELL 'EM THAT RIP M.D. HAS A DEAD FRIEND AND FAMILY HOME TO SAVE!!
I'LL CATCH UP WITH YOU LATER!
I'VE GOT A LITTLE UNFINISHED DEMANN BUSINESS TO TAKE CARE OF!
RIGHT!
IT HAD BEGUN TO RAIN BY THE TIME RIP REACHED THE DEMANN MANSION.
CAREFULLY AND CAUTIOUSLY, RIP CREPT UP TO A LARGE WINDOW AND PEERED INSIDE.
HIS HEART SANK.

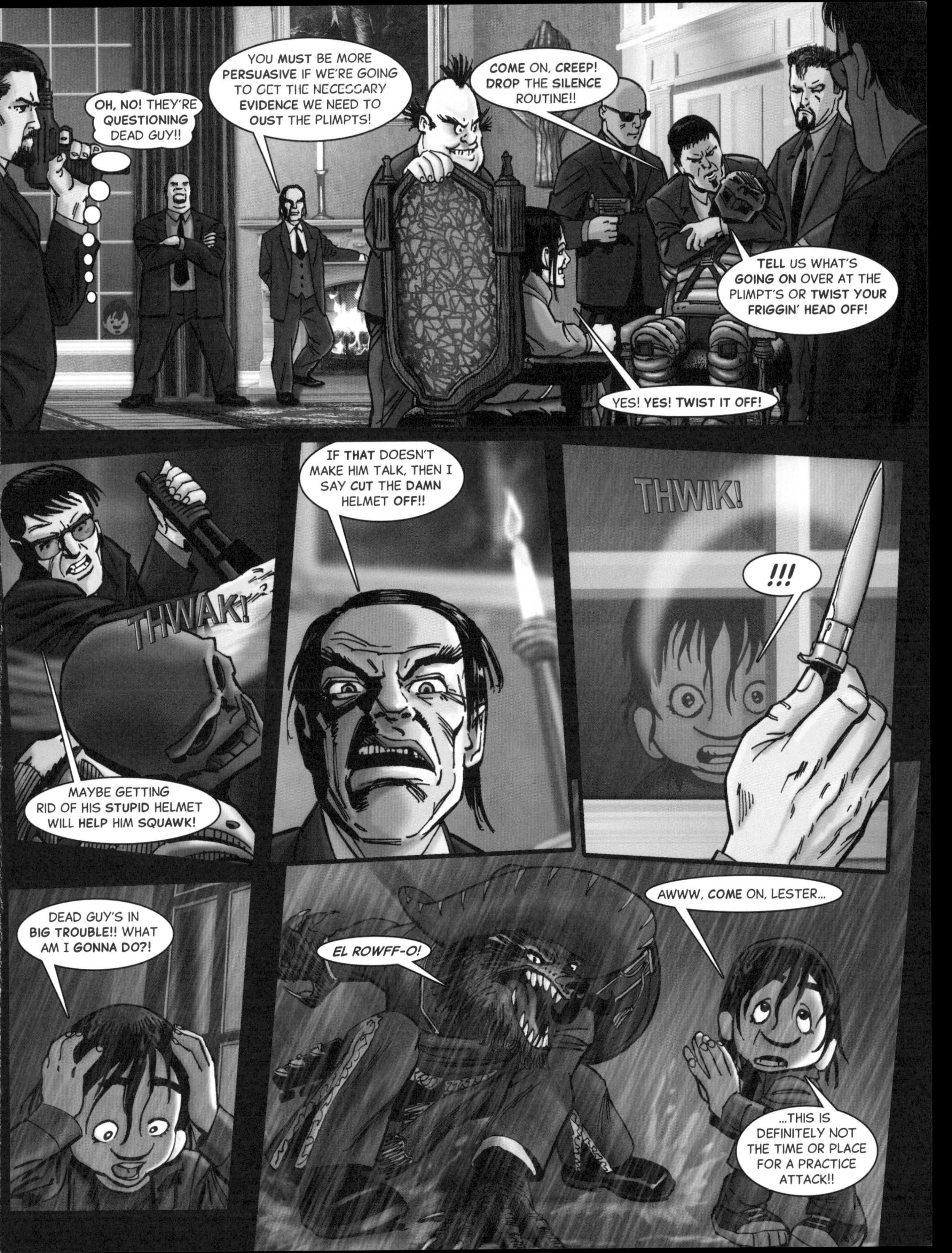
OH, NO! THEY'RE QUESTIONING DEAD GUY!!
YOU MUST BE MORE PERSUASIVE IF WE'RE GOING TO GET THE NECESSARY EVIDENCE WE NEED TO OUST THE PLIMPTS!
COME ON, CREEP! DROP THE SILENCE ROUTINE!!
TELL US WHAT'S GOING ON OVER AT THE PLIMPT'S OR TWIST YOUR FRIGGIN' HEAD OFF!
YES! YES! TWIST IT OFF!
THWAK!
MAYBE GETTING RID OF HIS STUPID HELMET WILL HELP HIM SQUAWK!
IF THAT DOESN'T MAKE HIM TALK, THEN I SAY CUT THE DAMN HELMET OFF!!
THWIK!
!!!
DEAD GUY'S IN BIG TROUBLE!! WHAT AM I GONNA DO?!
EL ROWFF-O!
AWWW, COME ON, LESTER...
...THIS IS DEFINITELY NOT THE TIME OR PLACE FOR A PRACTICE ATTACK!!

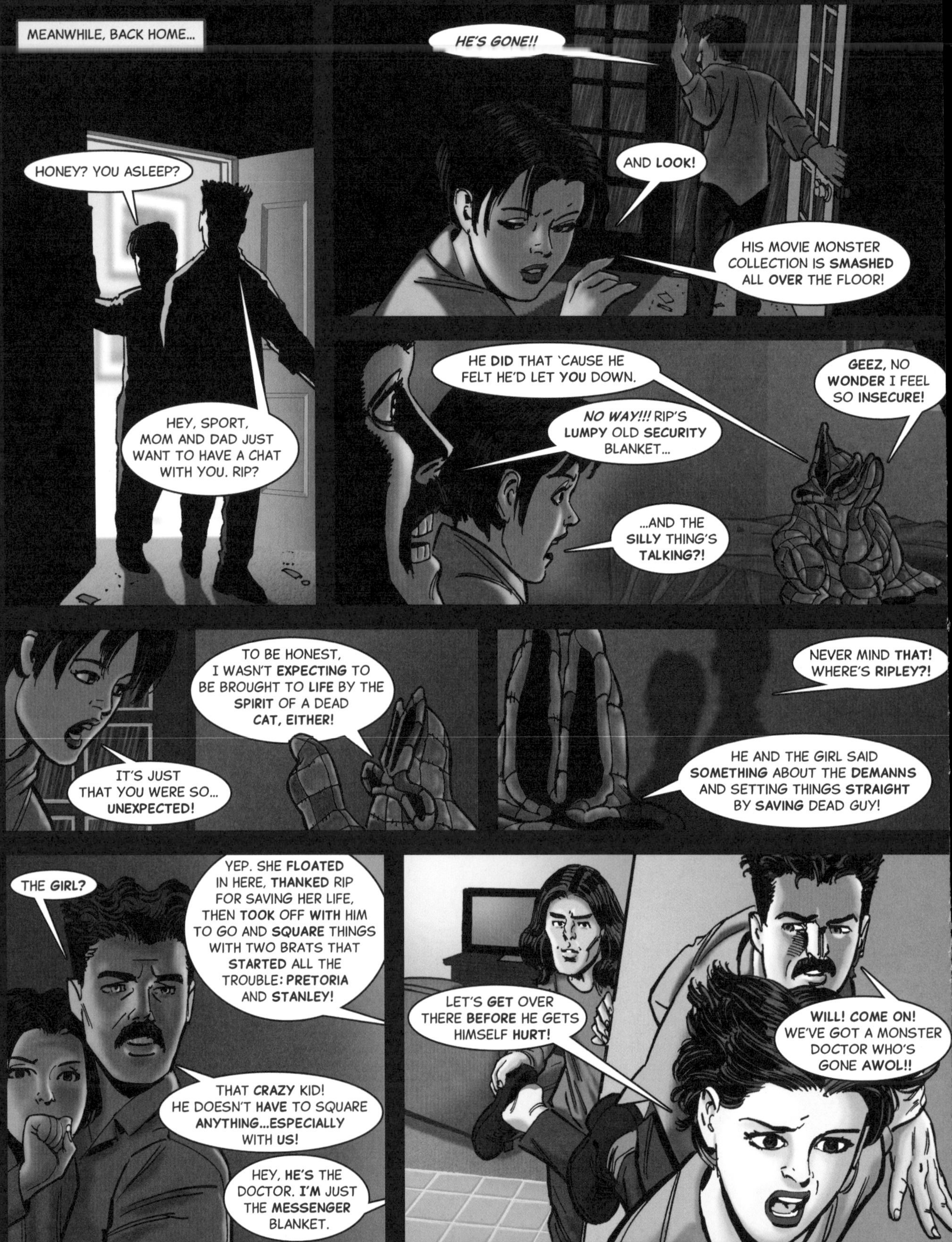
MEANWHILE, BACK HOME...
HONEY? YOU ASLEEP?
HEY, SPORT, MOM AND DAD JUST WANT TO HAVE A CHAT WITH YOU. RIP?
HE'S GONE!!
AND LOOK!
HIS MOVIE MONSTER COLLECTION IS SMASHED ALL OVER THE FLOOR!
HE DID THAT 'CAUSE HE FELT HE'D LET YOU DOWN.
GEEZ, NO WONDER I FEEL SO INSECURE!
NO WAY!!! RIP'S LUMPY OLD SECURITY BLANKET...
...AND THE SILLY THING'S TALKING?!
TO BE HONEST, I WASN'T EXPECTING TO BE BROUGHT TO LIFE BY THE SPIRIT OF A DEAD CAT, EITHER!
IT'S JUST THAT YOU WERE SO... UNEXPECTED!
NEVER MIND THAT! WHERE'S RIPLEY?!
HE AND THE GIRL SAID SOMETHING ABOUT THE DEMANNS AND SETTING THINGS STRAIGHT BY SAVING DEAD GUY!
THE GIRL?
YEP. SHE FLOATED IN HERE, THANKED RIP FOR SAVING HER LIFE, THEN TOOK OFF WITH HIM TO GO AND SQUARE THINGS WITH TWO BRATS THAT STARTED ALL THE TROUBLE: PRETORIA AND STANLEY!
THAT CRAZY KID! HE DOESN'T HAVE TO SQUARE ANYTHING...ESPECIALLY WITH US!
HEY, HE'S THE DOCTOR. I'M JUST THE MESSENGER BLANKET.
LET'S GET OVER THERE BEFORE HE GETS HIMSELF HURT!
WILL! COME ON! WE'VE GOT A MONSTER DOCTOR WHO'S GONE AWOL!!

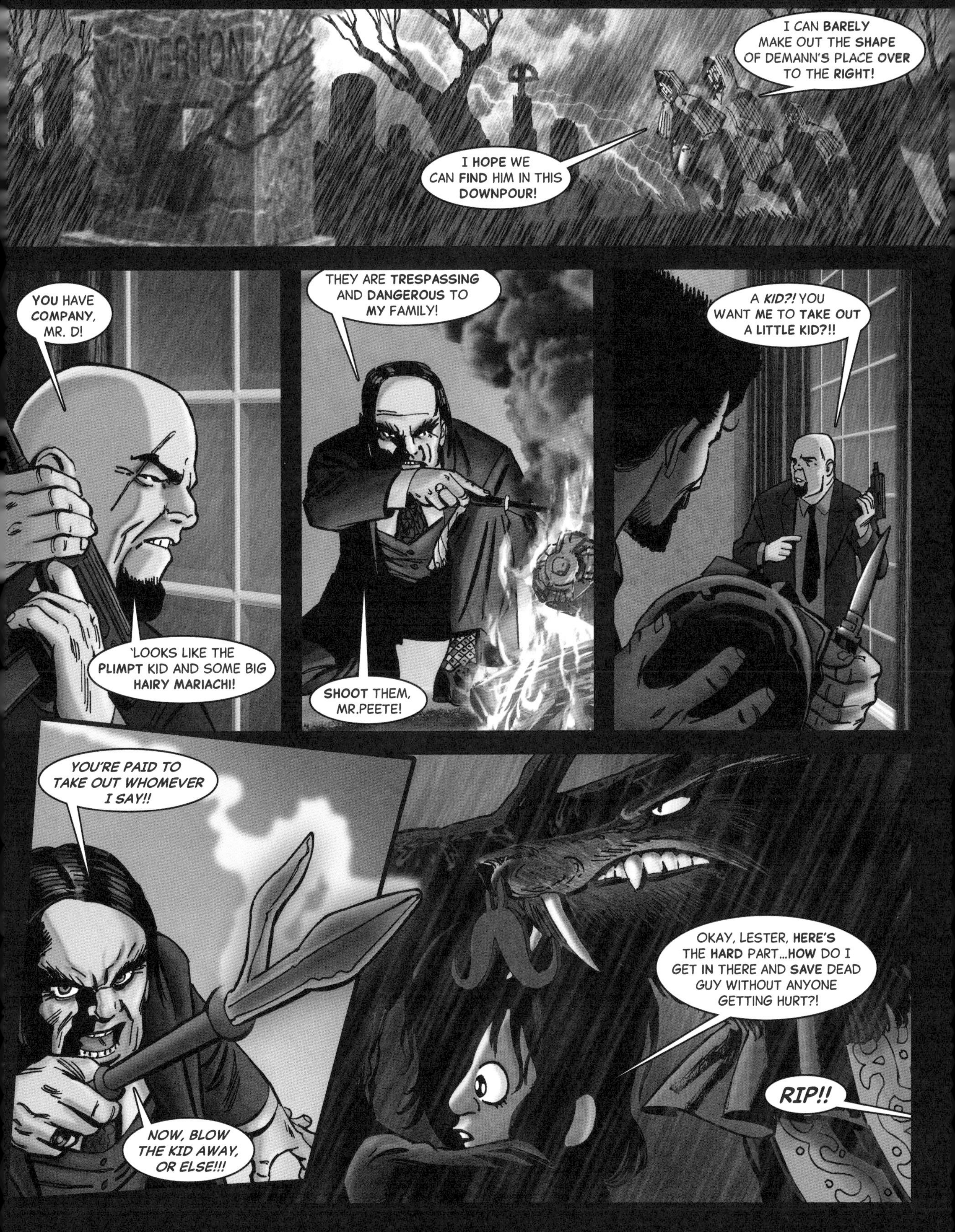
HOWERTON
I CAN BARELY MAKE OUT THE SHAPE OF DEMANN'S PLACE OVER TO THE RIGHT!
I HOPE WE CAN FIND HIM IN THIS DOWNPOUR!
YOU HAVE COMPANY, MR. D!
'LOOKS LIKE THE PLIMPT KID AND SOME BIG HAIRY MARIACHI!
THEY ARE TRESPASSING AND DANGEROUS TO MY FAMILY!
SHOOT THEM, MR.PEETE!
A KID?! YOU WANT ME TO TAKE OUT A LITTLE KID?!!
YOU'RE PAID TO TAKE OUT WHOMEVER I SAY!!
NOW, BLOW THE KID AWAY, OR ELSE!!!
OKAY, LESTER, HERE'S THE HARD PART...HOW DO I GET IN THERE AND SAVE DEAD GUY WITHOUT ANYONE GETTING HURT?!
RIP!!

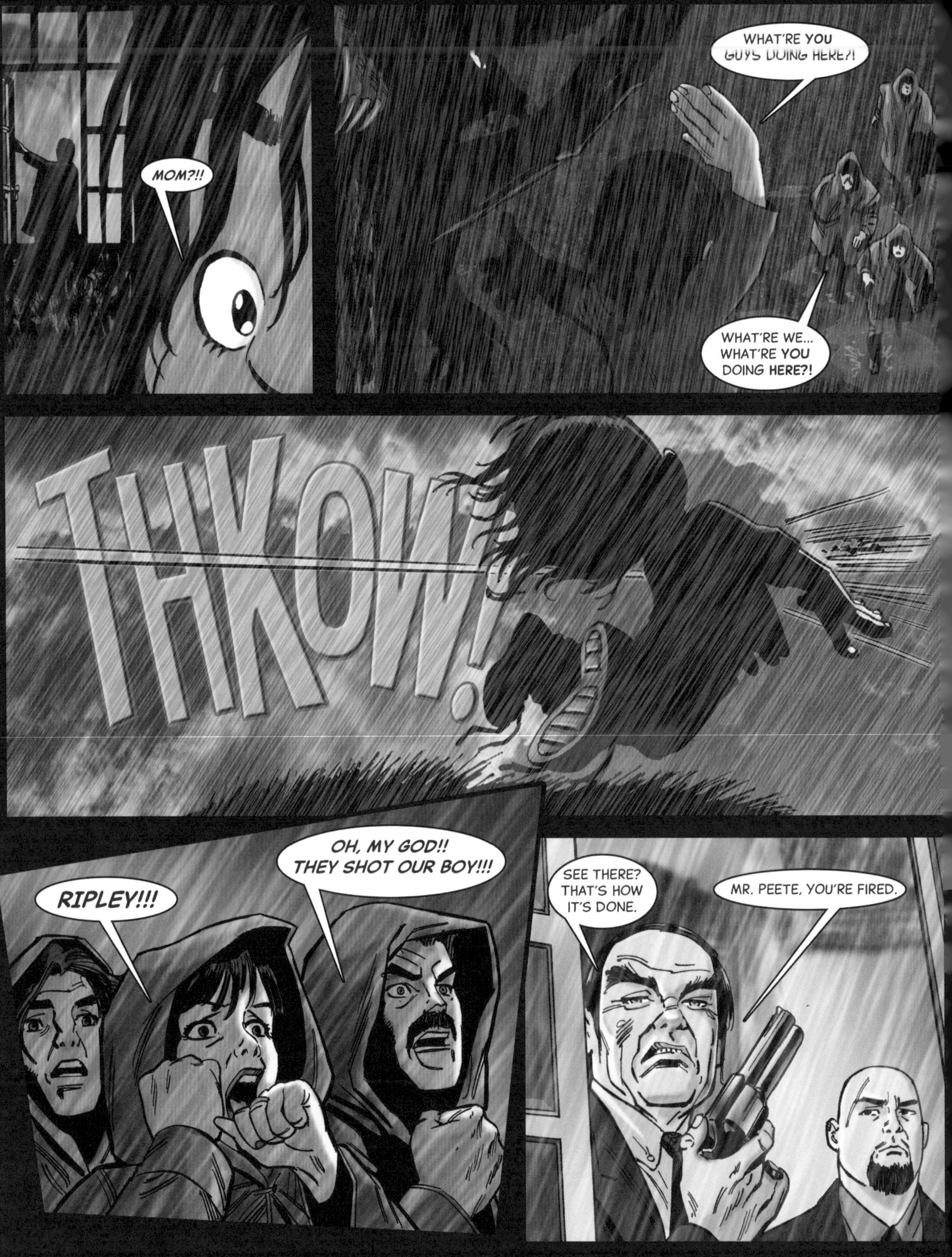
MOM?!!
WHAT'RE YOU GUYS DOING HERE?!
WHAT'RE WE... WHAT'RE YOU DOING HERE?!
THKOW!
RIPLEY!!!
OH, MY GOD!! THEY SHOT OUR BOY!!!
SEE THERE? THAT'S HOW IT'S DONE.
MR. PEETE, YOU'RE FIRED.

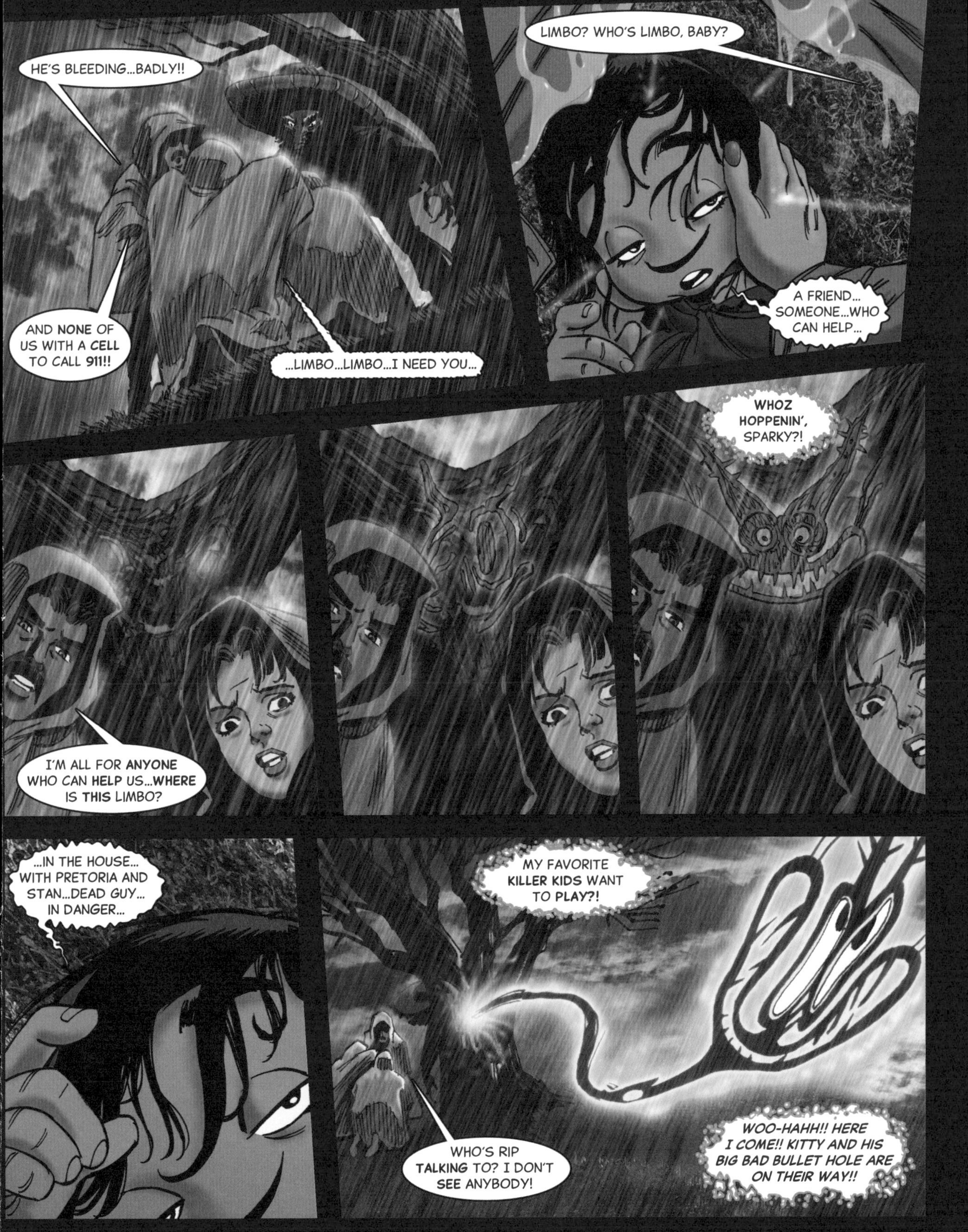
HE'S BLEEDING...BADLY!!
AND NONE OF US WITH A CELL TO CALL 911!!
...LIMBO...LIMBO...I NEED YOU...
LIMBO? WHO'S LIMBO, BABY?
A FRIEND... SOMEONE...WHO CAN HELP...
I'M ALL FOR ANYONE WHO CAN HELP US...WHERE IS THIS LIMBO?
WHOZ HOPPENIN', SPARKY?!
...IN THE HOUSE... WITH PRETORIA AND STAN...DEAD GUY... IN DANGER...
MY FAVORITE KILLER KIDS WANT TO PLAY?!
WHO'S RIP TALKING TO? I DON'T SEE ANYBODY!
WOO-HAHH!! HERE I COME!! KITTY AND HIS BIG BAD BULLET HOLE ARE ON THEIR WAY!!

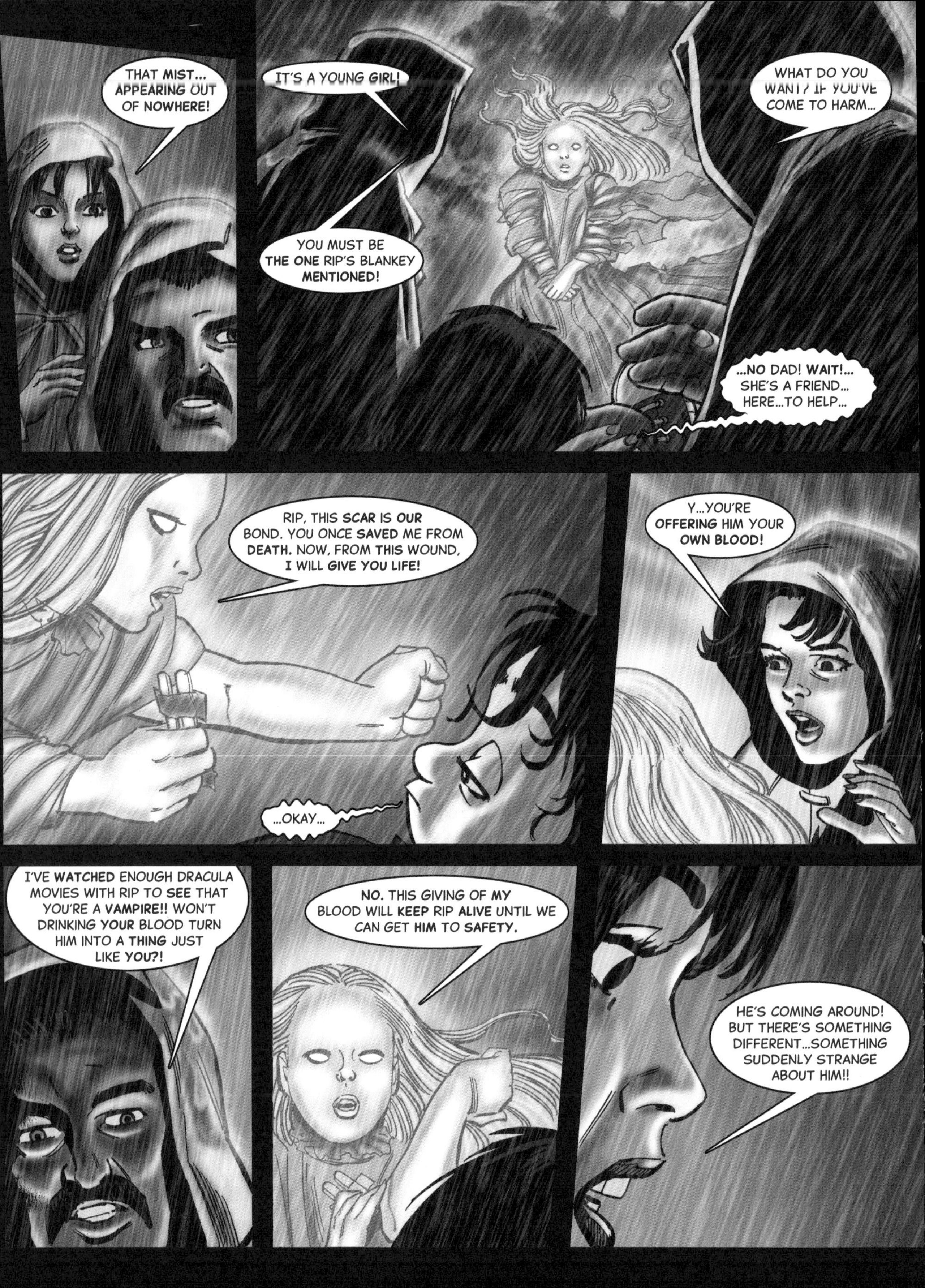
THAT MIST... APPEARING OUT OF NOWHERE!
IT'S A YOUNG GIRL!
YOU MUST BE THE ONE RIP'S BLANKEY MENTIONED!
WHAT DO YOU WANT? IF YOU'VE COME TO HARM...
...NO DAD! WAIT!... SHE'S A FRIEND... HERE...TO HELP...
RIP, THIS SCAR IS OUR BOND. YOU ONCE SAVED ME FROM DEATH. NOW, FROM THIS WOUND, I WILL GIVE YOU LIFE!
...OKAY...
Y...YOU'RE OFFERING HIM YOUR OWN BLOOD!
I'VE WATCHED ENOUGH DRACULA MOVIES WITH RIP TO SEE THAT YOU'RE A VAMPIRE!! WON'T DRINKING YOUR BLOOD TURN HIM INTO A THING JUST LIKE YOU?!
NO. THIS GIVING OF MY BLOOD WILL KEEP RIP ALIVE UNTIL WE CAN GET HIM TO SAFETY.
HE'S COMING AROUND! BUT THERE'S SOMETHING DIFFERENT...SOMETHING SUDDENLY STRANGE ABOUT HIM!!

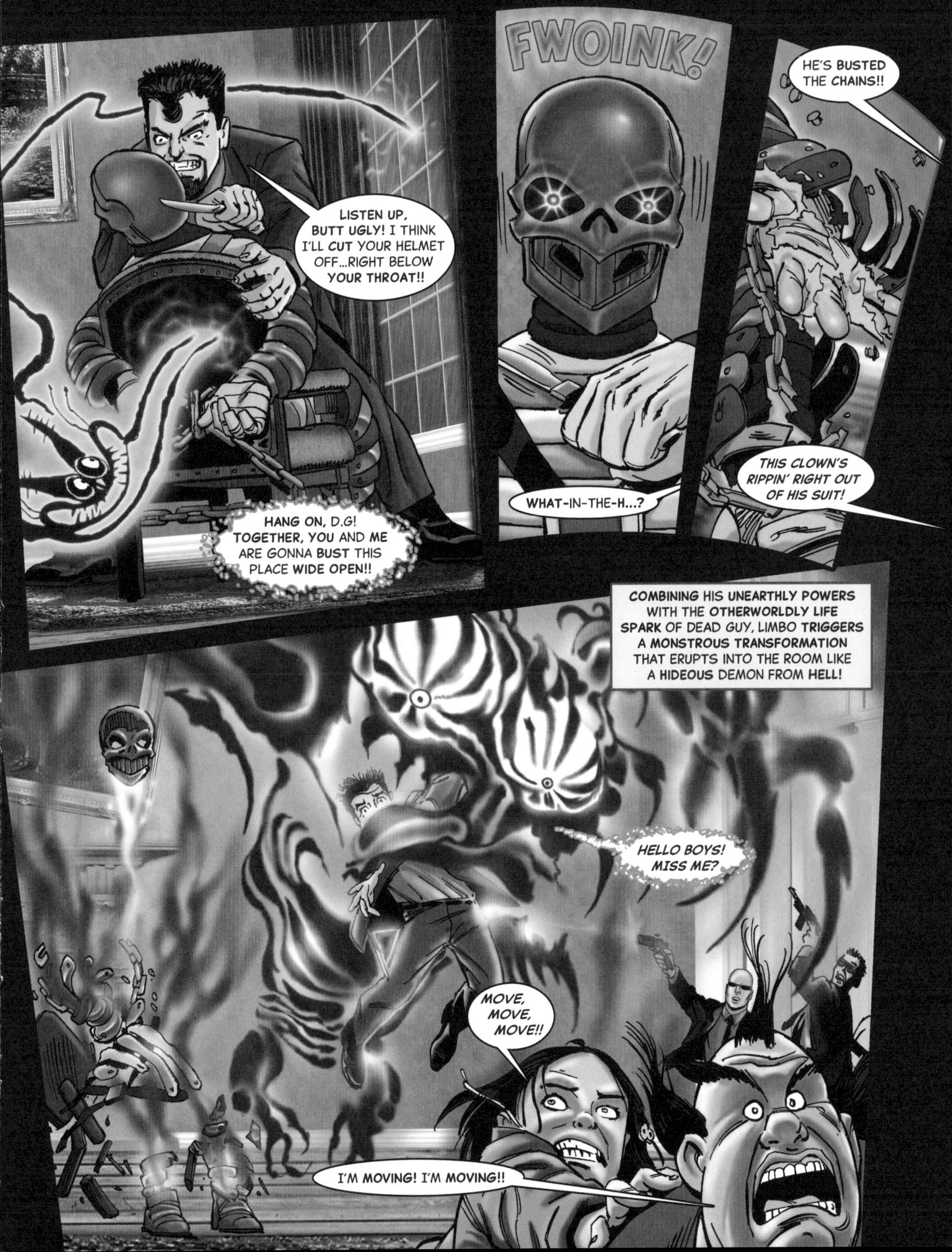
LISTEN UP, BUTT UGLY! I THINK I'LL CUT YOUR HELMET OFF...RIGHT BELOW YOUR THROAT!!
HANG ON, D.G! TOGETHER, YOU AND ME ARE GONNA BUST THIS PLACE WIDE OPEN!!
FWOINK!
WHAT-IN-THE-H...?
HE'S BUSTED THE CHAINS!!
THIS CLOWN'S RIPPIN' RIGHT OUT OF HIS SUIT!
COMBINING HIS UNEARTHLY POWERS WITH THE OTHERWORLDLY LIFE SPARK OF DEAD GUY, LIMBO TRIGGERS A MONSTROUS TRANSFORMATION THAT ERUPTS INTO THE ROOM LIKE A HIDEOUS DEMON FROM HELL!
HELLO BOYS! MISS ME?
MOVE, MOVE, MOVE!!
I'M MOVING! I'M MOVING!!

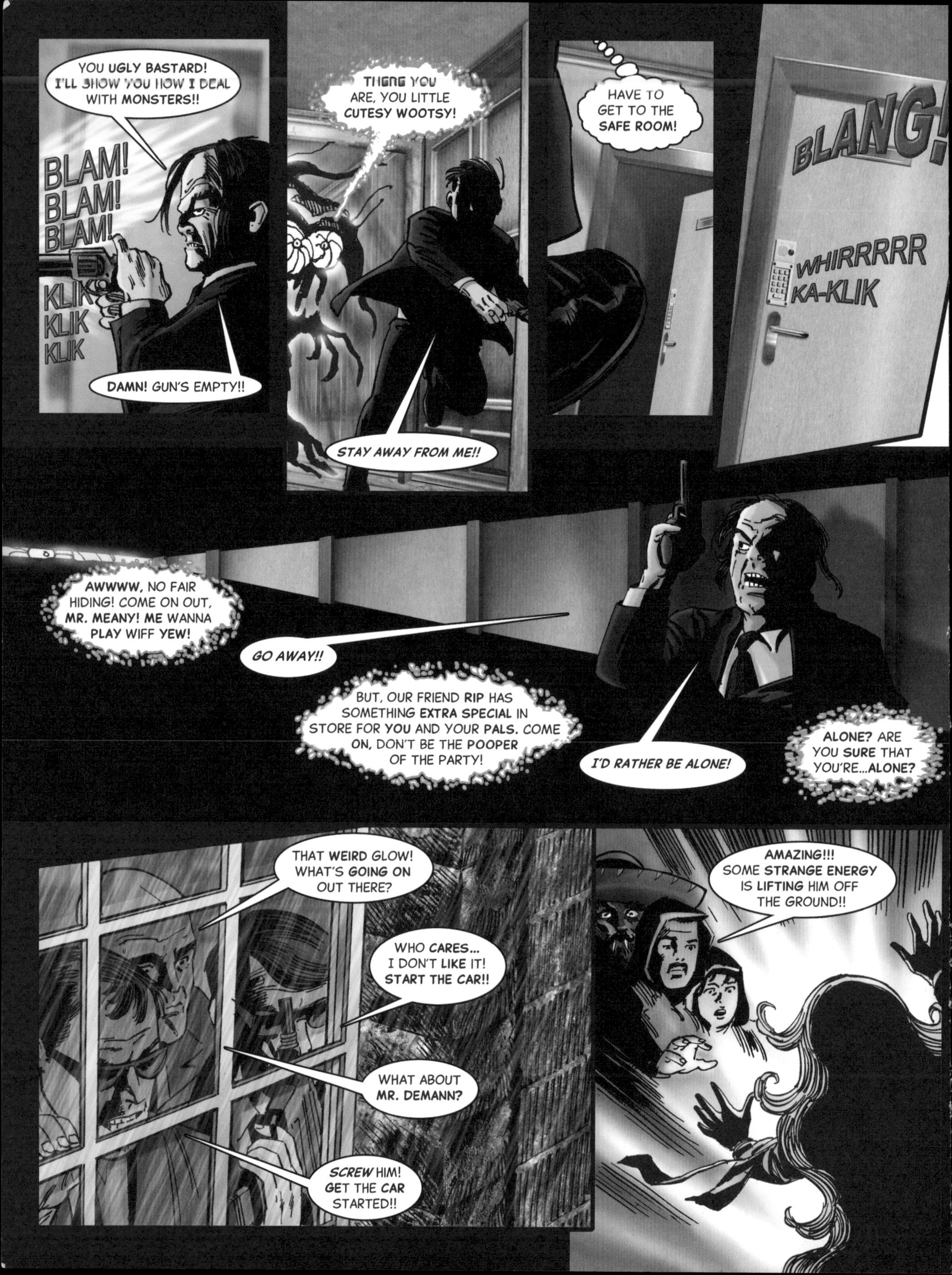
YOU UGLY BASTARD! I'LL SHOW YOU HOW I DEAL WITH MONSTERS!!
BLAM! BLAM! BLAM!
KLIK KLIK KLIK
DAMN! GUN'S EMPTY!!
THERE YOU ARE, YOU LITTLE CUTESY WOOTSY!
STAY AWAY FROM ME!!
HAVE TO GET TO THE SAFE ROOM!
BLANG!
WHIRRRRR
KA-KLIK
AWWWW, NO FAIR HIDING! COME ON OUT, MR. MEANY! ME WANNA PLAY WIFF YEW!
GO AWAY!!
BUT, OUR FRIEND RIP HAS SOMETHING EXTRA SPECIAL IN STORE FOR YOU AND YOUR PALS. COME ON, DON'T BE THE POOPER OF THE PARTY!
I'D RATHER BE ALONE!
ALONE? ARE YOU SURE THAT YOU'RE...ALONE?
THAT WEIRD GLOW! WHAT'S GOING ON OUT THERE?
WHO CARES... I DON'T LIKE IT! START THE CAR!!
WHAT ABOUT MR. DEMANN?
SCREW HIM! GET THE CAR STARTED!!
AMAZING!!! SOME STRANGE ENERGY IS LIFTING HIM OFF THE GROUND!!

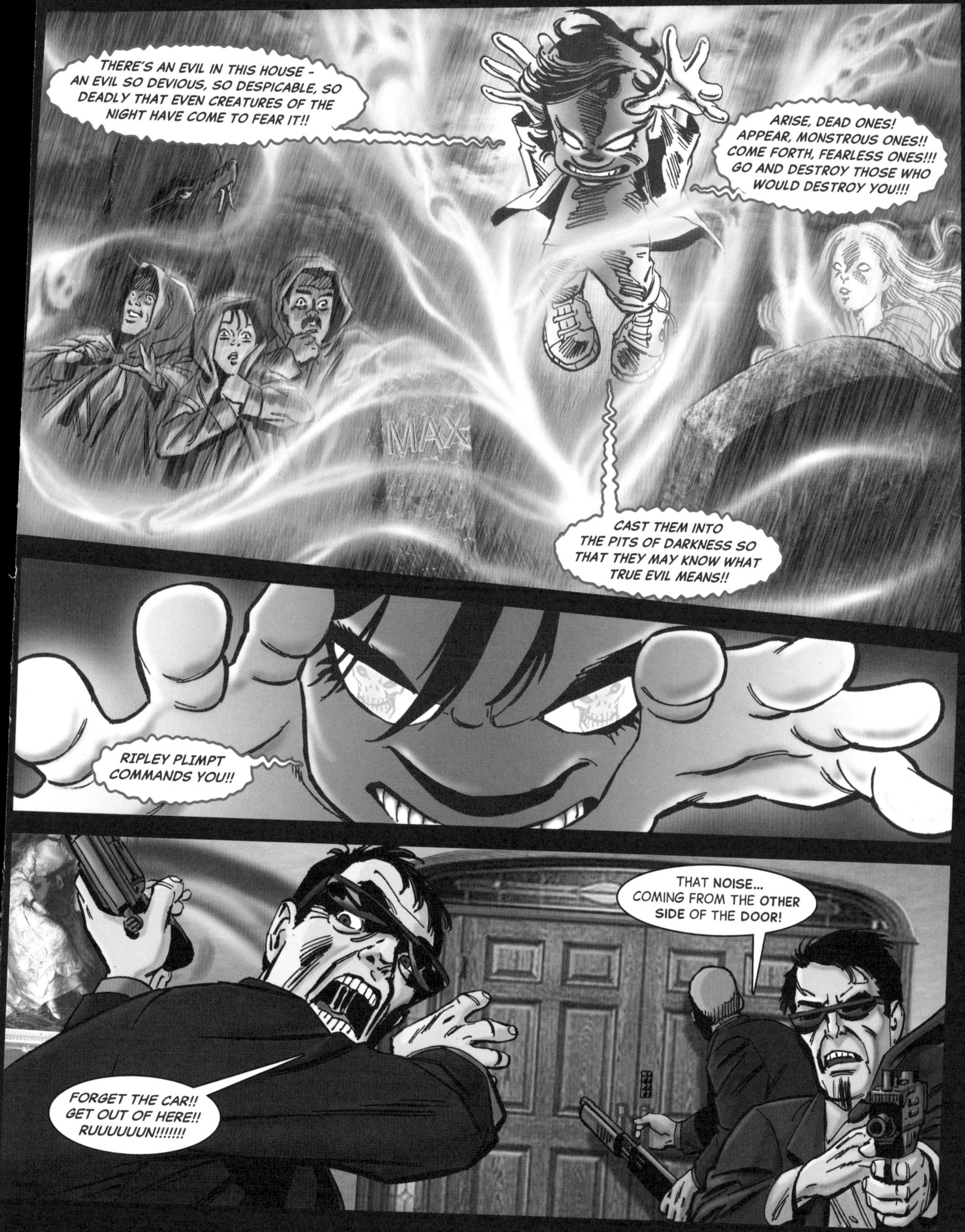
THERE'S AN EVIL IN THIS HOUSE - AN EVIL SO DEVIOUS, SO DESPICABLE, SO DEADLY THAT EVEN CREATURES OF THE NIGHT HAVE COME TO FEAR IT!!
ARISE, DEAD ONES! APPEAR, MONSTROUS ONES!! COME FORTH, FEARLESS ONES!!! GO AND DESTROY THOSE WHO WOULD DESTROY YOU!!!
MAX
CAST THEM INTO THE PITS OF DARKNESS SO THAT THEY MAY KNOW WHAT TRUE EVIL MEANS!!
RIPLEY PLIMPT COMMANDS YOU!!
THAT NOISE... COMING FROM THE OTHER SIDE OF THE DOOR!
FORGET THE CAR!! GET OUT OF HERE!! RUUUUUUN!!!!!!!

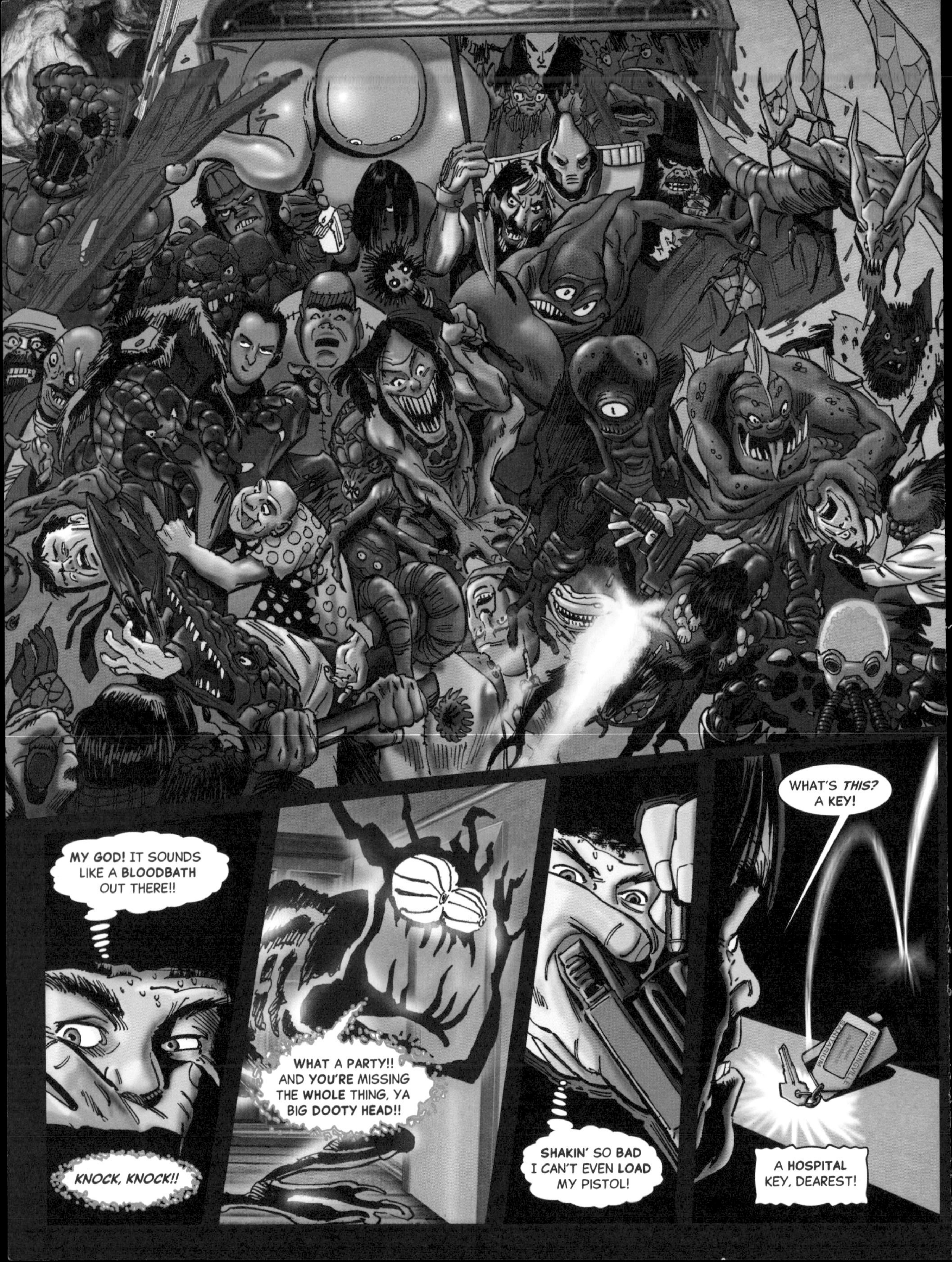
MY GOD! IT SOUNDS LIKE A BLOODBATH OUT THERE!!
KNOCK, KNOCK!!
WHAT A PARTY!! AND YOU'RE MISSING THE WHOLE THING, YA BIG DOOTY HEAD!!
SHAKIN' SO BAD I CAN'T EVEN LOAD MY PISTOL!
WHAT'S THIS? A KEY!
BROWNINGVILLE SANITARIUM
A HOSPITAL KEY, DEAREST!

ELSPETH?! BUT I SAW TO IT THAT **YOU** WERE **DIAGNOSED INSANE** AND **LOCKED AWAY** FOR GOOD!

I **KNOW** YOU DID, MY **HUSBAND** - JUST SO **YOU** AND OUR **CHILDREN** COULD TAKE **ALL** OF MY FAMILY INHERITANCE FOR **YOURSELVES**!

THEN, LIKE A **GOOD OMEN**, A TINY **BAT FLEW** IN THROUGH MY HOSPITAL WINDOW!

A TINY **BAT**?

YES, AND LIKE **MAGIC**, IT TURNED INTO THE **SWEETEST** AND **PRETTIEST** LITTLE **GIRL**! SHE **FREED** ME SO I COULD **COME** AND BE WITH **YOU**!

ELSPETH, YOU **BELONG** IN THE HOSPITAL!

MY **MONEY** HAS KEPT YOU LOOKING **WELL**, ARTEMUS – **ALMOST** AS YOUNG AS WHEN WE **EXCHANGED** OUR **WEDDING** VOWS, REMEMBER?

THAT DAY, YOU GAZED **PASSIONATELY** INTO MY EYES...

...AND SAID THAT WE'D BE TOGETHER "UNTIL **DEATH** DO US **PART**."

SO?

SO, **YOU GO FIRST**!!

ELSPETH, NO!!!

NOOOOOOOOOOOOOOO-

...THUK!

THOSE **AWFUL** SCREAMS! WHAT'S HAPPENING IN **THERE**!!

TRUST ME, MRS. PLIMPT, IT'S **BEST** YOU **DON'T KNOW**! RIP'S POWER IS **WEARING OFF**!

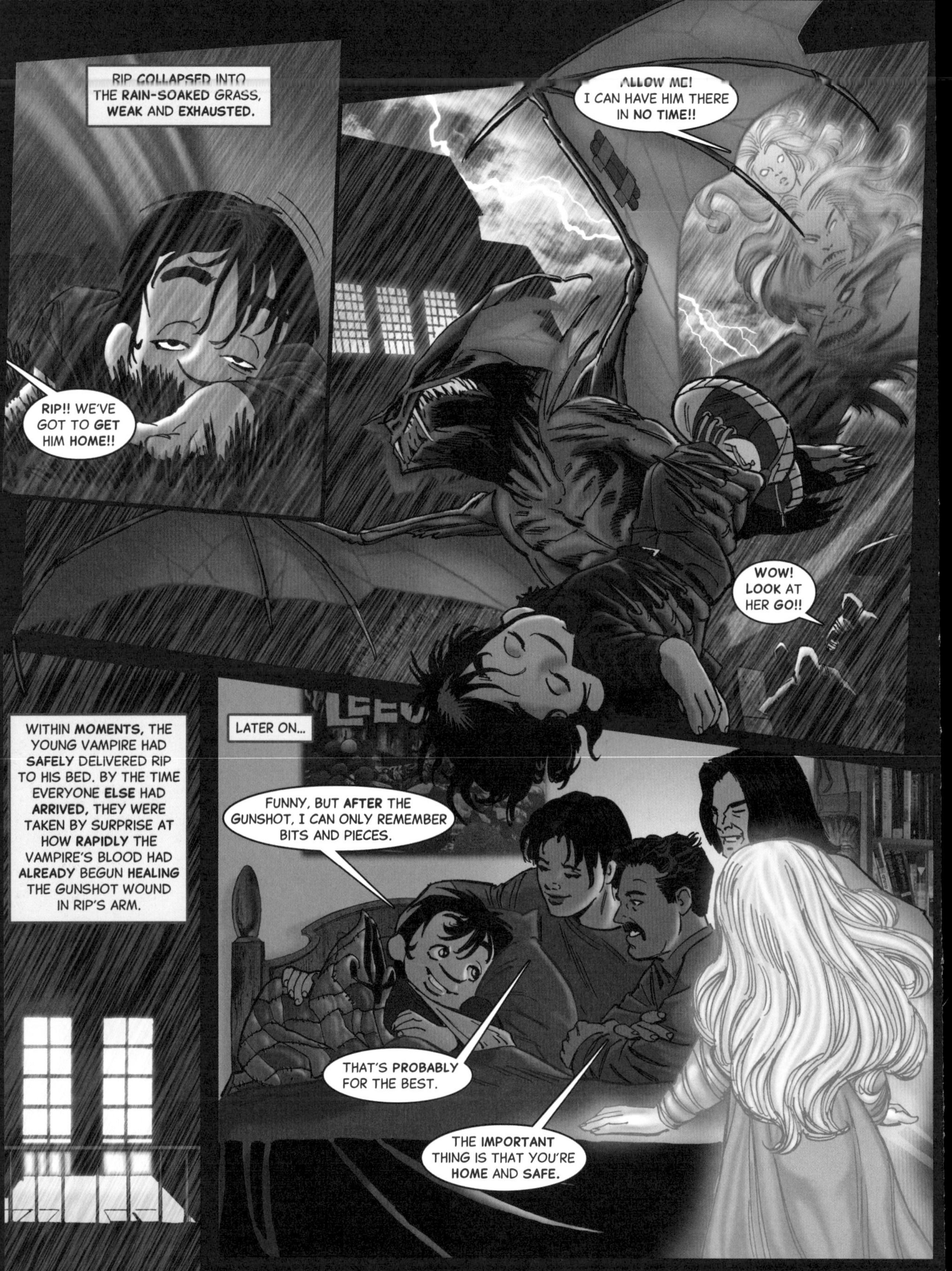
RIP COLLAPSED INTO THE RAIN-SOAKED GRASS, WEAK AND EXHAUSTED.
RIP!! WE'VE GOT TO GET HIM HOME!!
ALLOW ME! I CAN HAVE HIM THERE IN NO TIME!!
WOW! LOOK AT HER GO!!
WITHIN MOMENTS, THE YOUNG VAMPIRE HAD SAFELY DELIVERED RIP TO HIS BED. BY THE TIME EVERYONE ELSE HAD ARRIVED, THEY WERE TAKEN BY SURPRISE AT HOW RAPIDLY THE VAMPIRE'S BLOOD HAD ALREADY BEGUN HEALING THE GUNSHOT WOUND IN RIP'S ARM.
LATER ON...
FUNNY, BUT AFTER THE GUNSHOT, I CAN ONLY REMEMBER BITS AND PIECES.
THAT'S PROBABLY FOR THE BEST.
THE IMPORTANT THING IS THAT YOU'RE HOME AND SAFE.

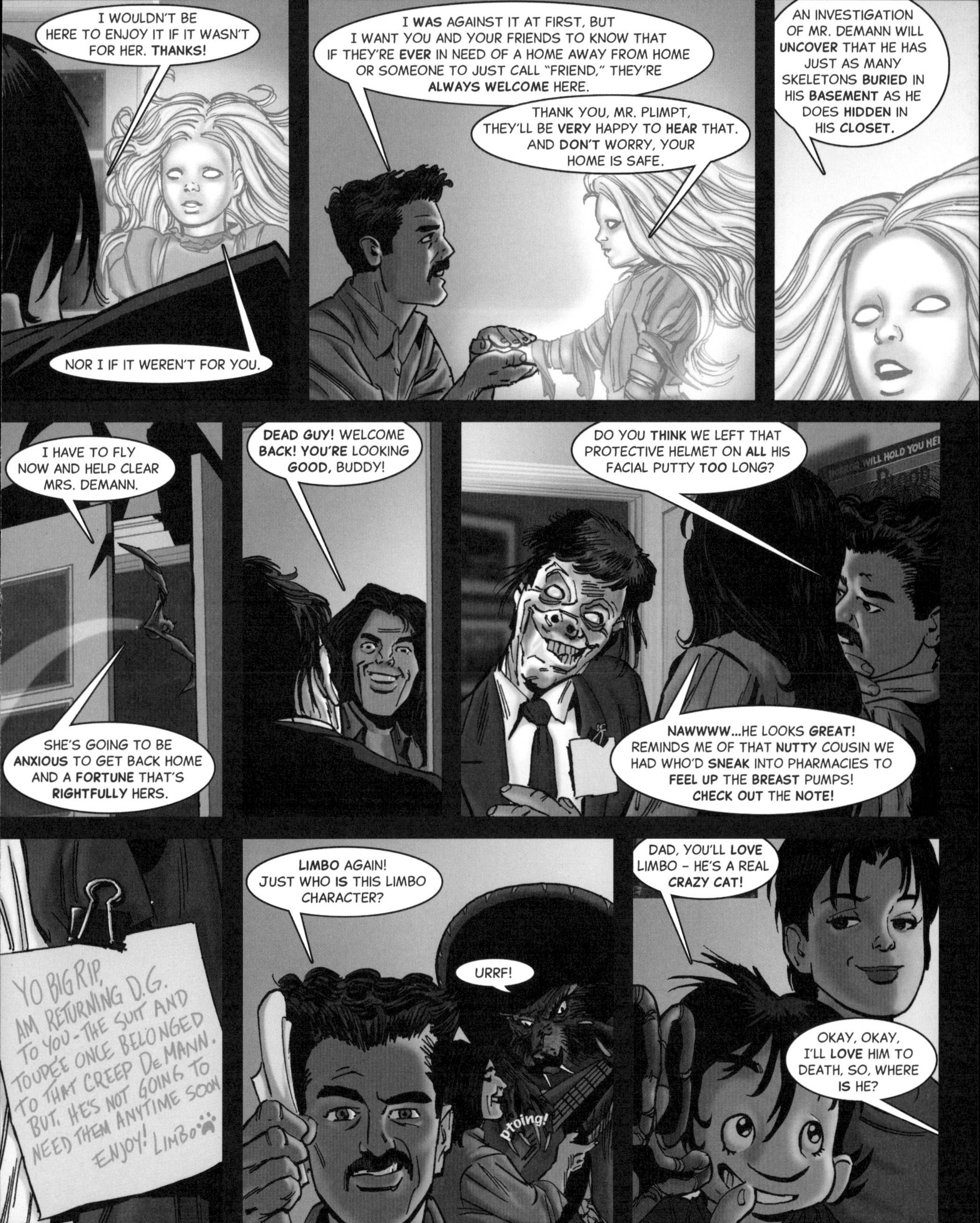
I WOULDN'T BE HERE TO ENJOY IT IF IT WASN'T FOR HER. THANKS!
NOR I IF IT WEREN'T FOR YOU.
I WAS AGAINST IT AT FIRST, BUT I WANT YOU AND YOUR FRIENDS TO KNOW THAT IF THEY'RE EVER IN NEED OF A HOME AWAY FROM HOME OR SOMEONE TO JUST CALL "FRIEND," THEY'RE ALWAYS WELCOME HERE.
THANK YOU, MR. PLIMPT, THEY'LL BE VERY HAPPY TO HEAR THAT. AND DON'T WORRY, YOUR HOME IS SAFE.
AN INVESTIGATION OF MR. DEMANN WILL UNCOVER THAT HE HAS JUST AS MANY SKELETONS BURIED IN HIS BASEMENT AS HE DOES HIDDEN IN HIS CLOSET.
I HAVE TO FLY NOW AND HELP CLEAR MRS. DEMANN.
SHE'S GOING TO BE ANXIOUS TO GET BACK HOME AND A FORTUNE THAT'S RIGHTFULLY HERS.
DEAD GUY! WELCOME BACK! YOU'RE LOOKING GOOD, BUDDY!
DO YOU THINK WE LEFT THAT PROTECTIVE HELMET ON ALL HIS FACIAL PUTTY TOO LONG?
NAWWWW...HE LOOKS GREAT! REMINDS ME OF THAT NUTTY COUSIN WE HAD WHO'D SNEAK INTO PHARMACIES TO FEEL UP THE BREAST PUMPS! CHECK OUT THE NOTE!
YO BIG RIP, AM RETURNING D.G. TO YOU - THE SUIT AND TOUPEE ONCE BELONGED TO THAT CREEP DeMANN. BUT, HE'S NOT GOING TO NEED THEM ANYTIME SOON ENJOY! LIMBO
LIMBO AGAIN! JUST WHO IS THIS LIMBO CHARACTER?
URRF!
ptoing!
DAD, YOU'LL LOVE LIMBO – HE'S A REAL CRAZY CAT!
OKAY, OKAY, I'LL LOVE HIM TO DEATH, SO, WHERE IS HE?

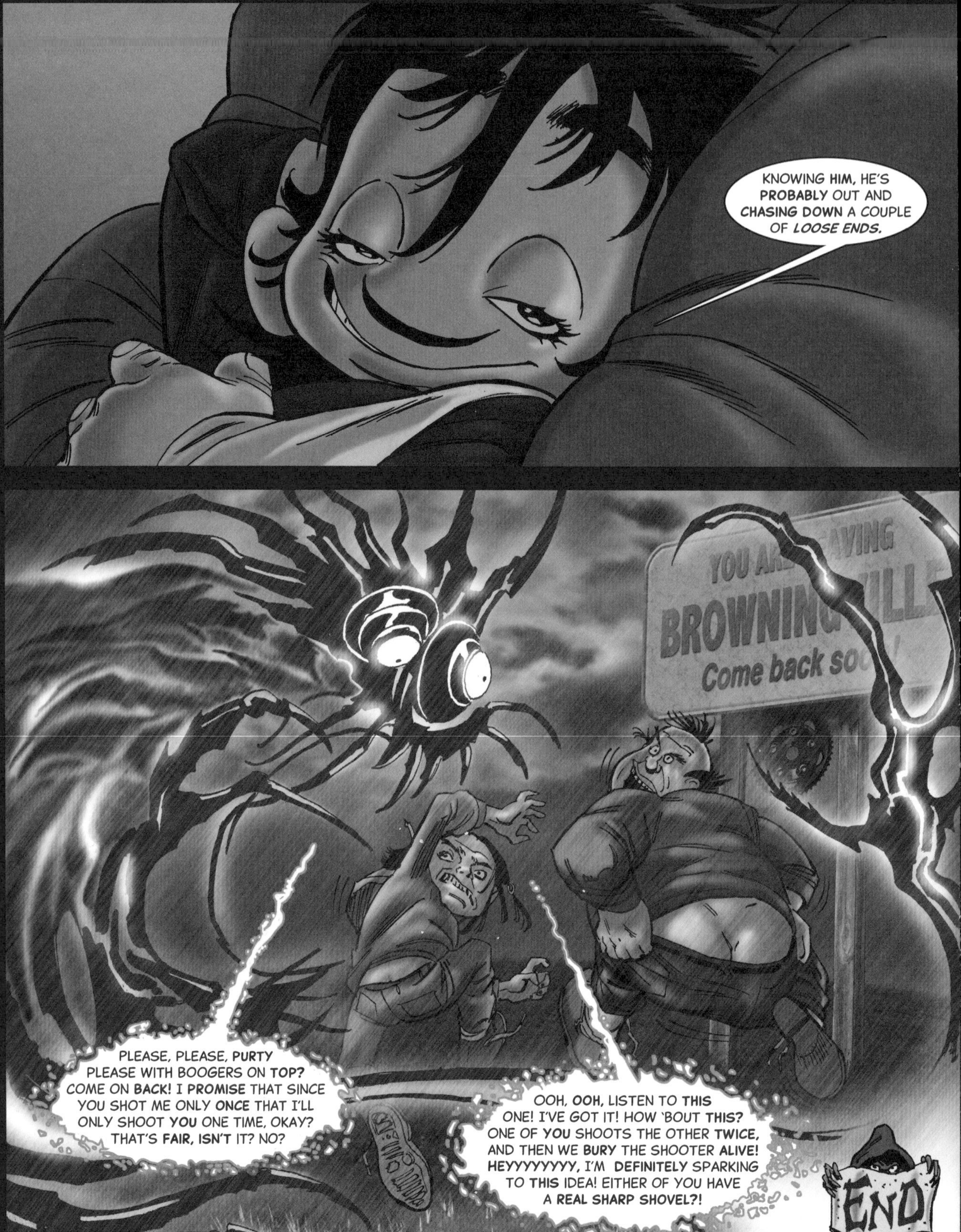
KNOWING HIM, HE'S PROBABLY OUT AND CHASING DOWN A COUPLE OF LOOSE ENDS.
PLEASE, PLEASE, PURTY PLEASE WITH BOOGERS ON TOP? COME ON BACK! I PROMISE THAT SINCE YOU SHOT ME ONLY ONCE THAT I'LL ONLY SHOOT YOU ONE TIME, OKAY? THAT'S FAIR, ISN'T IT? NO?
OOH, OOH, LISTEN TO THIS ONE! I'VE GOT IT! HOW 'BOUT THIS? ONE OF YOU SHOOTS THE OTHER TWICE, AND THEN WE BURY THE SHOOTER ALIVE! HEYYYYYYYYY, I'M DEFINITELY SPARKING TO THIS IDEA! EITHER OF YOU HAVE A REAL SHARP SHOVEL?!
END

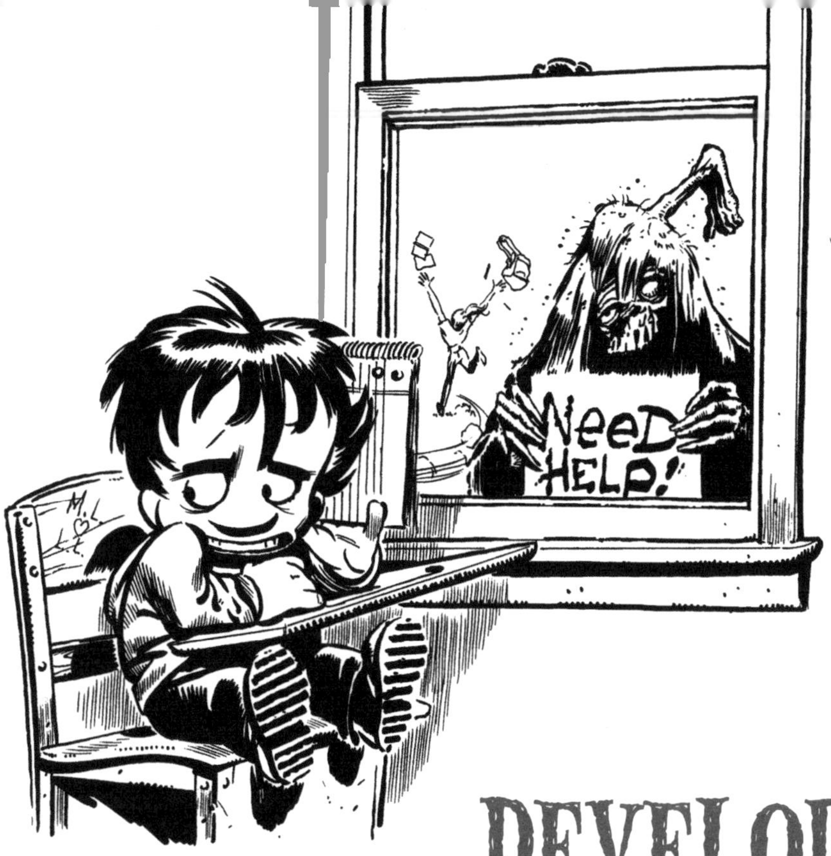
NeeD
HELP!

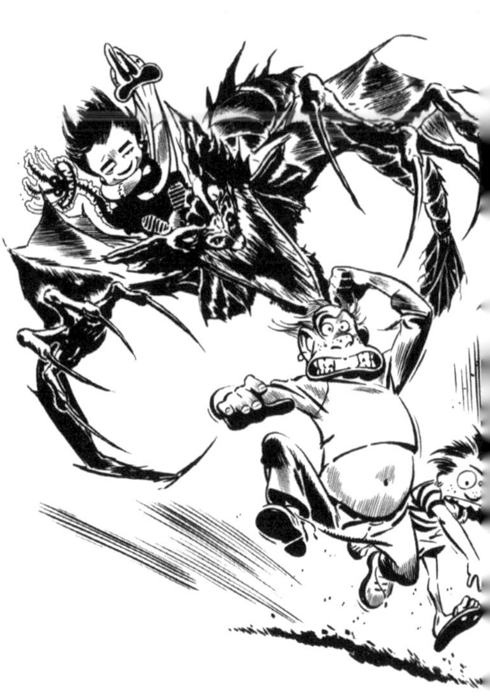

DEVELOPMENT ART

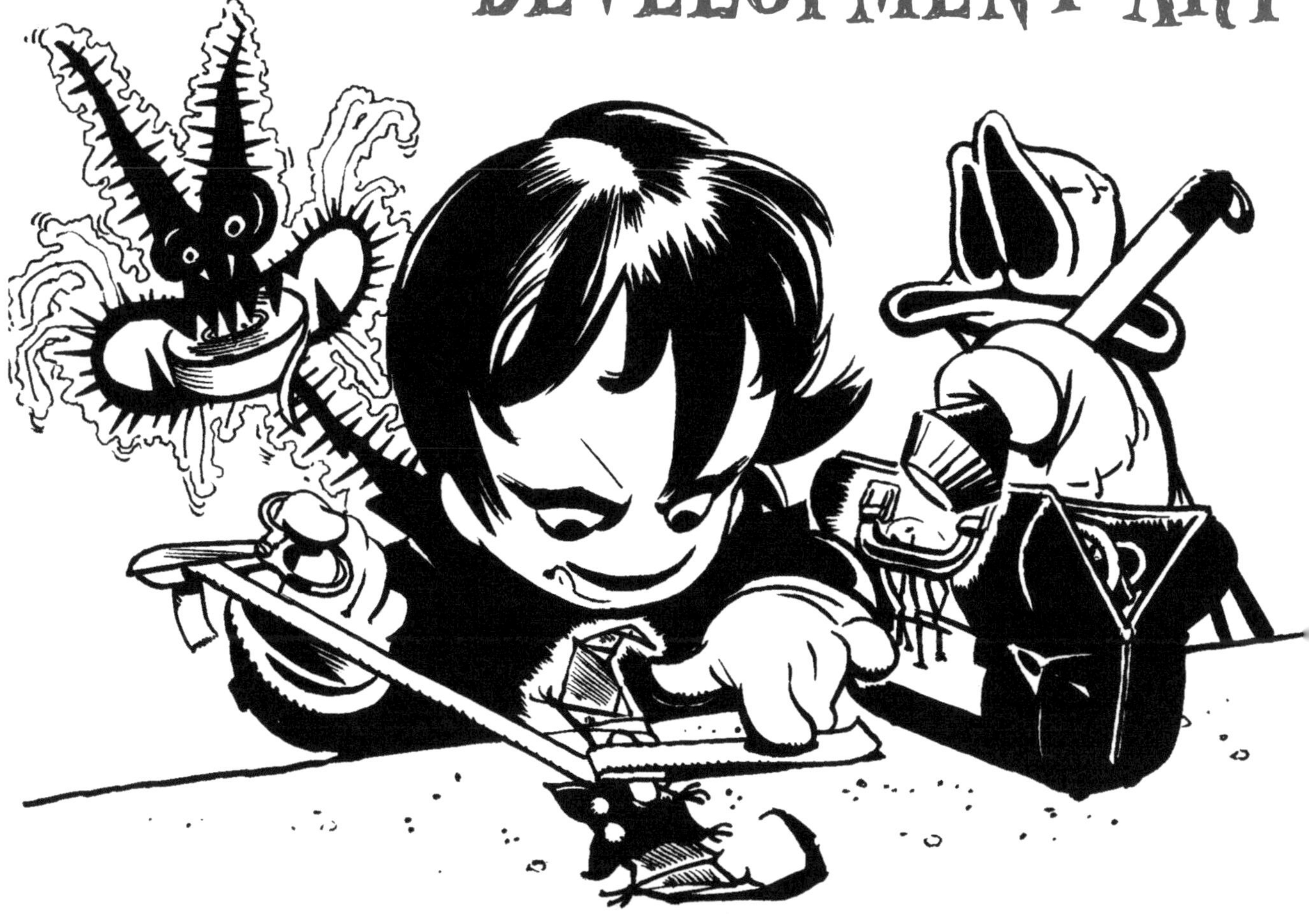

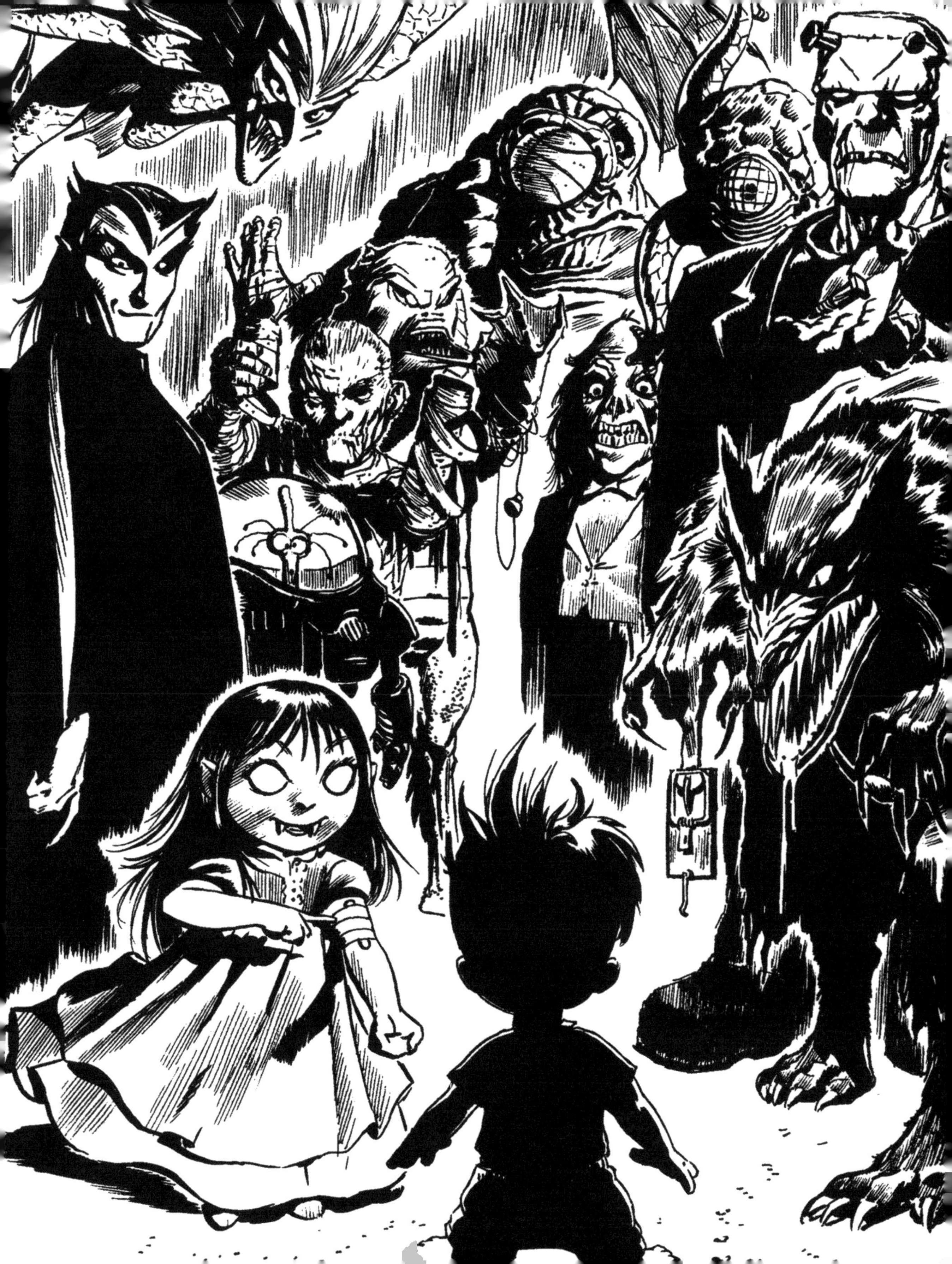

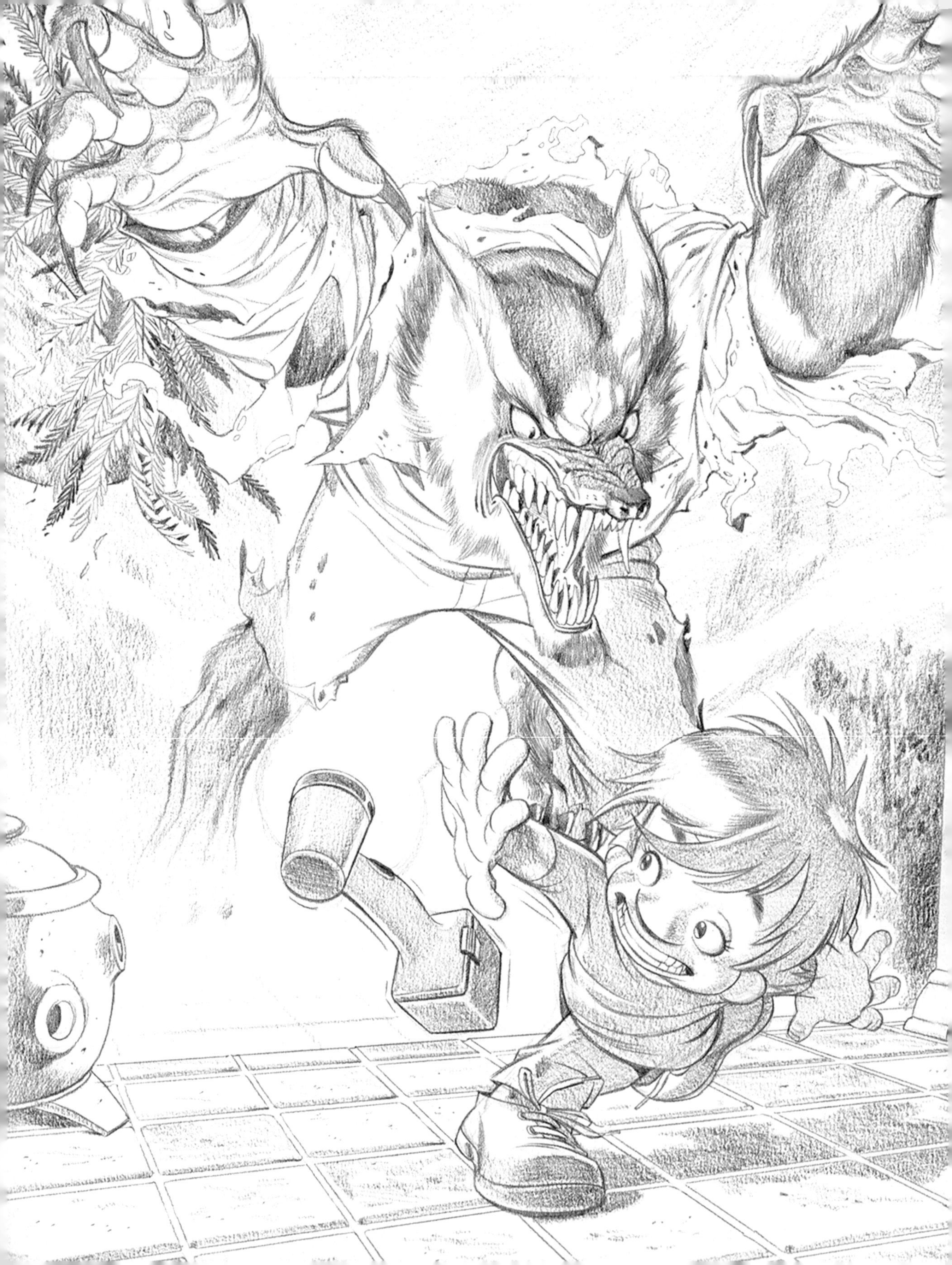

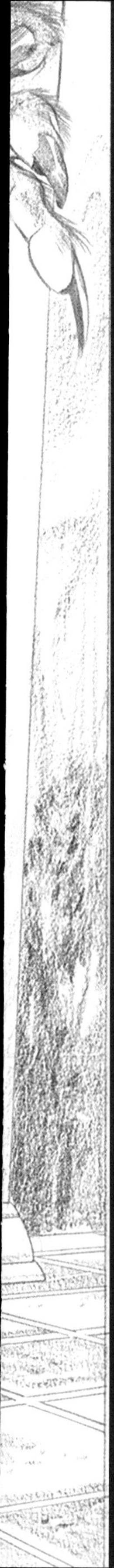

RIP M.D.

AND HOW IT CAME TO BE

LINCOLN BUTTERFIELD, LLC WAS FOUNDED BY VETERAN animation director Robert Hughes and his business partner Joseph Walker in Traverse City, Michigan. When the time came to move the business to Los Angeles, Robert asked Mitch Schauer and Michael Lessa to join the company. The three had known each other for many years. Rob had worked with Mitch and Mike on the Nickelodeon series *The Angry Beavers*. The show was created and Executive Produced by Mitch, Rob was a Director, and Mike was the Senior Producer. The three had also spent time working together in Berlin. When Mitch and Mike joined Lincoln Butterfield, Mitch brought several projects with him; one of these was *RIP M.D.*

When the opportunity arose to publish a graphic novel with Fantagraphics, it was decided that *RIP* would be the perfect property. Naturally, since Mitch created the project, he chose to write and pencil the story. Mike said 'if you draw it – I'll paint it'. Of course, realizing that it would actually have to be completed on a schedule, "I'll paint it" meant enlisting the help of Justin Yamaguchi, another Lincoln Butterfield artist/editor/production guy that they had lying around. Then all they needed to find was the right inker.

Several artists were considered. Knowing the cinematic look that Mitch wanted, they decided to ask Mike Vosburg if he'd like to ink the book. Vosburg, a veteran comic artist and storyboard artist for the *Narnia* films, is also an Emmy® Award winning director for the *Spawn* series. (We'll have to check but this may be the first graphic novel in history where two Emmy winners are the principal artists.) Mike Lessa had worked with Mike Vosburg about twenty years earlier and knew his love of movies and horror classics. When Lessa called Vosburg and he accepted, the crew was set.

RIP M.D. marks the first graphic novel produced by Lincoln Butterfield and after several months in the making – it's finally here. We hope you enjoy reading the book as much as we enjoyed creating it!

ABOUT THE CREATOR

WHILE ATTENDING ART CENTER COLLEGE OF DESIGN, MITCH SCHAUER began working in animation as a freelance storyboard artist for Filmation, Inc. Mitch turned his focus to producing animated series for Hanna Barbera in 1983, with such credits as *The 13 Ghosts of Scooby-Doo* and *Sons of the Pink Panther*. He joined Film Roman in 1988, where he designed and produced Howie Mandel's *Bobby's World*. In 1995, he earned an Emmy® Award for producing Warner Bros.' *Freakazoid!*, and created his own animated series *The Angry Beavers* for Nickelodeon the following year. Mitch designed the look of the show and its starring characters, wrote many episodes, composed several songs for the series and directed every voice recording session. Mitch's high standards of quality helped the 62 episode series earn numerous awards including "Best of Show" at Annecy. In 2007, he co-created the Jim Henson Company's live-action series *The Sam Plenty Cavalcade of Action Show Plus Singing!*

Mitch recently worked for two years in ⬚⬚⬚⬚⬚⬚⬚⬚⬚⬚⬚⬚ Companie. It was during this time that Mitch originally conceived *R⬚⬚⬚⬚⬚⬚⬚⬚⬚⬚⬚⬚⬚⬚* ⬚g Director for Marvel/Film Roman's *The Super-Hero Squad Show* and serves as the Creative Supervisor at Lincoln Butterfield.